Caring for People in the Community
The New Welfare

of related interest

Assessment and Care Management for Adults in Residential and Supported Accomodation
A Handbook for Care Managers and Social Care Staff
Philip Seed and Gillian Kaye
ISBN 1 85302 227 6

Dementia
New Skills for Social Workers
Edited by Alan Chapman and Mary Marshall
ISBN 1 85302 142 3

Handbook of Theory for Practice Teachers in Social Work
Edited by Joyce Lishman
ISBN 1 85302 098 2

Introducing Network Analysis in Social Work
Philip Seed
ISBN 1 85302 034 6 hb
ISBN 1 85302 106 7 pb

Caring for People in the Community
Community
The New Welfare

Edited by Mike Titterton

Jessica Kingsley Publishers
London and Bristol, Pennsylvania

 in the United Kingdom in 1994 by
a Kingsley Publishers Ltd
116 Pentonville Road
ondon N1 9JB, England
and
1900 Frost Road, Suite 101
Bristol, PA 19007, U S A

Library of Congress Cataloging in Publication Data
A CIP catalogue record for this book is available from the Library of
Congress

British Library Cataloguing in Publication Data
Caring for People in the Community:New
Agenda for Welfare
I. Titterton, Michael
362.1

ISBN 1-85302-112-1

Printed and Bound in Great Britain by
Biddles Ltd, Guildford and King's Lynn

Contents

Notes on Contributors

Jacqueline Atkinson is a lecturer in the Department of Public Health, University of Glasgow.

Rosemary Bland is a lecturer in Applied Social Work at the University of Stirling.

David Challis is Assistant Director and Reader in Social Work and Social Care, Personal Social Services Research Unit, University of Kent.

Anne Connor is Senior Research Officer at the Central Research Unit of the Scottish Office.

David Hunter is Professor and Director of the Nuffield Institute for Health, University of Leeds.

Lawrence Elliott is a researcher with the Department of Public Health, University of Glasgow.

Alison Petch was formerly Senior Research Fellow at the Social Work Research Centre, University of Stirling and is now Nuffield Professor of Community Care, University of Glasgow.

Philip Seed is Senior Research Fellow at the Department of Social Work, University of Dundee.

Paul Simic was formerly Research Fellow at the Social Work Research Centre, University of Stirling and is now Research Fellow at the Centre for Primary Care Research, University of Manchester.

Mike Titterton is a freelance trainer and consultant with Training, Research and Evaluation Consultants (TREC) and with Inter-Change, c/o Scottish Council for Voluntary Organisations in Edinburgh.

Gerald Wistow is Professor and Director of Community Care, Nuffield Institute for Health, University of Leeds.

Introduction

Mike Titterton

The 1990s and beyond will see new challenges facing the welfare state in Britain as the changes of the last decade start to take effect. These changes include major shifts in recent policy developments in community care, embodied in the appearance of Sir Roy Griffiths' report on community care, the Government's White Papers on Community Care and the NHS and the 1990 Act. However, a great deal of uncertainty presently exists about the implications of the changes. It is evident that the White Paper and Griffiths Report presuppose a profound revolution in professional and social attitudes to care, with respect to such changes as the rise of the new care manager, the creation of the 'enabling' authority and the development of a mixed economy of care. This book aims to examine critically the new agenda of welfare and to assess the implications for change for policy makers, formal and informal carers and consumers.

The book includes:

- critical surveys of new policy developments
- assessment of recent trends in patterns for priority groups
- examinations of key topics such as care planning and case management
- evaluations of service developments and innovations

The book falls into these sections. The first section deals with policy, planning and management issues. The first chapter has been written by the editor and it deals with the challenges confronting caring agencies for managing innovation and change in community care. Only by seizing learning opportunities and by responding imaginatively to the tasks of implementation will the caring agencies be in the vanguard of change. The author describes a recent interdisciplinary training initiative which attempted to stimulate change in thirteen localities across Scotland. He concludes that local authorities and other caring agencies must fully engage key stakeholders in the change process and take seriously the challenge of involving users and carers if they are to develop as enabling authorities.

These findings will provide music to the ears of the next two contributors who have contributed much to the policy analysis of health and social care policies within the UK, namely David Hunter and Gerald Wistow.

In this chapter on the impact of the NHS reforms on community care, David Hunter looks critically at the important implications of these reforms. He analyses key issues that have been raised of late: numbers in health care, long-term care, responsibility for health and social care, consumer choice, etc. He concludes that the NHS will not be able to withdraw from involvement from community care even if it wanted to. The guidance from central government is for health authorities to get even more closely involved and to develop the necessary dialogue.

Gerald Wistow in his chapter deftly picks up the baton and analyses inter-agency relationships between health and social service agencies. This issue is vital to the success of community care, yet Wistow detects a range of problems in facing up to the challenges of working together. He concludes that unless they are capable of demonstrating the will and capacity to work together there will be strong pressure towards retaining the old configuration of services. The new emphasis on user-centred services demands a radically different approach to problems such as organisational design.

The next section moves on to look at the development of community care services for vulnerable people. The example of mental disability has been used here, since it is one of the most deprived areas of service provision.

In his chapter, Philip Seed, who has for many years written extensively on issues to do with adults with learning disability, reviews some of the major changes which influenced perceptions and directions of service evolution. He looks at changing attitudes towards people with learning difficulty and the impact they are making. He deals with a variety of key issues such as social networking. He concludes that the rhetoric and practice result in many people still leading lives in older models of care, especially those with the most profound disabilities.

One of the most pressing issues and most difficult to pin down is the quality of life of those who have moved out of long-stay institutions into the community. In his chapter, Paul Simic provides a carefully researched study of the experience of adults moving out of a long-stay ward in the Royal Edinburgh Hospital. The study involved 24 patients who were discharged and followed up in the course of the study. Simic found that there was an improvement in the quality of life of some still experiencing severe mental health problems. The importance of new forms of provision, especially supported accommodation, is underlined.

It is precisely this theme which Alison Petch addresses in her very helpful research of eleven supported accommodation projects across Scotland. Many of the residents in these projects had severe mental health problems but experienced an improvement in their quality of life. The effectiveness of this supported housing is, she argues, cogently demonstrated and she rightly rejects the narrow view of housing as just 'bricks and mortar' in the Griffiths Report.

The next part of the book deals further with responses to perceived need and in particular addresses issues of management of care and the improvement of outcomes.

David Challis provides a valuable review of key issues in case management within the UK and in an international context, in particular the USA and Australia. Pointing to a similarity in trends, he argues that case management has become a central component for the development of community care. He outlines definitions and core elements and reviews some schemes in the UK, along with some problems for implementation. Challis concludes that clarity about target populations, models and direction for practitioners is essential.

Scotland has seen a number of innovations in this area and Rosemary Bland provides an interesting account of one such experiment in Central Region. The Elderly People in Care (EPIC) Project, set up by the social work department and health board, aimed to help frail older persons, by supporting them in their own homes and helping those caring for them. With a devolved budget and care package amounting to two-thirds of the cost of residential care or long stay hospital bed, a multi-disciplinary team with three helpers performed a range of personal and home care tasks with a comparison group. A number of key issues emerged – especially the extent to which case managers can really be free to act as advocates and brokers. Strenuous efforts will be required to engage older persons in planning and delivery of care. She concludes that service providers face a challenge of fundamentally altering the way they respond to need.

The final part looks at two issues of great importance for community-based strategies of care, namely the contributions of voluntary agencies and consumer involvement in assessing the nature and quality of services.

Anne Connor, in a wide-ranging and systematic piece of research, examines the key role which the voluntary sector has to play in the new set up for community care. This is based on research she conducted at the Scottish Office of the Care in the Community literature which ran in Scotland from 1985 to 1988. She produces a range of useful findings for the range of user groups. She suggests that things could develop in two ways – either an extension of the role of voluntary organisations in close partnership or for them to become more divorced in the world of contracts and ever tightening resources, with the most likely way lying in between.

This is followed by Jackie Atkinson and Lawrence Elliott in a perceptive chapter on the relationship between consumers and evaluation. After noting how important evaluation has become and the growing emphasis on consumer views, they provide a stimulating discussion of key issues in what is admittedly a complex area. They draw on their own research of 130 users of mental health services and their carers; this considered opinion of different services where the user was asked which in their view was helpful and which made their problem worse. They conclude that there are no easy or straightforward answers but suggest some helpful guidelines for evaluation.

The conclusion by the editor sets out a new agenda for action based on these contributions.

CHAPTER ONE

Managing Innovation and Change in Community Care

Mike Titterton

INTRODUCTION

Caring agencies are at present faced with the challenge of how to manage innovation and change in community care. They must now consider how best to imaginatively expand their repertoire of responses to the tasks of implementation, in the wake of the NHS and Community Care Act 1990. This chapter looks at this challenge and describes a training and development initiative designed to stimulate change in Scotland.

THE CHALLENGE

While the policy assumptions of the Government's White Papers, *Caring for People* and *People First*, have been the subject of critical scrutiny, the vision remains a compelling one (Secretaries of State for Health, Social Security, Wales and Scotland 1989, Department of Health and Social Services, Northern Ireland 1990; for critical discussion see Titterton 1990, House of Commons Welsh Affairs Committee 1992, House of Commons Health Committee 1993, Walker 1993). This embraces the development of a community care system where local authority social service and social work departments become enabling agencies, creating quality services tailored to the needs of users and carers. One of the principal challenges of the next decade will be the managing of change and innovation required to bring about the 'community revolution' (Audit Commission for Local Authorities and the National Health Service in England and Wales 1992).

The tasks may be summarised as follows. Under the NHS and Community Care Act 1990 and guidance, local authorities and other caring agencies must address these issues: assessment and care management; inspection; quality assurance; community care planning; new financial arrangements for residential care; a move towards a mixed economy of welfare; contracting and commissioning; separation of purchasing and providing; user and carer involvement; hospital discharge arrangements; better multidisciplinary working; including working with GPs (see policy and practice guidance issued by Department of Health, Department of Health and Social Services, Northern Ireland, the Scottish Office and Welsh Office; see also Neate 1993).

THE POSITION IN SCOTLAND

The challenge described above applies equally to the four countries of the UK. It must however be recognised that the four countries – England, Wales, Scotland and Northern Ireland – have differing policy contexts and administrative arrangements, Hunter and Wistow 1987, Titterton 1993). Scotland faces particular difficulties in moving from a hospital-based system of care to a community-based one (Titterton 1991; see also Chapter 5).

A paper prepared by the Scottish Office in 1992 acknowledged that the implementation of community care required major changes in practice and the deployment of professional skills and services. Staff managing and providing services in social work, health care and the private and voluntary sectors had to work together more effectively to improve the delivery of services to users and carers. It was recognised that gaps existed in the range of learning opportunities; the development and maintenance of effective working relationships across professional and agency boundaries required special attention.

An interdisciplinary training initiative was launched by the Scottish Office Community Care Implementation Unit and the Management Development Group of the Scottish Health Service in October 1992. Short-life funding was made available and tenders were sent to training and development organisations, inviting them to create and carry out a programme designed to tackle these issues.

THE INTER-CHANGE INITIATIVE

The Inter-Change consortium consisting of the Dundee University Community Care Studies Unit, the Scottish Council for Voluntary Organisations, four independent consultants and an administrator successfully tendered to carry out the programme. A monitoring group was set up to oversee the programme, consisting of representatives from the Management Development Group, the Community Care Implementation Unit, the Inspectorate and other staff from the Scottish Home and Health Department and the Inter-Change consortium. Following this, the Scottish Office wrote to local authorities, health boards and some voluntary groups who were invited to bid for projects.

The remit to develop a training and development was a broad one and the consortium faced some tough choices about direction and choice of projects. To guide the work, the consortium members outlined their commitment to these principles:

- training for staff who are implementing community care policies must itself reflect the principles and values which underpin those policies

- effective training will enable participants to improve their own and their agency's services to users and carers
- training must be tailored to meet actual needs; this necessitates negotiation with service providers to fine tune proposed initiatives
- training must be flexible and must accept the importance of minimising the absence of key staff from their work base
- training must make best use of resources and be cost effective
- training must be well planned and well evaluated

The consortium sought to develop a portfolio of local collaborative projects based on these principles. It also tried to ensure that initiatives chosen for inclusion met the following criteria:

- the work focused on specified issues which people needed to tackle in the near future. There were clear benefits to service users and/or carers resulting from the project
- the way the project was to be planned and managed would itself contribute to strengthening local networks and local ownership of the problem
- service providers from the voluntary or independent sector were to be actively involved
- people involved in the project would be better equipped to tackle similar problems next time
- people involved in the project were to consider new ideas
- the project had potential to be applied in a wider context and in this way to multiply its impact on practice
- the projects were further based on an assumption that it was essential that the process linked together the senior management, service management and practitioner levels
- users' and carers' involvement was considered to be another key requirement

THE PROJECTS

A considerable range and diversity of projects was put forward by agencies. In selecting the final portfolio, the Inter-Change team attempted to achieve good national coverage in Scotland and a balance of urban, rural and island locations. As far as possible, a reasonably coherent range of topics was sought.

The range of key issues tackled in the local projects is set out in the table.

Despite many other significant pressures, especially the rapid pace of change being experienced by agencies, there was a sense of urgency and commitment among key staff groups which enabled good early progress to be made. In particular, the initiative gained the support of a number of training officers whose commitment and enthusiasm was important to the launch and development of several of the projects.

Issue	Locality
User and carer involvement	Highland/Borders/Ayrshire & Arran
Assessment and care management	Shetland/Tayside/Western Isles
Contracting and commissioning	Central/Borders
Hospital discharge arrangements	Central/Lothian
Community care planning	Borders/Highland
Local needs analysis	Fife/Argyll and Clyde/Highland
Quality assurance	Central
Advocacy	Western Isles
Mental health developments	Highland/Lothian
Moving from hospital to community setting	Central/Lothian
Joint working	Glasgow/Shetland
GP involvement	Highland/Lothian

MANAGING THE INITIATIVE

Each of the projects moved through three phases:

(a) a consultation phase in which the role of the consultants was to develop a consensus on the nature of the problem to be tacked

(b) an implementation phase which varied in scale from project to project

(c) project review often assisted by the drafting of the project report and development of proposals for future action.

Three locality projects failed to get off the ground; initial work in Orkney and in West Lothian and on a GP training project did not prove successful. Staff changes and the pressure of time were major factors here.

The process of managing the projects was a difficult one and the choice of the Scottish Council for Voluntary Organisations in Edinburgh as a base proved fortuitous. There was great pressure on all involved to delivery a quality product within a timeframe of eight months and within a tight budget.

KEY ISSUES

Inter-Change tried very hard to move beyond simply providing a series of separate training events. The initiative sought to:

• contribute to the process of change demanded by care in the community

• identify common problems

• propose common solutions

It also sought to:

- assist in building a network of change agents in local projects and nationally

Inter-Change attempted to work with and widen the participation of important stakeholders in the local projects. The programme did seek to 'design in' participation by the major agencies and specified user and carer involvement. Some actors proved difficult to engage, particularly GPs and housing departments; both have been the subject of recent studies (Arnold and Page 1992, Leedham and Wistow 1992).

The participation of GPs was not as widespread or as thorough as one hoped, despite extraordinary efforts in some localities. In those areas where a GP was involved this was valued by colleagues. In one project in Kelty, Fife a GP played a lead role and was clearly a crucial information holder in this locality who had not been used in community care planning till that point. Participation by voluntary organisations should have been stronger. The process whereby initial proposals were submitted militated against this, and efforts were later made to pull in voluntary sector projects. Other important issues might have moved centre stage in a better balanced programme.

- reach an agreed definition of the current problem or situation

Some inter-agency groupings were more ready to use external help in developing a 'diagnosis' of the problems faced. Similarly some groupings more easily achieved consensus on the specific issue that could best be addressed within the current Inter-Change programme.

- guide stakeholders through a process of learning about what a better situation might look like

The consortium members used their extensive networks and knowledge base to provide some project briefing papers that suggested a range of options. In some cases, consultants and experts from outside were brought in to try to give a fresh perspective.

The members consistently suggested people to talk to and, equally important, helped groups to be clear about what they needed to find out. They tried to generate new ideas and fresh perspectives on old problems – with varying degrees of success.

In some projects it became clear that there was a disjunction between the agenda and priority list of local people/users and that of the major statutory agencies. The priority issues for people with disabilities in the Borders project concerned access and the physical environment. For them, community care planning could not be divorced from these issues and they felt that second round plans would need to look very different. Local people in Lockerbie, in Kelty and in Caithness similarly raised issues that were not considered in community care planning, for example local transport, that for them were crucial factors in being able to live independently or be supported in one's own home.

- support those involved in the change effort

The Inter-Change projects were for the most part small and fragile change initiatives. There were definitely some very positive outcomes both for staff involved and for users and carers. There was very popular feedback from the carers who attended the workshops in Ayrshire and Arran, and from carers and staff attending events in Central; the Borders Liberty group was supported through its early development in part by Inter-Change; both the users and staff at Bangour reported that the project had been valuable and there are plans to repeat the course both for people returning to the community in future and as part of staff training.

 • ensure learning is shared

One of the strengths of the consortium approach has been an ability to disseminate project findings both informally through networks and more formally.

The following outputs were produced: regular written reports for the Scottish Office Monitoring Group; three issues of a widely circulated bulletin, *Inter-Action*; short articles for *Caring Scotland*; briefing packs with up-to-date material from the literature for several projects; a network conference with international speakers; a training module on contracting and commissioning; a video on assessment; and reports for each of the locality projects.

KEY LESSONS FROM THE INTER-CHANGE INITIATIVE

Though Inter-Change was funded as a short-life project, the implementation of community care presents a continuing challenge to agencies, staff, users and carers. The organisation and cultural changes are still working their way through the system and there is a further structural change on the horizon with the plans for local government reorganisation in Scotland.

Inter-Change tried in its work with agencies to keep a focus on the effect of all this change on the services and supports provided to people who use services. There is little doubt that agencies and staff want to see a better deal for users. They want to see high quality, responsive, non-segregated services which mesh together in helping users to get on with their own lives as part of the community.

However, making progress on the changes needed is a long and complex process. There is no working package to be bought off the shelf. Agencies are often so busy with short-term development and adjustment that it is hard to spend time clarifying and holding on to the long-term vision of better human services.

It is important not to lose sight of two key factors. Firstly, community care can only be done together – not just health and social work together, but together with users, carers, voluntary agencies (not just community care service providers), and most importantly with communities. Secondly, the key resource in all this is the human resource. People's skills, personal networks, wisdom and commitment, and the way that managers at all levels of the system develop and direct this human resource; this is what will make a difference between doing community care well and doing it badly.

CONCLUSIONS

The implications for managing change and innovation in community care are these. First, local authorities must be prepared to show leadership in the change process. They have a responsibility to lead developments, but good leadership does not mean excessive control of events. It means being prepared to stimulate change and to let go of the process when the occasion demands it. Second, they must be prepared to build a common agenda for action, taking partnership seriously – moving beyond consultation to engage with hospital and community-based health care staff, GPs, housing agencies, voluntary and independent groups and users and carers. This will involve a lengthy process of learning on all sides. Third, senior managers from social services, health and the independent sectors must be prepared to get involved in training and development exercises, along with frontline staff and with staff from other agencies, but also with users and carers. Only when those receiving services and their carers are fully engaged will social service agencies truly become enabling authorities.

ACKNOWLEDGEMENTS

The author gratefully acknowledges the assistance of his colleagues in the Inter-Change consortium: Denis Rowley of the Community Care Studies Unit, University of Dundee who formerly acted as coordinator; Cathy Maclean, John Leggate and Geraldine Faulds of SCVO; and Brian Coyle, Eddie Palmer and Pete Ritchie. He would also like to thank the members of the Scottish Office Monitoring Group: Billy Gorman and Stanley Bonthron of the Community Care Implementation Unit; Douglas Peace of the Management Development Group; Dr Brian Potter, Evelyn Hide and Margaret Reed of the Home and Health Department; and Linda Hunt of the Social Work Services Inspectorate.

LIST OF INTER-CHANGE PROJECT REPORTS

Developing Multi-Disciplinary Arrangements for Long-Stay Hospital Discharges

Contracts in Community Care: Problems and Opportunities in Central Region

Ensuring Quality in Community Care for Older Persons: A Case Study Approach

Assessment, Risk-Taking and Advocacy for Older Persons in the Western Isles

Developing Community Mental Health Services in Caithness

Developing Inter-disciplinary Locality Team Approaches to Mental Illness in Glasgow

Closing a Hospital Well: A Programme of Seminars for Staff and Residents of East Lothian Care and Accommodation Project

Carers as Users of Social Work and Health Board Services, a Practical Workshop

Providing Services to Island Communities

A Comparison of the Community Care Needs of Two Communities in Fife

Developing a Discharge Protocol for a General Hospital

'Moving to the Community': A Course for Residents of Bangour Village Hospital

'Opening Gates': A Conference for Carers, Practitioners, Managers and Planners Organised by the Dementia Interest Group, Grampian

The Inter-Change Programme: Final Report to the Scottish Office

For further information, please contact the author at Inter-Change, c/o SCVO, 18/19 Claremont Crescent, Edinburgh EH7 4QD. Tel. 031 556 3882.

REFERENCES

Arnold, P. and Page, D. (1992) *Housing and Community Care: Bricks and Mortar or Foundation for Action?* Hull: Humberside Polytechnic School of Social and Professional Studies.

Audit Commission for Local Authorities and the National Health Service in England and Wales (1992) *The Community Revolution: The Personal Social Services and Community Care.* London: HMSO.

Department of Health and Social Services, Northern Ireland (1990) *People First: Community Care in Northern Ireland for the 1990s.* Belfast: HMSO.

House of Commons Welsh Affairs Committee (1992) *Community Care: The Elderly, Volume 1, Session 1991–92.* London: HMSO.

House of Commons Health Committee (1993) *Community Care: The Way Forward, Volume I, Session 1992–93, Sixth Report.* London: HMSO.

Hunter, D. and Wistow, G. (1987) *Community Care in Britain: Variations on a Theme.* London: King Edward's Hospital Fund.

Leedham, I. and Wistow, G. (1992) *Community Care and General Practitioners, Working Paper No. 6.* University of Leeds: Nuffield Institute for Health.

Neate, P. (ed) (1993) *Implementing the Community Care Act: the 8 Key Tasks.* Sutton: Community Care Publication.

Secretaries of State for Health, Social Security, Wales and Scotland (1989) *Caring for People: Community Care in the Next Decade and Beyond.* London: HMSO.

Titterton, M. (1990) *Caring for People in Scotland: A Report on Community Care in Scotland and the Implications of the NHS and Community Care Bill.* Report submitted in evidence to the House of Commons Social Services Committee.

Titterton, M. (1991) Caring for mentally disabled people in Scotland. *Social Policy and Administration, 25, 2, 136–48.*

Titterton, M. (1993) Community care policy in the United Kingdom: conformity and diversity. In Open University Community Care Course Workbook 2, *Community Care: History and Policy.* Milton Keynes: Open University.

Walker, A. (1993) Community care policy: from consensus to conflict. In J. Bornat *et al* (eds) *Community Care: A Reader.* Basingstoke: Macmillan.

CHAPTER 2

The Impact of the NHS Reforms on Community Care

David Hunter

Much of the comment on the changes under way in community care has focused on the White Paper, *Caring for People*, and subsequent policy and practice guidance emanating from the Department of Health/Social Services Inspectorate in England and the Scottish Office/Social Work Services Group in Scotland. However, the NHS reforms will have a marked impact on developments in community care and it is therefore the purpose of this chapter to describe the principal changes already under way in the NHS and their likely impact on community care provision. A brief description of the NHS reforms is followed by a more detailed assessment of the interface between the changes in the health service and those under way in community care. The changes in the NHS have gone much further and faster in England than in Scotland. In Scotland NHS hospital trusts have just started to come on stream since April 1993 and there is a mere handful of them compared with the 200 or so trusts in England. The position is much the same in respect of GP fundholders, where only a few exist in Scotland in contrast to the position in England.

THE NHS REFORMS

By general agreement, the outcome of the NHS review which resulted in the 1989 White Paper, *Working for Patients*, and the 1990 NHS and Community Care Act, has amounted to the most formidable programme of reform in the history of the Service (Harrison, Hunter, Johnston and Wistow 1989, King's Fund Institute 1989). While the Government has been quick to acknowledge the virtues of the NHS, it has also sought to establish that much-needed and long overdue improvements are necessary. The key problems that it believes demand attention are:

- inexplicable variations in clinical practice which can result in patients receiving immediate treatment in one hospital while waiting in another

- variable performance between health authorities in respect of avoidable deaths and their general performance
- marked variations in referral rates among GPs
- over-prescribing of expensive drugs by GPs
- concern over quality and standards of care among doctors and other provider groups
- a lack of responsiveness to consumers by service providers with choice either limited or non-existent.

While there may be good reasons for many of the variations that exist, and while it would be quite wrong, for example, always to equate shorter length of stay with better quality care, there is no denying that the existence of marked variations in practice prompts questions directed at both the efficiency and efficacy of particular procedures.

The response to the problems set out above has comprised the following principal changes:

- separation of purchasing from provision in order to stimulate competition and provide a market so that inefficient practices can be rooted out
- self-governing hospitals, or trusts, and GP fundholders, which will encourage a more efficient use of resources through competition and tackle GPs' idiosyncratic referral behaviour
- indicative drug budgets to reduce drug costs and over-prescribing among GPs
- medical audit for hospital doctors and GPs
- resource management initiative roll-out beyond the pilot sites to all areas
- reform of consultants' distinction or merit awards system
- tighter management of consultants' contracts
- increased choice for consumers.

Whether the prescription can successfully address the diagnosis has been the subject of heated debate since the White Paper was published in 1989 and the subsequent NHS and Community Care Act became law in 1990. The arguments have become more intense since the changes were introduced in April 1991. Many observers would not wish to take issue with the broad diagnosis of the NHS's ills and the need for modernisation (e.g. Klein 1989). As far as it goes, it is a reasonable assessment of the position, comprising as it does problems which have dogged the NHS for many years and have survived several reorganisations. Some commentators, however, have expressed serious reservations about the extent to which the reforms, taken as an integrated package, will successfully address the problems identified (Harrison *et al.* 1989, Social Services Committee 1989). A major criticism of them is their remarkably isolationist nature. Little mention is made in the NHS White Paper of the primary health care changes or of the changes under way in community care. Moreover, few in the NHS have given much attention to these matters, concentrating instead on what they regard as their main business, namely, acute hospital services. As some commentators have suggested, the reforms, however unintentionally, seem to equate the NHS with acute hospital services and GP medical services. The thrust of the proposals is directed at sickness or treatment services, and not at those for the chronic long-term sick.

If the 1991 reforms proved to be a turning point in the NHS's evolution then so did the first major reorganisation of the Service in 1974. In marked contrast to the present reforms, the 1974 NHS reorganisation was firmly (if imperfectly) based on an explicit philosophy concerning the nature of health care. Although it did not go far enough for some, the theme of *integration*, the hallmark of the 1974 changes, was a recognition of the fact that health care had to consist of more than merely hospital services (Hunter 1980). Accordingly, an attempt was made to bring primary, hospital and community health services closer together in order to achieve improved coordination and planning. The frontier problems confronted in 1974 were not successfully resolved, either between agencies or between professionals, and subsequent reforms have amounted to a progressive retreat from integration. But the principle remains no less valid. Progress was slightly more encouraging in Scotland where, since 1974, primary care has been integrated with secondary care and is organised as part of the health board structure rather than through separate agencies.

There is a danger that the 1991 NHS reforms could undermine what little integration remains and act as a spur to further fragmentation and the creation of new boundaries and barriers between services. As we move through the 1990s, the inter-agency and interprofessional problems evident in the early 1970s remain very much alive. But it has to be conceded that the NHS reforms do in some respects offer real and exciting opportunities to tackle persistent problems that have defeated successive governments. In particular, separating purchasing from provision could free up health authorities to concentrate on health planning and on identifying and meeting the needs of local communities through an approach which emphasises health gain rather than simply the provision of health care services regardless of whether they are effective or not (Harrison and Wistow 1992). The 1992 White Paper in England, *The Health of the Nation*, and its Scottish counterpart, marks an attempt to provide a strategic framework for the Service which it has hitherto lacked. Indeed, through SHAPE in 1980 and SHARPEN in 1989, Scotland has fared rather better in this regard. Released from the distractions of providing services directly, where the urgent forever drives out the important, health authorities are now in a position to improve and refine their strategic and analytical skills.

Of course, this is not the only scenario which has been put forward. A 'worse case' scenario sees health authorities adopting a conservative, narrow, risk averse, coercive approach that is primarily concerned with policing contracts in a highly restrictive and repressive manner. If, as many believe could happen, managers of calibre desert purchasing authorities in search of new challenges in the heartland of the future hospital service (i.e. NHS trusts) then the skills necessary to grasp the opportunities which will fall to commissioning authorities will not be in abundance and those available for imaginative health planning will not be taken up. The present rhetoric and hype suggest otherwise but health authorities must be judged according to their actions and these have been less impressive to date.

It is also the case that the tasks demanded of managers by the NHS reforms require skills that are not widely evident at the present time. While marketing and income generating skills are being developed, the reforms call for skills in business planning, communication, contracting and monitoring, which are vital if a 'worse case' scenario is to be avoided. In many respects, the changes seek to build on the 1984 general management reforms and, like the first Griffiths report, are chiefly concerned with *process* rather than *structure*. While there are major structural changes arising from the reforms it is fair to say that they are largely about changing the chemistry and power relations between key groups within the health service. The ultimate purpose of the changes is to reconfigure the balance of power between those providing services, principally doctors, and those managing them. The intention is that the changes will result in a redrawing of the boundary between management and medicine in favour of the former (Harrison 1988, Harrison, Hunter and Pollitt 1990).

There are two principal themes running through the reforms which are worth focusing on in a little more detail: the consumer dimension and markets in health care. It is desirable to examine these and look briefly to the wider agenda before turning our attention to the implications of the NHS changes for the community care reforms whose implementation commenced in 1991 and culminated in 1993 with the transfer of resources to local authorities from income support.

The Consumer Dimension

A central concern of the NHS reforms is to provide patients with better quality care and wider choice. Developments such as the Patient's Charter are an extension of the consumerist theme. In her foreword to the NHS White Paper, the then Prime Minister was emphatic that 'all the proposals in this White Paper put the needs of patients first'. The strategy for consumers evident in the NHS changes maintains that patients' needs will become paramount in health services organised and delivered through the vehicle of an internal market, whereby health authorities will become the purchasers of care but not the direct providers of it. Four principal developments are intended to show the government's commitment to the quality and choice of services available:

- removing restrictions on patients' ability to change their GP
- increasing the proportion of GP income derived from capitation fees
- separating responsibility for purchasing and providing hospital services
- introducing GP budgets for larger practices.

The underlying rationale of the reforms is that GPs will compete for patients and that hospitals will compete for business from GPs, if fundholders, and health authorities. In both cases, service providers are expected to respond to direct incentives to provide care which is more responsive to the needs and preferences of patients. Patients are intended to have greater opportunities to take their custom elsewhere if dissatisfied. This framework for enhancing patient choice and service quality is being supplemented by two further initiatives:

- introduction of medical audit throughout the NHS as a mechanism for safeguarding quality
- the provision of more information to enable patients (and their GPs) to make informed choices.

For the most part, patient choice will be expressed indirectly rather than directly. The main exception will be in the choice of GP. Restrictions on changing GPs will be removed and choice will be informed by practice leaflets, which all practices will produce as a condition of service. In all other cases, choice will be exercised by GPs on behalf of patients. Moreover, the extent to which consumers will in practice be able even to exercise a choice of GP will be geographically related and least available to those who live in rural areas. Such choices will also become progressively more restricted if practices combine to become eligible for practice budgets.

Despite the principle of choice figuring strongly in the NHS proposals there is some doubt over the extent to which it will be possible for genuine choice to be exercised. The choice offered by the changes is largely the surrogate choice of GPs which will be further mediated through contractual arrangements very largely restricting them to batch, rather than individual, referral arrangements. The increased flow of information to patients is similarly restricted, being concentrated on details of facilities and services offered. GPs are to be provided with more information on, for example, waiting times, and the results of medical audit are to be made available in a generalised form. It is questionable whether this information will enable consumers to exercise an informed choice based on performance criteria.

The changes display an approach to consumerism which emphasises providing information *to* consumers rather than obtaining it *from* them. The favoured model of consumerism is restricted to the former and firmly paternalistic approach. The proposals show no commitment to mechanisms for developing and delivering services to individuals and groups in ways which incorporate their own perceptions of their needs. The situation could change as health authorities experiment with ways of consulting the public using a variety of instruments including surveys, focused group interviews, rapid appraisal and so on. Many of these initiatives are in their infancy but the NHSME's 'local voices' initiative has been influential (NHSME 1991, Sykes *et al*. 1992).

Markets in Health Care

In the early days of the reforms there was much talk of competition and markets in health care. More recently, the business and commercial language has been toned down to reflect a shift in the government's belief that the changes are chiefly about introducing market mechanisms into the NHS. Nevertheless, it remains the government's intention to set up a system of competition within the health service in order to allow health authorities to purchase care from a variety of provider sources, rather than be dependent on those which happen to be within their area.

A problem with the internal market notion is that competition can, in the aggregate, be wasteful. That is, competitive behaviour entails maintaining surplus capacity and transaction costs which may not be offset by the benefits of competition. Incentives provided by the reforms could stimulate the over-provision of sophisticated medical technology in an attempt to attract patients and contracts with general practitioners. Such a temptation will be especially acute for trust hospitals and it is far from clear that the proposed financing limit and control of supra-regional technology will control this. Similarly, it is certain that the proposals for better information and better management will lead to increased administrative expenditure without any guarantee of its being offset by increased efficiency. A further set of consequences is that, since most of the knowledge in the possession of participants in the market will concern costs and processes rather than efficacy of treatments, competition will tend to occur on the former, rather than the latter, dimension. Indeed, it is possible that one may operate at the expense of the other.

It is far too soon to make any definitive judgement on such matters or to conclude that the reforms are destined to fail on these counts, but there is a recognition that they exist and this possibly accounts for a somewhat belated switch of attention from providers in the shape of trusts to the purchasing or commissioning role. Until recently this had been overlooked. But effective purchasing is now seen as central if the purpose of the reforms to improve the health of local communities is to be realised. The problem is that the vast majority of purchasers lack the skills required to perform their task adequately. In particular needs assessment skills are poorly developed (see below).

A circular to general managers in Scottish Health Boards in 1991 made it clear that boards had three main functions: to assess the health needs of the populations they serve and prepare a strategic plan to meet them, the negotiation of contracts to purchase health care, and to manage directly managed units appropriately (SHHD 1991). The pace of reform is much slower in Scotland and the notion of markets and competition is not evident in the official circular and guidance to the same degree as in England where much is made of influence of the market in health care in achieving greater efficiency and improved performance (The Scottish Office 1991, NHSME 1992).

The Wider Agenda

Because of their focus on acute hospital services, as has been noted above, there is a danger that the reforms will lead to increased fragmentation in the provision of care and that they will not provide the seamfree services which people whose needs embrace both health and social care demand. These problems become especially acute in relation to the issue of assessment of need. It is an area of concern with which health authorities in their new purchasing role are having to come to terms. To some extent, the assessment of need is the responsibility of directors of public health. However, they are not equipped to perform the task single-handed. Even less can they be expected to be competent in specifying services to the degree required in negotiating contracts for services. Planning services for mentally ill people serves to illustrate the point. Currently such a service is planned, notionally at least, by those professionals providing it (who may be located in health, social services and other agencies), planners (also located in different agencies), including community physicians and representatives of local authorities, and voluntary bodies. But as the Audit Commission (1986, 1992) and others have pointed out *ad nauseam*, attempts to bring about integrated plans and services are already riven with professional and agency factionalism, in addition to profound differences in the way particular professions view the same problem (Rowbottom 1992). Getting agreement cannot be assumed and has to be worked at. How appropriate or inappropriate the 'contract culture' will prove to be in such a setting remains to be seen.

If the intended effect of the NHS reforms is to shift the balance of power from the providers to the purchasers, then the possibility of such a shift is largely dependent upon the purchasers being able adequately to specify their requirements. This is proving slower than initially expected in the first year or two of the reforms. If purchasing is to mean anything other than maintaining the status quo then it is going to be necessary for purchasing authorities to be able both to assess need and to specify those services required to meet it. An issue is whether it is reasonable to expect purchasers to undertake these tasks without the involvement of the providers. All the evidence suggests that defining need is not an activity which is independent of the means of delivering services intended to meet that need. It is not possible to be concerned with means without simultaneously being concerned with ends, even if this occurs implicitly rather than explicitly.

The planning role envisaged for health authorities is implicit in the functions set out in the NHS reforms. The role will contain two key elements: needs analysis and outcome monitoring/evaluation; and service planning. The former element will need to draw substantially upon epidemiological and research-based skills which are currently in short supply. Both elements imply strengthening precisely those parts of the planning process which are currently the most underdeveloped throughout the human services. The notion that service development should be needs-driven rather than norms-led represents a shift of such magnitude that the lead time for developing appropriate tools and attitudes cannot be underestimated. This reservation has even more power if mechanisms for obtaining consumer views of need are to be promoted in line with the emphasis on 'putting patients first'. Precisely similar considerations arise in relation to outcome monitoring and evaluation, with respect to both the skills and consumer dimensions of those tasks.

The second element of the health authority planning task is service planning, in which is included designing the shape of individual services and also the balance of services to be funded by the health authority as a whole. Health authorities will be required to make an assessment of the extent to which health and related needs are being met across the service system as a whole. As such, planning will need to maintain a strong inter-agency focus. Health authority planning will continue to relate to that of whichever agency is responsible for purchasing community care services in order to ensure that, for example, the transition to community-based provision is phased in with

the decommissioning of hospitals. Such inter-agency planning will also continue to be necessary to secure an appropriate level and mix of health and
other provision within new community-based models. Intersectoral collaboration will similarly be required in the planning of health promotion policies
and activities as set out in *The Health of the Nation* White Paper.

Perhaps even more crucial is the role which health authority planners will
play in relation to the providers of both acute and priority services. The central
issue here is how far purchasers will need access to specialist expertise about
service models and procedures they are considering for purchase. The extent
to which the reforms create a purchaser- or a provider-driven market will turn
on the respective capacity of the health authorities to purchase what they
define as necessary to meet need and of providers to determine what they
will supply. Where do the community care reforms fit in?

THE HEALTH REFORMS AND COMMUNITY CARE

The Griffiths report on community care (1988, para 4.12) argued that 'acute
hospitals and community care are complementary'. The absence of any
recognition of this interdependence, or, indeed, of community care as a serious
agenda item for the new model NHS, is one of the more remarkable omissions
from the NHS White Paper and much of the subsequent thinking about the
health care reforms. Ministers have chosen to review the future management
of community care and of acute health services sequentially rather than in
tandem and, implicitly if not explicitly, to view the latter as being of greater
importance.

The government's delay in responding to the report of Griffiths' inquiry
into community care has been well documented elsewhere (Hunter and
Wistow 1987). Somewhat ironically, the NHS White Paper, which made no
mention of community care, served to hasten the need for a response to the
Griffiths report. It became the missing piece in the grand strategy to improve
health care services. Speculation became rife on where lead responsibility for
community care services would go. Moreover, detailed work on the NHS
proposals was being severely hampered by the deafening silence on community care. When the government did finally respond to the Griffiths report it
conceded that its community care policy had not been spectacular in respect
of progress made and that in particular 'the rapid growth of residential and
nursing home care has been unplanned and largely based on the availability
of social security benefits'. While not altering the nature or responsibilities of
community health services, the government accepted that 'the best way
forward would be to build on local authorities' existing responsibilities'.
However, the government's approach has not avoided considerable uncertainty as to what respectively remain health service and local authority
responsibilities.

The decision to phase in the community care reforms over a period of three
years between 1991 and 1993 has only served to fuel anxiety about their likely
outcome and the government's faith in its own policy. With reform of local
government now underway with all that this implies for the future location
of social services and for the emergence of common boundaries between

health and local authorities, it becomes decidedly unclear as to where responsibility for community care will finally end up. Few observers believe the present solution to be stable or sustainable for long.

There is no disputing the valiant attempts being made by many local and health authorities to get on with the job and to avoid becoming victims of yet another outbreak of 'planning blight'. But far from the thrust of policy being on course, as Ministers would have us believe, there is growing concern about the destination of the reforms. If the policy itself is looking increasingly precarious, then the activity surrounding implementation will cease to have any real meaning. Perhaps in recognition of these concerns, Ministers are insisting that the reforms represent a programme of change for a decade and that a gradualist approach will prevail. Contrary to expectations there was no 'big bang' on 1 April 1993 (Department of Health 1992a). It is also possible to detect a shift in the NHS's stance with the NHSME emphasising that health authorities and provider units cannot afford to ignore the community care changes (Department of Health 1992b).

But observers continue to speculate on the longer term. Although considered and dismissed by Griffiths in his review of community care, the notion of integrated primary health and social care agencies could be resurrected and would seem attractive at a time when, in England, many Family Health Services Authorities are assuming responsibility for community health services. In addition, as of 1 April 1993 GP fundholders are now able to purchase community health services. It might seem logical to bring social care provision under the control of such authorities. Indeed, there are experiments beginning which take service development one step further along this route. In one area, for example, local GP practices will act as the gateway, i.e. serving as a one-stop shop, into a range of health and social care provision.

Another option which has begun to receive public attention is taking community care into the NHS and putting it under the control of the new purchasing authorities at district level. This option was particularly attractive to Regional Health Authorities in England during the interregnum between the appearance of the Griffiths report and the government's response to it. The option was rejected on the grounds that the NHS was undergoing sufficient turbulence arising from its own reforms. But if the present changes in community care are not going to come fully 'on stream' for several years it could be argued that many of the present changes in the NHS will have begun to bed down by then and that it could assume responsibility for community care.

The NHS is already directly involved in the community care reforms in at least two respects: the production, in collaboration with local authority social services departments (SWDs in Scotland), of community care plans which in some areas are taking the form of integrated single plans; and the 'triggering' of the specific grant for the development of social care services for people with a mental illness. The grant, which became available from 1 April 1991, is for social care agreed by social services and the appropriate health authority. The onus is on SSDs to agree with the health authorities, and if necessary FHSAs, what social care services should be funded. Once a formal agreement has been reached and confirmed to the Regional Health Authority in each case, the

RHA will trigger payment by notifying the Department of Health who will pay the local authority direct. In Scotland, the arrangements are slightly different in that the regional role will be undertaken by the Scottish Office which will devolve decisions on expenditure to health and local authorities. This mechanism gives the NHS a measure of control over the development of social care in respect of a particular care group, which does not apply to other groups. If it is decided that the NHS should have a greater say over the development of community care services, if only to ensure that its own reforms do not come unstuck, then conceivably this specific grant mechanism could be applied more widely. Such a move would have the effect of blunting further the lead responsibility for community care granted local authorities (and feared by many health authorities) but would avoid the need for major structural surgery. While not a long-term solution, it could have considerable short-term appeal to those anxious about local government's capacity to deliver.

The problem with all this intense speculation over what precisely the government's policy is concerning community care is that it diverts attention and makes developments difficult to plan, finance and implement because no one dare do so with any confidence. Managing uncertainty is one thing. Managing political vacillation on a grand scale is quite another. Whether it is a case of 'holding the line' as Ministers and officials in the Department of Health insist or a new policy for community care will be fashioned which, while not excluding local government altogether, will result in a very different organisational configuration from that set out in the community care White Paper, *Caring for People*, is hard to say. It is too early to judge the issue but it seems that the government is quite prepared to experiment with other ways of bringing together primary care, social care and health care – ways which do not necessarily involve local authorities retaining their lead responsibility. On the other hand, the announcement of the amount of money to be transferred to local authorities from income support does demonstrate the government's commitment to its own policy.

In the longer run, there are serious questions to be raised about the issue of continuing or long-term care within the NHS. Long-term care is increasingly being seen as social rather than health care and therefore not the responsibility of the NHS. Health authorities have, against the specific instructions of the NHSME, been closing continuing care beds and generally withdrawing from this sector (Department of Health 1992b). Budgets in long-term care have been raided to support or develop acute services. Once social security funds are transferred to local authorities and decisions on assessment for services are transferred to social workers and a new breed of care managers, it will almost certainly become more difficult for the NHS to discharge patients into nursing home facilities. Decisions about who will be able to get access to care will be taken by social workers rather than by health care providers, except in respect of mentally ill people, where the care programme approach is centred on the consultant psychiatrist retaining a pivotal role.

A further area of concern and speculation is the future of community services and NHS trusts. The issue is not one confined to community health service trusts but to all NHS Trusts. It will be essential for acute hospitals to be able to discharge patients promptly into the community if they are to maintain appropriate levels of patient throughput and income generation. It will not be in the interests of hospitals to have patients languishing in beds beyond their need for specific health services. As soon as their needs become social, rather than health, hospital trusts will be anxious to discharge such patients into the community. Under the new arrangements, they will be dependent upon local authority social services to make decisions about taking people into care. Many trusts feel that this will mean unnecessary delay and a possible silting up of their beds. Trusts are, therefore, looking for ways of providing their own community services by adopting an outreach, or in reach, approach, thereby enabling them to have control over discharge arrangements for patients requiring care. For local authorities, strapped for cash, it will be in their interests to give most attention to people in need of support who are already living in the community, rather than attend to the needs of those individuals who are in hospital but who may be better provided for in the community. Local authorities, while sympathising with their plight, will take the view that if such people are in hospital then they are at least getting some form of support and care, which will not be the case in respect of those living in the community who are lacking any support. Difficult decisions will need to be taken in respect of priorities and the allocation of resources. In this situation it is virtually certain that the NHS will not be able to withdraw from any involvement in community care even if it would like to. This is certainly the strongly held view of the NHS Management Executive which sees it as vitally important that health authorities get involved in community care issues and open a dialogue with their local authorities if they have not already entered into one.

REFERENCES

Audit Commission (1986) *Making a Reality of Community Care*. London: HMSO.

Audit Commission (1992) *The Community Revolution: Personal Social Services and Community Care*. London: HMSO.

Department of Health (1992a) Community care reforms. *Caring for People*, Issue No. 10. London: DoH.

Department of Health (1992b) *Implementing Caring for People*. EL(92)65. London: DoH.

Griffiths, R. (1988) *Community Care: Agenda for Action*. London: HMSO.

Harrison, S. (1988) *Managing the NHS: Shifting the Frontier?* London: Chapman and Hall.

Harrison, S., Hunter, D.J., Johnston, I. and Wistow, G. (1989) *Competing for Health: A Commentary on the NHS Review*. Leeds: Nuffield Institute for Health Services Studies.

Harrison, S., Hunter, D.J. and Pollitt, C. (1990) *The Dynamics of British Health Policy*. London: Unwin Hyman.

Harrison, S. and Wistow, G. (1992) The purchaser–provider split in English health care: towards explicit rationing. *Policy and Politics, 20*, No. 2.

Hunter, D.J. (1980) *Coping With Uncertainty: Policy and Politics in the NHS*. Chichester: John Wiley and Sons.

Hunter, D.J. and Wistow, G. (1987) *Community Care in Britain: Variations on a Theme*. London: King's Fund.

King's Fund Institute (1989) *Managed Competition: A New Approach to Health Care in Britain*. Briefing Paper 9. London: King's Fund Institute.

Klein, R. (1989) *The Politics of the NHS. Second edition*. London: Longman.

NHS Management Executive (1991) *Local Voices: The Views of Local People in Purchasing for Health*. London: NHSME.

NHS Management Executive (1992) *NHS Reforms: The First Six Months*. London: NHSME.

Rowbottom, J. (1992) *Seamless Services – A Stitch in Time: Care in the Community*. London: Institute of Health Services Management.

Scottish Home and Health Department (1991) *The Functions and Structure of Health Boards*. NHS Circular No. 1991(GEN)2. Edinburgh: SHHD.

The Scottish Office (1991) *Framework for Action*. The NHS in Scotland. Edinburgh: The Scottish Office.

Social Services Committee (1989) *Resourcing the NHS: The Government's Plans for the Future of the NHS, Eighth Report, Session 1988–89*. London: HMSO.

Sykes, W., Collins, M., Hunter, D.J., Popay, J. and Williams, G. (1992) *Listening to Local Voices: A Guide to Research Methods*. Leeds: Nuffield Institute for Health Services Studies and Public Health Resource Centre.

CHAPTER 3

Community Care Futures
Inter-Agency Relationships – Stability or Continuing Change?

Gerald Wistow

INTRODUCTION

Ministers have consistently emphasised that the implementation of the community care changes depends fundamentally upon improved inter-agency working. For example, the importance of 'partnership' was one of the three core themes of the then Secretary of State's address to the 1991 Social Services Conference. As he underlined, 'Caring for people puts a premium on health and local authorities working together effectively' (Waldegrave 1991a). Moreover, his predecessor had argued that the government's new framework for the organisation and delivery of community care would make such interservice coordination easier to achieve (Clarke 1989). This paper starts from that framework and analyses the extent to which it is likely to meet such a goal. It then moves on to consider possible developments in patterns of interservice relationships in the context of the NHS as well as the community care changes which began to be implemented in April 1991. Relatively little attention is given to inter-agency relationships with users, voluntary organisations and the private sector: rather, the intention is to explore the relative stability of the meta-organisational framework within which relationships with non-statutory interests must necessarily be organised and conducted.

THE NEW CONTEXT FOR INTER-AGENCY WORKING

It is universally recognised that joint working of all kinds has been an area of major disappointment and failure in the recent history of community care. Compared with the, perhaps over-optimistic, expectations of the mid-seventies, achievements have been modest (Wistow 1988 pp.13–15, Secretaries of State 1989 para 6:9). Thus, the White Paper *Caring for People* aimed to provide a new context for inter-agency working based upon 'strengthened incentives and clearer responsibilities' (Secretaries of State 1989 para 6:1) and containing four essential characteristics.

1. Clarification of 'who does what' through the more explicit recognition of the distinction between health and social care as the basis for funding health and social services, respectively.

2. Allocation of responsibility to social services departments for ensuring that assessment and care management processes take place, and within a multi-disciplinary context where appropriate. This provision also implies the designation of individual responsibilities for specific individual cases.

3. Re-definition of joint planning through an emphasis on outcomes (i.e. results) rather than machinery. The two key steps emphasised here were the simplification of joint planning machinery and the substitution of specific planning agreements for generalised joint plans. A clear statement of the outcomes for users and carers that such planning agreements were intended to secure was also provided by the White Paper.

4. Strengthened financial incentives for joint working through the transfer of social security funds to social services departments and the creation of new specific grants.

It may be argued that the differences between the new and the old frameworks for collaboration are less than substantial. For example, the distinction be-tween health and social care is neither straightforward in practice nor is it immune from the influence of financial pressures which encourage health and local authorities to define their respective responsibilities as narrowly as possible (Wistow 1990a). Nor is it clear how the institution of assessment and care management processes will, by themselves, remove or erode the differ-ences in professional perspectives and status which have bedeviled multi-dis-ciplinary working in the past. Moreover, the distinction between health and social care purchasing responsibilities does not extend to nursing home care (see below). In addition, that distinction does not apply to provider functions: NHS units and trusts are empowered to provide social care; by contrast, local authorities may not provide health care. Overall, then, there are grounds for questioning whether the new framework for inter-agency working remains closer to what Griffiths (1988) called the 'discredited refuge of exhorting collaboration' rather than his own framework for ensuring that it was nor-mally present. More particularly, it remains to be seen whether the rejection of Griffiths' proposals to link resource allocation to the submission of com-munity care plans will prove to be an especially serious weakness.

There is, however, another side to this balance sheet. The White Paper proposals provided stronger financial incentives for joint working, together with a more systematic framework for planning and monitoring than has hitherto existed. The transfer of social security funds increases the incentive for health authorities to work with social services departments in order to retain access to such resources. Unilateral care in the community develop-ments and early discharge procedures from acute beds using the private and voluntary sectors will be much less likely unless health authorities use their own resources to fund such initiatives.

As a result, therefore, social services have been dealt an important new bargaining card in their relationships with the NHS. Moreover, health and local authorities are operating under new obligations to produce community care plans and will be subject to a common national and regional monitoring process which will, in part, be concerned to establish how effectively they are working together.

The requirement to consult on and publish such plans may provide further external pressures on authorities to work together. At the same time, the move towards a commissioning/enabling role for both health and local authorities can be expected to encourage a stronger sense of common interest in identifying the needs of a shared population and ensuring that those needs are appropriately met. In all of these respects, therefore, there does seem to be real potential for improving the quality of joint working. Moreover, the Audit Commission has argued that the shift from provider-centred to needs-led services will itself create pressures for closer coordination:

> as authorities go back to basics it will be necessary for them to do so together... it will simply not be possible for authorities to work out what they are going to do unilaterally without regard for the actions of others. There are too many potential gaps and overlaps. (Audit Commission 1992 para 59)

Whether or not that prediction proves to be well-founded, the potential influence of another factor ought not to be neglected: the last fifteen years' experience of collaboration enables health and local authorities to be better prepared for their new roles than they were in the mid-seventies. The record since then has not been uniformly poor and the degree of learning which has taken place can easily be overlooked in the disappointment with progress overall (Wistow 1990b). Indeed, it is already possible to detect a renewed understanding of the importance of inter-agency working and the sense that the White Paper did at least provide an opportunity for a fresh start. For example, a common theme in responses to the Department of Health's draft policy guidance during mid-1990 was the need to give much greater emphasis to the importance of joint working. There is some evidence which suggests that the requirement to produce community care plans has been accompanied by a revitalisation of inter-agency planning arrangements (Wistow, Swift and Hallas 1991). This is a significant achievement. However, it is easier to establish planning mechanisms and secure in principle agreements about the future of cross-boundary planning than to reach agreement about funding and service responsibilities. As is argued below, it is only now that some of the real tensions inherent in the new arrangements are becoming more evident.

For all these reasons, therefore, it is unclear whether the new framework created by the White Paper, the 1990 Act and the subsequent policy and practice guidance will in fact make inter-agency coordination easier to achieve. Such uncertainties are, however, now beginning to be overtaken by even more fundamental ones about whether the White Paper has proved to be merely the beginning, rather than the end, of a process of organisational change. The remainder of this paper examines whether the White Paper and Act provide a stable framework within which to develop and extend inter-agency relationships or whether that framework will itself be superseded by further change in structures and service responsibilities.

A STABLE OR CHANGING FRAMEWORK FOR INTER-AGENCY RELATIONSHIPS?

Four major sources of uncertainty about the future of the new community care framework may be identified:

- lingering doubts about whether the changes implied by the Act will be implemented in full

- tensions at the interface of acute and community care which are now becoming more fully apparent in the wake of the implementation of the Act

- an emerging process of rolling structural change in the NHS

- the promise of structural change in local government.

The implications of each of these areas of uncertainty for future community care arrangements are considered below.

Will the Community Care Changes be Implemented?

Ministers and the Department repeatedly emphasised their commitment to implement *Caring for People* in full and by April 1993 (see, for example, Waldegrave 1991a and 1991b). However, at least some health and local authorities retained a degree of scepticism about this commitment, particularly following the reluctance of central government to add to the financial responsibilities of local government in 1990. Such doubts were reinforced by the subsequent announcement of proposals for major change in local government finance and organisation. They were not been allayed by the apparently slow progress in agreeing how funds will be transferred from the Social Security budget. Although officials had been working on this issue for a year, Mrs Bottomley told the Social Security Committee in June 1991 that it was still too early to make final decisions on, for example, the balance between the housing and care elements of the new arrangements (House of Commons, 1991a Q252). Since then, however, an interdepartmental group of officials and representatives of the local authority associations has been created to establish 'the algebra but not the arithmetic' of the social security transfers and this has led to a fuller flow of information and debate around such issues.

While it would be wrong to over-emphasise the importance of doubts about the full implementation of the proposals of the White Paper, it would also to be wrong to ignore the consequences of such feelings for the strength of commitment to the community care changes. With so many change agendas to manage, local authorities – and even more especially health authorities – might be forgiven for giving relatively less weight to change about which the centre's commitment is in question. It would, however, be shortsighted of local authorities to allow continuing uncertainties about the transfer arrangements to prevent them from preparing even outline purchasing strategies from 1993–94 onwards. It is in their own interests, as well as those of users, to ensure that thinking is well-advanced on the broad parameters within which they will be making purchasing decision between sectors and services from April 1993. To that end, progress in establishing the algebra of the transfers could go a considerable way to creating more confidence about implementation.

Against this background, an important and welcome development in March 1992 was the issue of a joint letter by the Deputy Chief Executive of the NHs Management Executive and the Chief Inspector of the Social Services Inspectorate. This document not only reaffirmed that the government remained 'fully committed to the objectives of the *Caring for People* policy, but it also specified more explicitly what was required of authorities in the year up to the April 1993 implementation date (Foster and Laming 1992). Thus local and health authorities were notified of eight key tasks on which they would need to concentrate during 1992/93 in order to meet the requirements of the NHS and Community Care Act. This positive contribution to the change process was clearly designed to remove authorities' lingering doubts about the government's commitment to the 1993 implementation timetable, even though neither the algebra nor the arithmetic of the financial transfers could not yet be answered.

Will Implementation Encourage Instability in Inter-Agency Relations?

Because the funds transferred from the social security budget are not ring fenced, they may be allocated between different local government functions according to locally determined needs and priorities. Health authorities will, of course, have a direct interest in whether or not the funds are allocated wholly to community care; but it is not clear whether they will understand, or accept, the concept of local discretion which apparently lies at the heart of the government's decision not to ring fence the transfers. It must be anticipated, therefore, that local authorities will be criticised for diverting funds from community care into other areas of their responsibility just as local authorities have alleged that the NHs diverts resources from priority services to the acute sector. Thus, it is conceivable that the process of allocating social security resources to and within local government will, itself, not be conducive to promoting the mutual respect and understanding which the policy guidance rightly sees as the foundation of effective inter-agency relationships (Department of Health 1990 para 1:7).

A second and related issue is whether social services departments will perceive strong enough incentives to spend such increased funds as they do receive in ways which directly or indirectly support NHS objectives. The implementation of the 1989 Children Act in England and Wales alongside the community care changes has intensified competition for resources within social services departments, especially given the evidence of pressures on services to children and families. For example, increasing numbers of London (and at least some other) authorities were reported to be unable to allocate social workers to all children on their Child Abuse Registers (House of Commons 1991b). Moreover, conflicting demands have also become evident in the field of community care, itself. For example, in determining the balance of investment between institutional and home-based care, departments have to decide whether they are able and willing to meet demands for their services which originate in the NHS due to changing lengths of hospital stay and rates of hospitalisation. The experience of de-hospitalisation in the long-stay sector suggests that local authorities give greater priority to community-based need than that originating from the health service (Wistow 1987). Indeed, it was precisely this barrier to inter-agency collaboration which led to the introduction of the Care in the Community arrangements enabling resources to be transferred with patients moving from hospital to social care (DHSS 1983). That initiative was effectively overtaken by the use of social security payments to fund care in the community developments (see Audit Commission 1986, Glennerster and Korman 1990, Hardy, Wistow and Rhodes 1990). Such payments have also contributed to acute sector throughput, effectively removed the need for the NHS to invest in nursing home services beyond a pilot programme in three authorities, and have also helped to make possible an absolute reduction in geriatric bed numbers (Laing 1991).

Two new factors are now at work in this context; first, the de-hospitalisation of long-stay services is being followed by an increasingly rapid de-hospitalisation of acute services. Reduced lengths of stay, increased rates of day surgery and other developments are increasingly shifting the boundary between hospital and other forms of care (Marks 1991). Moreover, this process still has far to go. As Chapman (1991) noted, 'six years after... the College of Surgeons suggested that 50 per cent of all surgical procedures could be performed as day cases, the UK rate stands at 17 per cent, about one-third of the rate in Canada and the US'. The scope for increasing that rate was further identified by the Audit Commission (1991a) in what was, significantly, one of its first NHS studies. A subsequent study from the same source suggested that 'if all districts reduced their lengths of stay to those of the lowest 25 per cent (after allowing for the effect of age), and matched bed numbers more closely to their use, the current level of medical treatment in England could be provided with 27,000, or almost a third, fewer beds' (Audit Commission 1991b p.2).

The implementation of these recommendations on the use of acute medical beds can, therefore, be expected to place greater demands on community services. Indeed, all these developments in the acute sector necessarily have implications for the level of demand on both health and local authority services in the community. However, it is by no means clear that *Caring for People* gave sufficient attention to this increasingly important interface between acute and community care services. Rather, its focus was shaped by the policy concern to avoid 'unnecessary' admissions and expenditures on residential care and hence to target public resources on services which enable dependent individuals to live in their own homes. In short, its preoccupation was with the interface between residential and home-based care, thereby reflecting definitions of problems and solutions historically located within the personal social services rather than at their boundary with acute medical services.

A second, and closely related, issue is the degree of ambiguity surrounding responsibility for funding nursing home care under the terms of *Caring for People*. The White Paper refers to the responsibility of health authorities for purchasing 'continuous residential health care in parallel with the provision of nursing care by the independent health sector' (para 4.20). At the same time, its provisions meant that social services departments are now responsible for purchasing nursing as well as residential care from that independent sector with funds transferred from the social security system. Thus, there is apparently ample scope for confusion, if not conflict, about the nature and extent of the authorities' respective responsibilities for this function.

Significantly, the health and local authority associations each tended to emphasise the responsibility of the other service for funding nursing home care when giving evidence to the Health of Commons (1991b) Social Security Committee during the summer of 1991. Another example of the potential for disagreement is provided by the reported case of a District General Manager in North London who threatened to charge local authorities up to £130 a day for patients who do not receive medical care but remain in hospital because of the inadequacy of community services (Eaton 1991).

The same social security changes also raise questions about the viability of business planning in the NHS and thus the operation of the internal market. Such planning by provider units necessarily involves the making of implicit if not explicit assumptions about the level of services in the community. Early discharge from, as well as inappropriate admissions and readmissions to, acute hospital beds are all influenced by the adequacy and quality of such services. A survey conducted by Trent RHA found that 50 per cent of all admissions to private nursing homes and 28 per cent of all admissions to private residential homes were from NHS hospitals. The Department of Health suggested that among the 100,000 people who, under current funding arrangements, might be expected to enter publicly funded long-stay residential or nursing home care in England during 1993/4, 40,000 would have been discharged from hospitals (Laming 1992).

As was argued above, in a difficult financial climate, it is not clear what, if any, incentives local authorities will perceive to meet the costs of nursing or residential home care for such former patients. They do not appear to be under a statutory obligation to do so and there are likely to be many other calls on the resources transferred from the social security budget. Yet, the National Association of Health Authorities and Trusts (1991) has argued that private and voluntary nursing home provision 'now represents a vital component of the mixed economy of health care. Were it to fail the NHS would not... be in a position to cater, in hospital beds, for those displaced from nursing homes.'

As the above analysis demonstrates, there is considerable scope for tension between the acute sector and personal social services now that the social security changes have taken effect. As a result, hospital discharge procedures promise to be an area with high potential for conflict and cost-shunting strategies between health and local authorities. Unless firmly addressed, the spill-over consequences from this issue seem likely to threaten the establishment of productive inter-agency relationships on a broader front. The government's response has been to urge 'a smooth transition' from the existing to the new arrangements, most particularly by regarding 'the current broad pattern of funding through social security support... as an implied commitment for 1993–94 by the local authority in respect of new clients requiring residential or nursing home care after April 1993' (Foster and Laming 1992). This emphasis on a managed process of change is an important development, but two uncertainties remain. First, how authorities will nego- tiate a path from the existing service pattern towards one based on individual needs assessment while maintaining supplier confidence and thus continuity of care for those currently in the service system. The social care market is an 'external' rather than an internal market and less susceptible to control. Moreover, social services departments have little expertise in, or even knowl- edge of, market management (Wistow, Knapp, Hardy and Allen 1992). Unless any variations in demand, such as the reduction of institutional services in favour of community based care, are managed with care, there are real dangers of market failure. A gradual transition to new patterns of care is designed to reassure independent sector proprietors that the supply of fund- ing will not suddenly dry up and, perhaps, allow them time to diversify into other areas such as day and domiciliary services.

A second, and related, area of uncertainty is whether health and local authorities will be able to make – and keep – agreements to use the social security transfers in ways suggested by the guidance. Although the arrange- ments for 'smooth transition' were monitored on a six-monthly basis by RHAs and the Social Services Inspectorate, it remains to be seen whether present arrangements will overcome the influence of budgetary pressures and com- peting agency priorities as countervailing forces at local level to central requirements. Moreover, the apparent duplication of responsibilities for pur- chasing long-term care remains to be addressed. The Parliamentary Under Secretary for Health did refuse early in 1992 to permit the closure of long-stay beds in Northumberland on the grounds that DHAs had purchasing respon- sibilities for such care under para 4.20 of *Caring for People* to which we referred above (Dobson 1992). Although this is a potentially significant precedent, the Foster/Laming letter did not refer explicitly to NHS purchasing responsibili- ties in this field. However, it did seek to prevent any further unilateral withdrawal by the NHS from the funding and provision of long-term care: 'we would not expect a health or local authority to change the current (March 1992) pattern of provision or the commitment which each is making except on the basis of prior agreement which should be properly reflected in their community care plans' (Foster and Laming 1992).

It would appear, therefore, that the respective purchasing responsibilities of health and local authorities in this field have been left to local negotiation, with the Department of Health drawing a line at March 1992 service patterns. Inevitably, this approach will be more readily accepted by health authorities and appear less welcome to local authorities in those localities where the NHS withdrawal from long-term care has proceeded furthest.

What Are the Implications of Continuing Change in the NHS?

It is already clear that the health reforms have initiated an unfolding process of structural change in the NHS. While this process originates in diverse NHS agendas, it is beginning to move in directions with potentially significant consequences for the organisation and management of community care. *Working for Patients* raised the prospect of mergers between DHAs and between DHAs and FHSAs. The former kind of merger has already taken place in order to maximise purchasing power as well as to use purchasing skills more effectively (*Health Service Journal*, 5th April 1990 and 19th September 1991). The wish to secure coterminosity with local authority boundaries is another factor supporting moves towards merger or joint purchasing between health authorities. In some localities (for example Leeds) authority mergers have already taken effect; in others (for example North Yorkshire and South East London) purchasing consortia were formed and constituent districts applied for whole district Trust status. Mergers between FHSAs and DHAs would require primary legislation. However, this does not preclude FHSA involvement in consortia arrangements with DHAs or the appointment (as in Doncaster) of the same person to serve as both DHA general manager and FHSA chief executive. The first study of joint purchasing cautioned against assuming that they should necessarily lead to mergers between DHAs. It also emphasised the need to give greater priority to locality purchasing in order to prevent 'remoteness and insensitivity on the part of those now charged with acting as champions of the people' (Ham and Heginbotham 1991 p.31). The Audit Commission (1992 paras 57–58) has seen the development of consortia arrangements as an opportunity to address the problems caused by the lack of boundary coterminosity between existing DHAs and SSDs. It should be noted, however, in view of the trend towards decentralised budgeting in Social Services Departments, that there are potential difficulties for collaboration if health authorities aggregate purchasing functions upwards while local authorities disaggregate them downwards.

Figure 3.1 Nursing in the Community: Management and Organisation Models

1. 'Stand alone' community trust or DMU
2. Locality management/neighbourhood nursing
3. Expanded FHSA or primary health care authority
4. Vertical integration or outreach
5. Primary health care team – GP managed

Alongside this redrawing of the NHS map are proposals for more fundamental reconfigurations of purchasing responsibilities. These were contained in the Roy report on the future of community nursing, published in December 1990, and the Foster report on family health service authorities, published in January 1991. Each of them identifies a number of options for structural change within the NHS which are summarised in Figures 3.1 and 3.2. This is not the place the discuss them in detail. However, the proposals do raise a number of issues relevant not only to the future organisation of primary and community health services but also to the organisation of community care, to the role of the personal social services and to that of local government more generally. They do, of course, begin from organisation needs and agendas within the NHS, including: the need to clarify the role of community health services and community nurses; the importance of integrating primary and secondary care; the clarification – and potential expansion – of the FHSA role; the need to strengthen primary and community health service contributions to health promotion and illness prevention; and the importance of strengthening purchasing functions in the NHS.

Figure 3.2 FHSA's – Today's and Tomorrow's Priorities:
Future Models

A. 'Dynamic status quo'

   • builds on strengths of existing DHA/FHSA arrangements

B. Health care purchasing organisation/Family health services provided

   • unified purchasing authority and family health service provider units/trusts, including responsibility for contractor management

C. Unified Commissioning

   • Single purchasing agency for HCHS and primary health care, including responsibility for contractor management (provider units include Social Care Management Units)

D. Primary health care authority

   • combines FHS with community health services purchasing, together with contractor management. Comprehensive health and social care (purchasing) organisations might ultimately be envisaged

---

At the same time, however, the organisational models identified in these reports have important implications for the personal social services and local government. At the most mundane level, any re-ordering of purchasing functions will redefine the agencies with which local authorities must relate in the community care planning and commissioning processes. At the furthest extreme, they could raise questions about the continuing existence of unified local authority social services departments on the Seebohm model. For example, under the 'expanded FHSA model' the Roy report (1990 p.13) raises the possibility of establishing in the longer term 'full-scale primary health care authorities (possibly including local authority functions).' Similarly, the Foster report's 'unified commissioning model' includes, but does not define, 'social care management units' within its list of providers. In addition the same report suggests that its 'primary health care authority' model might ultimately evolve into comprehensive health and social care purchasing organisations.

Notwithstanding these proposals, and without pre-judging their respective advantages or disadvantages, it is not clear that the reports have been discussed widely with or within local government. The Roy report was distributed to directors of social services but the Foster report (1991) sees RHAs, the Institute of Health Services Managers and the National Association of Health Authorities and Trusts as the focal point for discussion of its options and RHAs are expected to feed back responses to the centre. It is questionable, therefore, how much discussion there has been of the possible implications for local government of such proposals or, indeed, how much awareness there is of their content. Senior managers in social services departments are, however, undoubtedly conscious that the integration of health and social care purchasing functions is the logical and not undesirable consequence of making the purchaser/provider split; and some, at least privately, would welcome the freedom from local political control which would result if that process of integration took place within the NHS. The alternative of unifying health and social care purchasing responsibilities within unitary local authorities (Harrison *et al.* 1991) has yet to emerge as an option for serious consideration. However, the development of a broadly based strategy for health, as represented in *The Health of the Nation*, can be expected to extend an awareness about the contribution of local authority functions to a health gain strategy, including those such as housing and environmental health which, historically, have had a greater impact on health status than personal medicine (McKeown 1976, Royal Commission 1979). In the future, collaboration agendas are likely to be concerned with 'joint prevention' (Wistow 1982) no less than joint planning. Thus the shift towards a positive health strategy may be seen as another pressure towards closer cooperation between the NHS and local government.

What Future for Local Government?

Possible changes to the structure and finance of local government constitute a final source of uncertainty in the organisational context for community care. As in the health service, though in a more limited way, a process of organic change is already under way through the amalgamation of personal social services and housing functions. Such mergers are of crucial relevance to community care policies based on 'ordinary life' principles and it will be interesting to see how far the community care planning process identifies the importance of housing to high quality services consistent with the values and principles of the White Paper.

In the slightly longer term, it appears that local government will be reconstituted on the basis of the unitary authority model; the issue still to be resolved at local level is whether such authorities should be based on existing county councils, existing districts, or combinations of districts. As with NHS structural changes, this process will raise the issue of coterminosity because of the possibility that as NHS purchasing functions are amalgamated up to the level of the current social services authorities, the latter may be broken down into components corresponding, in some places, to existing health districts (see, for example, Coopers and Lybrand Deloitte 1992). Organisational consistency and coherence have rarely been features of the history of community care but the case for common boundaries, at least for purchasing agencies, should be taken into account in decisions to restructure both health and local authorities.

Finally, it might be observed that the initiative for change not only lies with the centre, as might be expected, but the role of local government has been a largely passive one. Yet, following the local management of schools initiative and the expected increase in numbers of schools applying for 'grant maintained' status, social services will be the last major service providing responsibility left to local government. Even so, local authority interests do not appear to have reacted with any degree of vigour to the proposals for NHS change which have such potentially important consequences for the future of the personal social services. The integrated community services model based on local authorities remains to be developed or advocated. Similarly, the implications of a health gain strategy for local authority involvement do not appear to have been positively taken up. If there is a case for preserving the local government role in the field of health and community care, it has yet to be stated. Yet, paradoxically, the *Caring for People* philosophy provides ample justification for such a statement, as we identify below.

THE TEMPLATE FOR ORGANISATIONAL CHANGE

If it is accepted that the White Paper's framework for inter-agency responsibilities and collaboration is an unstable one and likely to be the subject of further organisational change, what criteria should determine any future configuration of agency responsibilities? The logic of the White Paper was to start with the philosophy and objectives of community care rather than the interests of organisations and providers: as with the planning and delivery of care to individuals, the organisation of services should be needs-led rather than service-driven. Fortunately, *Caring for People* contains a clear statement of overarching aims (i.e. the promotion of choice and independence) and of more specific policy goals:

> ... enabling people to live as independently as possible in the community is at the heart of community care. (para 2.1)

> Community care means providing the right level of intervention and support to enable people to achieve maximum independence and control over their own lives. (para 2.2)

> Social care and practical assistance with daily living are key components of good quality community care... suitable good quality housing is essential and the availability of day care, respite care, leisure facilities and employment and educational opportunities will all improve the quality of life enjoyed by a person with care needs. (para 2.4)

Two consequences flow from this description of community care as the means of enabling people 'to live as normal a life as possible' (para. 1.8) in their own local communities. First, health care should be seen as part of a range of services which contribute to good quality community care; and, conversely, community care is rather more than an adjunct to the efficient operation of health services. The implication here is that the needs of the NHS should not dictate the structure of purchaser and provider functions for community care. This is not to say that no adjustments in responsibilities are required; it is questionable whether the White Paper's framework gave sufficient attention to the need for continuity of care following discharge from hospital or for ensuring cost effectiveness in the use of health service resources (see below).

The second consequence is that community care should be regarded as a corporate responsibility of local government and not merely as the province of the personal social services. The philosophy outlined by the White Paper can be realised only by extending the role of, and access to, mainstream services. Perhaps its most fundamental – and challenging – implications are for established social services functions as traditional residential care is replaced by housing-based alternatives and much day care is superseded by widening opportunities for leisure, education and employment. Eventually, an enabling social services department may come to be seen as one which not only stimulates a greater variety of providers but also one which enables individuals to use a much wider range of services than hitherto provided within the personal social services. More immediately, however, the realisation of the White Paper's underlying philosophy and service principles depends upon a more corporate commitment to community care than has been generally evident to date. For example, the Chief Social Services Inspector recorded his disappointment that a genuine authority-wide response to care in the community was evident in only a few areas and that there was little involvement by housing departments and associations in the run up to April 1993 (Laming 1992 para 4.8–4.9). Since April, it has become clear that numerous obstacles still inhibit participation by housing agencies. This has prompted recent calls for the integration of housing and social services (Bamford 1993).

Both the above considerations suggest the need to be cautious of placing too much weight too quickly on organisational solutions which originate in the needs of the NHS, however legitimate and important such factors are in the meeting of individual need and in securing the cost-effective use of NHS resources. What is required, therefore, is a broad-based review which gives due regard to NHS priorities and needs but does so within that wider concept of community care that the White Paper advanced.

STRUCTURING INTER-AGENCY RELATIONSHIPS:
OPTIONS FOR THE FUTURE

Three possible approaches to the structuring of inter-agency relationships may be drawn from the analysis in this paper of futures for community care:

(i) Unification

(ii) Redefinition

(iii) Collaboration.

In the language of the purchaser/provider split, these approaches might be better described as: the integration of health and social care purchasing (or commissioning) functions; redrawing the boundaries of purchasing responsibilities for health and social care, respectively; and the development of joint purchasing arrangements.

The first approach involves unifying health and social care budgets within a single management structure. Such unification might be more or less comprehensive in terms of the extent to which it encompassed responsibilities for hospital, community and primary health care, on the one hand, and personal social services, housing and other local authority functions on the other. It might also take place either within a framework of appointed or of locally elected authorities. Possible permutations range from combining all health and social care purchasing functions within an appointed health authority or elected local authority to the unification of a restricted number of such functions within NHS or local government structures (for example community health and/or primary care and/or personal social services). Whatever organisational designs emerged as a result of this process, their principal purpose would be to reduce the scope for cost shunting between separate agency budgets and to increase opportunities for substitution between different kinds of health and social care inputs.

A second approach would be to redefine the responsibilities of the NHS and local authorities as an act of explicit policy. In practice, the boundaries of health and social care have been progressively redrawn over time through a process of implicit policy making as services have been developed outside the hospital sector. Most recently, this process of implicit boundary redefinition has been fuelled by, on the one hand, the influence of cost improvement pressures to reduce hospital stay and, on the other hand, the unplanned growth of social security support for residential and nursing home care. These two developments have combined with the preparedness of social services departments' residential, day and domiciliary services to accept responsibility for people with increasing levels of dependency in order to prevent or delay moves into other care settings. The result has been a spontaneous rather than a structured and agreed process of adjustment in the responsibilities of health and social care agencies. Its consequence has been to shift the boundary between health and social care responsibilities strongly towards the latter. In effect, social services departments are not only routinely meeting long-term care needs which have inappropriately been met by the health service in the past but also routinely dealing with levels of dependency in which health needs are clearly an element. To take but one example, social services residential and domiciliary services regularly meet the needs of people suffering from incontinence, a condition which would seem more generally to be associated with health than social causes.

Against this background, the 1993 social security changes have raised the possibility of further exacerbating inter-agency tensions and conflicts, as was argued above. A possible route to defusing such conflicts would involve addressing directly this secular trend in the shift between agency responsibilities and boundaries with the intention of ensuring that the NHS should remain responsible for at least the immediate consequences of changes in clinical practice. In other words, the health service in general and the hospital sector more particularly should be required 'to consume its own fire'. The underlying principle of this approach would be to remove the incentive for cost-shunting from hospital to social (and community/primary health) care by unifying budgetary responsibility for in-patient, and, for a specified period, after care services. The latter period might be specified in relatively general terms or calculated more systematically using disease categories/DRGs as a basis for predicting the likely pattern of need for post-discharge care. While such care would be funded through the NHS, hospitals could subcontract with whatever agencies could provide such care appropriately and cost-effectively within the health, local authority and independent sectors. This concept would clearly need to be explored further and the location of responsibility for long-term care would also require further consideration, particularly with regard to whether budgets for the nursing and residential care sectors should be combined or separate. It is also implicit in this approach that the NHS would need funding appropriate to the range of responsibilities suggested here. However, this approach would have the advantage of securing greater continuity of care at the point of hospital discharge where so many difficulties have occurred in the past, not least because of the pressures to secure rapid throughput which dictate against time-consuming assessments of need.

However far budgets are unified or the responsibilities of individual agencies redefined and clarified, some degree of interface between health and other agencies will remain to be managed. In other words, some degree of joint working is likely to be necessary, no matter what, structural reorganisations take place. Thus, the third possible approach identified here is for collaboration between health and social care agencies, whether this be of a residual nature or of the substantial kind required by the current allocation of responsibilities of health and local authorities. Within the current framework, it is an approach which implies the development of joint budgets and joint commissioning arrangements. Such arrangements will not be straightforward given the differences in the interpretation of commissioning within health and local authorities and especially in the level at which the purchaser/provider split is being made in each service. Thus frontline professionals are potentially purchasers in social services departments but providers in the NHS. Such differences are likely to be particularly problematical in the context of multidisciplinary assessments (see Brown, Flynn and Wistow 1992 for a discussion of the implications of the NHS community care reforms for joint working in the field of learning disabilities).

The Audit Commission (1992 para 78) proposed a model of integrated purchasing through the adoption of care management in the NHS as a means of overcoming such potential problems. Given the difficulties of establishing collaboration at the strategic management level in the past, its effectiveness will depend crucially upon the extent to which the new framework for joint working does prove to contain stronger incentives and opportunities than that which it is replacing. As was argued above, there are indications of at least initial progress being made. It is also at least implicit in the argument advanced here that some 'fine tuning' of the new arrangements is likely to prove necessary if the potential for a new start to inter-agency relationships is to be fully realised. Unless such steps are taken, the new arrangements may not be able to sustain the weight placed upon them. In those circumstances, the demand for some form of budgetary and organisational integration seems likely to grow. Whatever approach is taken, however, it will be essential to take into account the values and principles of *Caring for People* if the major policy advances contained within that document are to be realised in practice.

CONCLUSION

There is always a tendency to look towards the 'next reorganisation' of health and social services, either because each major restructuring appears to leave behind an agenda of unfinished business or because, and against all the evidence of past experience, it appears to offer the possibility of resolving otherwise impervious problems. At the time of writing, it is impossible to do more than observe that the organisation and management of community services are subject to a process of unfolding change, whose end point is difficult to predict with certainty. Two points are clear, however. First, unless health and local authorities demonstrate the will and capacity to work together more constructively than in the past, there are likely to be strong pressures, especially within the NHS, towards unification rather than collaboration. The Chief Social Services Inspector has recently emphasised the need for fully agreed policies, practices and training arrangements to promote interagency collaboration (Social Services Inspectorate 1993). Second, the emphasis on user-centred services, which is one of the underpinnings of both the health and community care changes, demands a radically different approach to organisational design. As the Audit Commission (1992) has argued, 'organisations should follow needs as formulated by service commissioners – not the other way round' (para 79). That imperative should apply to the operation of the new framework for community care, no less than to any future arrangements which might subsequently be deemed necessary.

ACKNOWLEDGEMENT

An earlier version of this paper was delivered at a seminar on 'Community Care Futures' held at Cliveden in September 1991 and jointly sponsored by KPMG Management Consulting, Sheridan Systems Ltd and Bull UK. I am grateful for their permission to publish this revised version here.

REFERENCES

Audit Commission (1986) *Making a Reality of Community Care*. London: HMSO.

Audit Commission (1991a) *A Short Cut to Better Services: Day Surgery in England and Wales*. London: HMSO.

Audit Commission (1991b) *Lying in Wait: the Use of Medical Beds in Acute Hospitals*. London: HMSO.

Audit Commission (1992) *Community Care: Managing the Cascade of Change*. London: HMSO.

Bamford, T. (1993) 'Integration arguments'. *Community Care*, 30 September.

Brown, S., Flynn, M. and Wistow, G. (1992) *Back to the Future: Joint Working for People with Learning Disabilities*. Manchester and Leeds: National Development Team for People with Learning Disabilities and Nuffield Institute for Health Services Studies.

Chapman, R. (1991) It's better by day. *The Health Service Journal, 19 September*, pp.18–20.

Clarke, K. (1989) Secretary of State's Statement to Parliament on the Future Arrangements for Community Care. *Press Release 89/298*. London: Department of Health.

Coopers and Lybrand Deloitte (1992) Caring for the community: the role of local government. *The Review of Local Government Paper Number 9*. London: Association of County Councils.

Department of Health (1990) *Caring for People in the Next Decade and Beyond: Policy Guidance*. London: HMSO.

Department of Health and Social Security (1983) *Health Service Development: Care in the Community and Joint Finance, Circular HC(83)6/LAC(83)5*. London: HMSO.

Dobson, J. (1992) Confusion in the community. *Health Service Journal, February*, 11.

Eaton, L. (1991) Hospitals threaten £130 levy for 'Blocked Beds'. *Social Work Today, 25 July*, 5.

Foster, A. (1991) *Family Health Services Authorities: Today's and Tomorrow's Priorities*. London: NHS Management Executive.

Foster, A. and Laming, H. (1992) *Implementing Caring for People, EL(92)13/C1(92)10*. London: Department of Health.

Glennerster, H. and Korman, N. (1990) Success costs money. *Community Care, 20 April*, 30–31.

Griffiths, Sir R. (1988) *Community Care: Agenda for Action*. London: HMSO.

Ham, C. and Heginbotham, C. (1991) Purchasing together. *King's Fund College Papers*. London: King's Fund College.

Hardy, B., Wistow, G. and Rhodes, R.A.W. (1990) Policy networks and the implementation of community care policy for people with mental handicaps. *Journal of Social Policy, 19*, 2, 141–168.

Harrison, S., Hunter, D.J., Johnston, I.H., Nicholson, N., Thunhurst, C. and Wistow, G. (1991) *Health Before Health Policy, Social Policy Paper No. 4*. London: Institute for Public Policy Research.

House of Commons (1991a) *The Financing of Private Residential and Nursing Home Fees, Fourth Report of the Social Security Committee, Session 1990–91, HC121-II*. London: HMSO.

House of Commons (1991b) *Public Expenditure on Personal Social Services: Child Protection Services, Second Report from the Health Committee, Session 1990–91, HC570–I*. London: HMSO.

Laing, W. (1991) *Laing's Review of Private Healthcare 1990/91*. London: Laing and Buisson Publications.

Laming, H. (1992) Speech by Mr Herbert Laming (Chief Social Services Inspector) to the *Care Management and Assessment Seminar, London, 27 January 1992*. London: Social Services Inspectorate, Department of Health.

Marks, L. (1991) Home and hospital care: redrawing the boundaries. *King's Fund Institute Research Report No. 9*. London: King's Fund Institute.

McKeown, T. (1976) *The Role of Medicine: Dream, Mirage or Nemesis?* Oxford: The Nuffield Provincial Hospitals Trust.

National Association of Health Authorities and Trusts (1991). Evidence in House of Commons Social Services Committee. *The Financing of Private Residential and Nursing Home Fees, Fourth Report, Session 1990–91*. London: HMSO.

Roy, S. (1990) Nursing in the community. *Report of the NHS Management Executive Working Group on Nursing in the Community*. London: North West Thames RHA.

Royal Commission on the National Health Service (1979) *Report, Cmnd 7615*. London: HMSO.

Secretaries of State for Health, Social Security, Wales and Scotland (1989) *Caring for People: Community Care in the Next Decade and Beyond (CM 849)*. London: HMSO.

Social Services Inspectorate (1993) *Raising The Standard: Second Annual Report of the Chief Social Services Inspector 1992/93*. London: HMSO.

The Health Service Journal (1990) CHCs warn of merger dangers. *Health Service Journal, 5 April*, 5.

The Health Service Journal (1991) Primary care body on the cards. *Health Service Journal, 19 September*, 5.

Waldegrave, W. (1991a) Speech to *Social Services Conference, 27 September*.

Waldegrave, W. (1991b) Achieving the change, Speech to *Caring for People – Achieving the Change Conference*. London: Department of Health.

Wistow, G. (1982) Collaboration between health and local authorities: why is it necessary? *Social Policy and Administration*, 16, 1, 43–62.

Wistow, G. (1987) Joint finance: promoting a new balance of care in England?'. *International Journal of Social Psychiatry*, 33, 2, 83–91.

Wistow, G. (1988) Health and local authority collaboration: lessons and prospects. In G. Wistow and T. Brooks (eds) *Joint Planning and Joint Management*. London: Royal Institute of Public Administration.

Wistow, G. (1990a) Planning and collaboration in a mixed economy. In L. Wolstenholme, G. Wistow and D. Gilroy (eds) *Community Care in a Mixed Economy: Meeting the Challenge, Seminar Series 2*. London: Nuffield Institute for Health Services Studies.

Wistow, G. (1990b) *Community Care Planning: A Review of Past Experience and Future Imperatives, 'Caring for People' Implementation Document CC13*. London: Department of Health.

Wistow, G., Swift, J. and Hallas, J. (1991) Community care planning workshops. *Caring for People, No. 8*, 14–16. London: Department of Health.

Wistow, G., Knapp, M., Hardy, B. and Allen, C. (1992) *Social Care in a Mixed Economy*. Buckingham: Open University Press.

CHAPTER 4

Changing Services for People with Learning Disabilities

Philip Seed

INTRODUCTION

During the past 25 years the force of a social movement has brought a new quality of living to people with learning disabilities. A social movement has been defined as a collective enterprise to establish a new order of life (McLaughlin 1969). Changes that have taken place during this period in attitudes to, and services for, people with learning disabilities can usefully be viewed in this light.

Movements related to the development of services (or 'social service movements') are often characterised by the gap between rhetoric and practice, with over-ambitious claims and a tendency to oversimplify the issues. Social service movements typically go through phases from a heroic initial phase associated with charismatic personalities – e.g. Stanley Segal (1967), Sir Brian Rix, Peter Mittler (1979), Wolf Wolfensberger (1972) – to more routinised phases characterised by official regulations and procedures as innovative ideas become incorporated into the official practice guidelines and legislation such as the National Health and Care in the Community Act 1990.

It can, indeed, be claimed that the movement for better services for people with learning disabilities has influenced the vision for a better quality of care in the community generally. For example Community Mental Handicap Teams with key workers allocated to individual clients – representing a client needs approach – were in place ahead of similar practical schemes (as distinct from general calls for greater service coordination) for elderly people. Yet practice is uneven and often lags behind the best ideas (Glendinning 1986). Community Mental Handicap Teams, for example, have been very varied in what they have aimed to achieve and in how effective they have been (Seed 1990, Rollo 1992).

Movements are often international in character and the movement for change with regard to people with learning disabilities is no exception. The themes and the issues are largely common to many other countries, though different countries have individual traditions and starting points. Two main ideas have dominated the movement, nationally and internationally. The first is integration – meaning integration of children with special needs as far as possible into ordinary school and adults into ordinary living patterns in the community. The second idea is normalisation – making living situations as normal as possible. Each of these main ideas has developed since first enunciated. A stage beyond integration in school is referred to as inclusive schooling, meaning the same school setting for everybody. The stage beyond normalisation is recognising people's worth as members of the community.

We shall now explore these themes in more detail.

INTEGRATION

One of the main issues today so far as children with learning disabilities are concerned is integration. This means the integration of children with special needs into classes of ordinary children. Beyond integration is what is called 'inclusive schooling', defined as 'interdependent integrated education' (Stainback and Stainback 1990).

Inclusive schooling is the ultimate goal of the integration and mainstreaming process. Once this is achieved, integration and mainstreaming will no longer be necessary since there will no longer be anyone left out to be integrated or mainstreamed into regular educational settings. This is an extreme view and the merit of going this far, as well as the practicality, is questioned by some parents and many schools, especially for children with the most complex needs.

There are various 'stopping off' points along the route to integration in schools – the most common being a special unit within an ordinary school with flexible arrangements for attending mainstream classes depending on each child's needs. Such compromises with full integration raise problems too. In my experience, moves towards greater integration have been more successful in primary than in secondary settings but there are exceptions where good practice has been demonstrated – for example at Aboyne Academy in Scotland – even for children with severe difficulties (Seed 1988b).

The extent of successful integration in school will profoundly affect expectations of adult services. Parents and young adults alike will ask how it is that if they can attend class with ordinary children they should tolerate segregated adult services. I once fell into conversation with a young man in a train who showed me his disabled person's rail pass which enabled him to travel much of the day around his local town. When I asked him if he had ever been to a day centre he replied firmly, 'If you mix with the daft, you act daft.'

Integration, then, also applies as a goal for services for adults with learning disabilities. In this context integration means taking part in activities along with 'ordinary' people rather than being segregated from them in daily living. Use of ordinary swimming pool sessions, dental services and further education classes as distinct from special services or facilities are examples. Integration with the community also implies living in an ordinary house or flat, but the mere fact of living in an ordinary dwelling does not, in itself, constitute integration. Integration means that people's social networks will include contacts with people, attendance at places, and pursuit of activities in ways which are both 'ordinary' and shared with others who do not have learning disabilities.

'Contact' does not necessarily mean close friendship. Many people with learning difficulties may prefer to choose peer friendships from others with learning difficulties. The issue is whether they have the opportunity to choose.

NORMALISATION

Integration overlaps with the second theme which has particularly influenced services for people with learning disabilities during the past 20 years, namely normalisation. The best-known exponent of this idea, or set of ideas, is Wolf Wolfensberger (Wolfensberger 1972). Wolfensberger was the first to realise that the ideas needed clarification and while normalisation has stuck within the movement for better services, Wolfensberger himself sometimes preferred the phrase 'social role valorisation' – meaning valuing people's contribution to society.

The idea of valued roles overcomes the problems of defining what is 'normal' in society and whether the 'normal' is, in any case, worth aspiring to where it represents mediocrity.

Normalisation has been influential as a slogan with an immediate appeal, but how far it has been operationalised in Wolfensberger's terms of 'enhancement of social images' is much more questionable. The interpretation of normalisation, according to Wolfensberger, includes 'presenting, managing, addressing, labelling and interpreting individual persons in a manner that creates positive roles for them, and that emphasises their similarities to, rather than differences from, other (valued) persons' (Wolfensberger and Thomas 1981 p.11).

DIFFERENT APPROACHES

While integration and normalisation have widespread appeal as ideas, when it comes to practice there are very different approaches to providing services. In other words, there are separate movements within the general social movement to recognise the worth and potential of people with learning disabilities.

For example, contrasting views and approaches are represented by the Campaign for People with Learning Difficulties and, say, the Camphill Rudolf Steiner Movement. In their newsletter, the CPLD attacked residential communities like Camphill in the following terms:

> Most people do not want to live in communes, and most people who live in village communities are not there by choice. There may be Laura Ashley curtains at the windows, but inside the place is still an institution. (Campaign Newsletter 1990)

The Camphill communities themselves are unrepentant and are prepared to question some of the currently more fashionable ideas about integration and normalisation. They point out:

The major innovations in which the Camphill communities have been at the forefront might briefly be listed:

> (The) introduction of the term 'in need of special care' in place of then current classifications of 'idiot', 'imbecile', (1924); the provision of small scale domestic settings for those in need of special care (1940); insisting on the educability of all those with special needs and the integration of 'normal' and 'special' children in the same classes (1951); the provision of places for adults in integrated working communities (1954); the breaking up of pupil groups based on single classifications of handicap and the substitution of groups based around the complementarity of handicap (1964); the provision of formal further education for school leavers with special needs (in the schools from 1951, in separate colleges from 1973); provision of urban communities and half-way houses (from 1969).

CHANGES IN ATTITUDES

During the last 25 years there has been a general erosion of fear on the part of those of us who think we are relatively normal towards 'people with learning disabilities'. In place of fear one would like to think that acceptance has come about. I wonder how far professionals as well as the general public do really accept people with learning disabilities on their own terms, valued for their potential? There is a lot of evidence of patronage even as notions of integration and normalisation are embraced.

Changes in attitudes, however, have occurred in the following respects:

1.   A change from favouring segregation away from the community towards 'placement' within the community. There have been two main stages in interpreting what 'living within the community' means. During the first stage, ten or more years ago, it tended to mean living in hostels – typically catering for about 24 residents – instead of hospital wards. This has been criticised as simply moving from one institution to another, though there may be a case for smaller hostels to be used for a transitional move after leaving hospital. During the second stage of the development of ideas and policies 'living in the community' has been interpreted in various ways to mean more individualised support to people living in smaller houses or flats dispersed in the community. Financial considerations currently tend to favour the dispersal of people with fewer support needs at the expense of those who need 24-hour staff support and for whom the provision of accommodation for very small groups appears prohibitively expensive (Seed 1992a).

2.   A change from adopting a pathological approach to understanding learning disabilities, emphasising the abnormalities people manifest, towards recognising their abilities and potential. This is reflected in assessment instruments currently favoured – for example the Open University's 'Shared Action Planning' (Seed 1991a). This change is in line with more optimistic or hopeful expectations on the part of

parents. I realised this for myself after I had chosen the title *The Constant Hope* for a study of parental attitudes towards children with profound learning difficulties in 1986, juxtaposed with *The Constant Burden* which was the title of an earlier study by Margaret Voysey (Voysey 1975).

3. A change from a custodial approach to care to one which recognises a responsibility to provide support and services in response to an understanding of individual needs. This approach finds expression, for example, in Individual Programmed Planning.

4. Recognition of the right to greater self-determination and advocacy. This change is reflected so far in projects which tend to be outside mainstream services. There is still a long way to go in according people with learning disabilities the same rights as others when it comes to looking closely at practice affecting choices about marriage, employment, the right to live in a neighbourhood of choice and styles of daily living.

CARE IN THE COMMUNITY

I will now consider how these changes in attitudes affect key topics of care in the community as envisaged in the Griffiths Report, The National Health and Care in the Community Act 1990 and subsequent policy and practice guidelines (SSI 1991). A first key topic is assessment, a second care management.

Assessment

The changes in attitude which we have discussed – as well as their limitations – have influenced basic ideas about assessment of people with learning disabilities. It was not so very long ago that 'defectives' were 'graded' according to estimates of their intelligence quotient (IQ). In many instances this approach is maintained, especially in hospitals, although the terminology has changed. Assessments are often concerned with dependency levels rather than IQs, but many research papers still talk about low, medium and high 'grades'. If the researchers cannot get unhooked from these terms, what hope is there for the policymakers? Many assessment procedures still tend to be 'normative' – related to assumptions about what is the norm, for example in terms of adaptation, levels of dependency, stress, etc. (Hogg and Raynes 1987). Such tests tend to bring out 'deficits' in relation to the norm.

An alternative approach most in line with the ideals of care in the community can be called an opportunities approach. Such an approach assesses individual potential irrespective of what others can do (Seed 1992a).

There have also been changes in notions of where assessment should take place. Normative tests often take place in a controlled setting to enhance validity and reliability. But there is more acceptance now of the idea that people with learning difficulties can be more appropriately assessed in their living situation. There are problems if the living situation is, for example, a hospital ward where is a lack of opportunity to practise daily living skills such as cooking. The emphasis recently has been to remove the distance between the assessor and the assessed, and to concentrate on identification with the person with learning disability, getting to know him or her and sharing a view of the present and the future with them.

Changes in attitudes towards assessment partly draw impetus from an emphasis on 'quality of life'. It has been suggested that quality of life will take over from normalisation as the key idea of the 1990s (Schalock *et al.* 1989). To assess quality of life implies assessing the individual and the environment together. For example, it implies assessing not only what the person with learning difficulties can and cannot do in a group home but assessing the home as a setting which enriches the potential of the person concerned.

Quality of life is an attractive idea because it draws the person with learning disabilities into the arena of common human experience. The popularity of the notion of quality of life reflects the disenchantment shared by many about the values which dominate current society. These values are often not shared by people with learning disabilities, as Wolfensberger has pointed out (Wolfensberger 1988).

Care Management

At the time of writing it is still very much an open question how procedures in place for placement moves and programme planning for people with learning difficulties will fit into general procedures for care management. In recently completed research regarding adults with learning difficulties in supported accommodation (Seed 1990) I found the most sensitive and effective care management was in areas characterised by a localised rather than a centralised approach to resource allocation.

Care management means giving attention to the detail of what people want and need in self-care and daily living. This is easier to achieve where local knowledge is brought into play – for example, a knowledge of what ordinary housing is available and suitable, what employment prospects there may be, what care and leisure facilities there are and so on. The idea of a package of care means taking all of these things into consideration and helping people to develop their potential in the light of available opportunities.

Integration and normalisation should mean that people have choices to live where it is convenient for them to continue to develop opportunities and not where, for example, purpose schemes happen to be developed for them or where surplus accommodation is designated for their use. I know of more than one local authority children's home which was converted by stages to become a hostel or house for adults with learning disabilities – many of the staff remaining and, in one instance, some of the children! I have also seen many houses in the private sector in remote rural places chosen, it seems, to fulfil the ambitions of the proprietor for a quiet rural life rather than the needs of the residents. Or perhaps property was cheaper to buy in some rural areas than in towns.

Most people with learning disabilities continue to learn new skills and become more independent in self-management in adult life (Seed 1988a). This means that a level of support that is appropriate at one stage in their lives will not be necessary at another – and, for some, further support will become

necessary as they become elderly. Sometimes levels of staffing provision have
been very rigid. People's needs change.

There has also been a debate as to whether staffing levels should change
while residents remain in the same house or whether the residents should be
moved to accommodation offering different levels of support. The choice
should surely be for the individual concerned. Much of my research has
shown that large numbers of adults with learning difficulties wish to leave
hostels or other staffed accommodation to move into more independent flats
or houses on their own or with friends. Whichever way it is arranged there
should be flexibility and sensitiveness to changing needs.

There are a variety of ideas for accommodating adults with learning
difficulties. For example, in some areas there are schemes of supported
landladies. There are support schemes based on 'good neighbours'. In one or
two instances day services consistently provide a targeted support service in
residents' own homes. Then there are still 'village communities' and variations in the form of residential 'colleges'. There is nothing wrong with variety
provided it reflects an understanding of client needs and not the eccentricities
of the service providers.

A more radical idea I heard at a conference of the International Spastics
Association was that people with disabilities – and why not people with
learning disabilities? – should be able to employ their own support staff and
to dismiss them. It remains to be seen whether this is feasible within the
concept of care in the community for the future.

FURTHER EDUCATION AND OTHER ACTIVITIES

One of the most significant changes in the past few years in daytime activities
for people with learning difficulties has been the opening up of opportunities
in colleges of further education.

This is often overlooked in heated debates about what, if any, function
adult training centres, social education centres or resource centres – or centres
known by any other name – should fulfil or whether indeed they should be
abolished altogether. The problem about abolishing them is that there is little
so far to put in their place – except, as I have said, opportunities in colleges
of further education. There are some exciting projects promoting opportunities and support for 'real' wage-earning employment but these only meet the
needs of a small minority.

Day services and their uses have been more comprehensively studied in
Scotland than in England and Wales (Jackson and Struthers 1974, Goda 1981,
Baker and Urquhart 1987, Seed 1988a). There are also more centre places per
10,000 of the general population in Scotland. In *Day Care at the Crossroads*,
which is the most comprehensive evaluation of social work provision for
daytime activities in Scotland, no less than eight main aims were identified
for adult training centres (Seed 1988a).

These were:

1. To develop clients' potential.
2. Preparation for more independent forms of living (through a variety of means, varying from work preparation to preparation to take part in recreational activities).
3. Throughput to some specific activity outside the Centre at a later date.
4. The enrichment of people's pattern of living at home.
5. To provide social activities and opportunities for mixing amongst clients at Centres.
6. To provide respite for parents or other carers at home.
7. Simply to provide constructive forms of occupation.
8. To be a resource to clients, their families and to the wider community.

Some of these aims also apply to attendance at colleges of further education – most clearly the development of potential. The main difference between attendance at an FE college and attendance at a Centre is that the former is time-limited in terms of a course. Attendance at a Day Centre is nearly always indefinite and, whatever the stated intentions, the extent of throughput (which varies greatly from one centre to another) is on average less than 5 per cent per annum – after taking into account deaths and movement to other localities.

In *Day Care at the Crossroads* I recommend that local authority (or voluntary) day centres should follow one or another of three clear paths (Seed 1998a). The first is to provide explicit preparation for employment and support in employment. The second is to provide preparation for further education in collaboration with FE colleges. The third is explicitly to provide support to enable people to live more interdependent and richer lives in the community, whether with parents or on their own or in groups in the community.

PEOPLE WITH PROFOUND DISABILITIES

While there has been a steady improvement in the education of children with profound disabilities, the development of day services to follow on from school are usually lacking.

For many years such people were left out of daytime activities. Then, with development of special care units in some centres, often in a rather token way, they were cared for rather than 'trained' for anything very specific. In the last five years in particular there has been a developing movement to demonstrate that even those who are the most profoundly disadvantaged are capable of learning and benefiting but that this can only come about with the highest quality of service provision and the highest calibre of staff (Hogg 1991, Seed 1991b)

A number of new centres have been developed separate from the traditional adult training centre for this purpose including, for example, the Persondy Centre near Bridgend, the Carrisbrook Centre at Airdrie and the White Top Centre at Dundee – the latter associated with a Chair in Dundee University in Profound Disability. Others are shortly to be opened – for example a new small centre in Hamilton pioneered and managed by a local parents' group, known as AVEYRON (Seed 1992b).

The large majority of people with profound mental handicap also have physical disabilities and often some sensory impairments. A few, on the other hand, are physically fit and capable. The support needs of both groups are very high. but also very different in each individual case.

OTHERS WITH MULTIPLE DISABILITIES

Evidence from recent research (Seed 1992a) suggests the numbers of adults with multiple disabilities not included within the category of 'profound learning difficulties' may be greater than hitherto conceded. Partly this is because of the increasing number of elderly people with learning difficulties but also because the other disabilities, for example visual impairment and epilepsy – to name two of the most common – have tended to take second place in what could be called a hierarchy of labelling. The RNIB are very aware of this after undertaking their own research and have been campaigning to draw attention to the needs of people with visual impairments and learning difficulties (RNIB 1990).

OLDER PEOPLE WITH LEARNING DISABILITIES

Attention has recently been focused on the higher incidence of pre-senile dementia in cases of Down's Syndrome. However, for others with learning disabilities the evidence suggests a propensity for continuing to live an active life so long as opportunities are sustained. I recently came across a man of 72 who had been 'ordered' by his carers to stop cycling!

CHANGES IN ATTITUDES OF PARENTS

Parents often have a very poor set of experiences with professionals when their handicapped child is born. Even today, in spite of improvements, I come across recent stories of professionals failing to provide factual information to parents, and leaving them to guess what is wrong with their child. Of course, in medical terms, a diagnosis is not always easy, or straightforward. Down's Syndrome and other genetic conditions may be apparent at birth, but these are the exceptions rather than the rule. Often there is no specific medical diagnosis. It is the parent rather than the professionals who first perceives that something is amiss. During the early years such a parent will ask advice initially from Health Visitors and GPs. Frequently they will be falsely reassured not to worry and that he or she will develop normally in time. Then, finally, the professionals are convinced that something must be wrong and a fuller assessment takes place.

What often happens next is that the parents are presented with the worst scenario. They are told that he or she will never be able to do this or that – sometimes professionals go far outside their justified remit in prognosticating that he or she, for example, will never be capable of employment, will always need constant attention, and so on. Finally, the parents – and sometimes the professionals alongside them – slowly learn that a more optimistic scenario can unfold granted sufficient services and resources (Horobin and May 1988).

For some children whose difficulty is relatively mild or who are extremely neglected in primary school, all this happens not when the child is 2 or 3 but when he or she is 11 or 12.

Against the background of such experiences, parents often feel isolated and become protective. However, in recent years, parental attitudes have changed. Of course this is a generalisation. But in a number of recent surveys I have been surprised at the extent to which parents begin to think of their children living independently at a very early age and prepare for employment prospects when they are still at school. Parents tend to align themselves on one side or the other in the debate about integration into mainstream schools. Many stories have been produced by the National Foundation for Educational Research, for example, of parents fighting for the right to send their children to normal schools. Some research that I have done in contrast has shown examples of parents deliberately withdrawing their children from normal schools in favour of special education. What matters to the parent is the quality of educational experience and the level of individualised attention and support that is available. Of course other things being equal parents tend to want their children to mix with normal children, but many parents have also experienced neglect of their handicapped children in ordinary classes. The underlying point is that parents' expectations of services, whatever form these services take, has greatly increased in the last decade.

RESPITE

Amongst these expectations is the expectation of respite. If parents are expected to care for their children at home – and we seem to accept that they are – the need for respite to enable them to lead as normal a life as possible is important not only for themselves but for their child and other members of the family. Respite is perhaps an odd and misleading word because what is needed is positive support rather than simply relief. This can take various forms. Again there is a lot of passion and many different approaches. These range from residential respite centres, usually provided by Social Services Departments or voluntary agencies but sometimes by Health Boards, to shared family care schemes and sitter services. Parents vary in what they want and why (Holligan, Roberts and Seed 1991).

SOCIAL NETWORKS

Extensive research has been undertaken into the social networks of people with learning disabilities (Seed 1988b, 1988c). The point to note about the networks of children with special needs is that they tend, more than is normal, to be dominated by contacts with relatives. Correspondingly, they lack child–child relationships out of school. What relationships they do have with their peers tend to be in segregated settings. This will apply less in situations where children are genuinely integrated into mainstream schooling, with parental support and where the parents are active in seeking a normal life for their children out of school.

Granted that social networks are depleted compared with the networks of many non-handicapped children they enter adulthood with a disadvantage even when they have been brought up at home. If they had been brought up in residential settings such as hospital or other institutions this will apply even more with the added disadvantage that in this case they may not even enjoy regular contacts with relatives. All this applies especially to people with severe or profound learning difficulties.

A day service which promotes community involvement can compensate to some extent for a very limited and self-contained home-based network. But the real thrust for extending social networks, both quantitatively and quali-tatively, depends on home-based initiatives and impetus and there is no evidence that day services on the whole do anything to enhance these pros-pects. The same seems to apply to limited studies I have undertaken in this field in schools.

Networks in residential settings can vary enormously. It is interesting to find that the extent of contacts outside hospital can vary between individuals even in the same hospital ward. They tend, however, to be networks involving formal activities rather than the kind of informal spontaneous friendships in the community (apart from relatives) which most of us to some extent enjoy. Again, however, there are exceptions and some networks of individuals with learning disabilities that I have studied are extensive and rich in quality.

Networking, or helping people to develop and sustain social networks, should be a crucial part of the support that is offered to people with learning difficulties. The skills to do this are seldom taught, however. Parents are often involved in networking amongst themselves to form various kinds of support groups. Not all parents are interested in these kinds of activities – they have their own lives to lead and their own network of contacts at work or elsewhere. Other parents feel a sense of isolation and welcome the opportunity to make contact with other parents who have been through similar experiences.

Often parents' groups have formed a major pressure group for bringing new services into being.

THE FUTURE

The gap between rhetoric and practice is likely to remain. I read accounts about (and see for myself) adults in hostels or elsewhere sometimes leading very routine lives or attending day centres where routine is still the rule rather than the exception. Many are caught in a trap of second-best hostel-type accommodation where there seems no means to move elsewhere.

The need for more resources than are made available during a prolonged recession, coupled with the current emphasis on a market-oriented rather than a welfare-oriented approach to care in the community will block further progress. These factors will tend to disadvantage those with the greatest needs, especially those for whom 24-hour staff attention is required.

REFERENCES

Baker, N. and Urquhart, N. (1987) *The Balance of Care for Adults with a Mental Handicap in Scotland*. Scottish Office, Edinburgh: ISD Publications.

Campaign for People with Learning Difficulties (1990) *Newsletter, No. 62, Autumn.*

Glendinning, C. (1986) *A Single Door: Social Work with the Families of Disabled Children*. London: Allen and Unwin.

Goda, D.F. (1981) *A Training for Life*. Edinburgh: University of Edinburgh.

Hogg, J. and Raynes, N. (1987) *Assessment in Mental Handicap: A Guide to Assessment Procedures, Tests and Checklists*. London: Croom Helm.

Hogg, J. (1991) Developments in further education for young adults with profound learning difficulties. In G. Lloyd and J. Watson (eds) *Meeting Special Educational Needs: A Scottish Perspective. Vol 1: Innovatory Practice and Severe Learning Difficulties*. Edinburgh: Moray House.

Holligan, B., Roberts, D. and Seed, P. (1991) *Respite needs in Central Buchan*. Dundee: University of Dundee, Department of Social Work Book Distribution Service.

Horobin, G. and May, D. (1988) *Living with Mental Handicap, Research Highlights, No.16*. London: Jessica Kingsley Publishers.

Jackson, S. and Struthers, M. (1974) *A Survey of Scottish Adult Training Centres*. Glasgow: SSMH.

McLaughlin, B. (ed) (1969) *Studies in Social Movements: A Social/Psychological Perspective*. New York: Free Press.

Mittler, P. (1979) *People not Patients*. London: Methuen.

RNIB (1990) *New Directions. Towards a Better Future for Multi-handicapped Visually Impaired Children and Young People*. London: RNIB Publications Unit, 224 Great Portland Street, London W1N 6AA.

Rollo, T. (1992) Community mental handicap teams – An evaluation. Unpublished *MA Dissertation*, University of Dundee Social Work Department.

Schalock, R.L. *et al.* (1989) Quality of life: its measurement and use. *Mental Retardation, 27*, No.1.

Seed, P. (1988a) *Day Care at the Crossroads*. Tunbridge Wells: Costello. (Obtainable from Dundee University Department of Social Work Book Distribution Service.)

Seed, P. (1988b) *Day Services for People with Severe Handicaps, Case Studies for Practice, 2*. London: Jessica Kingsley Publishers.

Seed, P. (1988c) *Day Services for People with Mental Handicaps, Case Studies for Practice, 1*. London: Jessica Kingsley Publishers.

Seed, P. (1990) *Supported Accommodation and Day Services for People with Learning Difficulties*. Dundee: University of Dundee Department of Social Work, Book Distribution Service.

Seed, P. (1991a) *Assessment, Resource Allocation and Planning for Adults with Learning Difficulties in Supported Accommodation in Scotland: A Literature Review*. Dundee: University of Dundee Department of Social Work Book Distribution Service.

Seed, P. (1991b) The establishment of a day centre for young adults with profound learning difficulties. In G. Lloyd and J. Watson (eds) *Meeting Special Educational*

Needs: A Scottish Perspective. Vol 1: Innovatory Practice and Severe Learning Difficulties. Edinburgh: Moray House.

Seed, P. (1992a) *Assessment, Resource Allocation and Planning for Adults with Learning Difficulties in Scotland*. Dundee: University of Dundee Department of Social Work Book Distribution Service.

Seed, P. (1992b) *Assessment for Developing a Needs-Led Day Service for Adults with Profound Mental Handicap*. A Report commissioned by Aveyron (The Association of Parents and Carers of Profoundly Mentally Handicapped People, Hamilton and East Kilbride). Obtainable from University of Dundee Department of Social Work Book Distribution Service.

Segal, S. (1967) *No Child is Ineducable*. Oxford: Pergamon.

Social Services Inspectorate (Department of Health) and Scottish Office (Social Work Services Group) (1991) *Care Management and Assessment. Policy and Practice Guidelines*. London: HMSO.

Stainback, W. and Stainback, S. (1990) *Support Networks for Inclusive Schooling: Inter-dependent Integrated Education*. Baltimore, MD: Paul H. Brookes.

Voysey, M. (1975) *A Constant Burden*. London: Routledge.

Wolfensberger, W. (1972) *The Principle of Normalisation in Human Services*. Toronto: Toronto Institute of Mental Retardation.

Wolfensberger, W. and Thomas, S. (1981) The principle of normalisation in human services. In *Research Highlights, No.2*. Aberdeen: University of Aberdeen.

Wolfensberger, W. (1988) Common assets of mentally retarded people that are commonly not acknowledged. In *Mental Retardation, 26, No. 2*.

CHAPTER 5

Moving Out of Hospital into the Community

Paul Simic

INTRODUCTION

Over the period from November 1989 to December 1990, 24 younger adults who had been long-stay patients and who had experienced major psychiatric disorders were discharged from the Royal Edinburgh Hospital. They were mostly from the Thomas Clouston Clinic site, much of which was closed by the end of the study period. A collaborative study was conducted involving the Social Work Research Centre at Stirling University, the Royal Edinburgh Hospital and the Centre for Health Economics at York University. The study followed the discharged patients out into the community, interviewing them and those helping them, describing their circumstances and analysing outcomes for the group. A comparison group of patients who stayed in hospital was also followed up over the year. This is a discussion of some of the findings of that study.

THE ROYAL EDINBURGH HOSPITAL

The Royal Edinburgh Hospital (hereafter REH) has a catchment area population of 438,700 and consists of the Andrew Duncan clinic and professorial unit dealing with acute psychiatry, Mackinnon House dealing with long-stay psychogeriatric cases and forensic psychiatry, and the Jardine clinic for psychogeriatric patients. They are all based on one site in the centre of Morningside. There is also the Thomas Clouston Clinic (hereafter TCC), a mile or so away set in its own grounds, which housed wards for long-stay patients, psychogeriatric assessment and rehabilitation psychiatry. There are, furthermore, a number of hostels in the area at some distance away from the main sites in ordinary housing in the community.

Major changes were occurring at the hospital over the lifetime of this study, under a major plan to rationalise and reorganise the hospital system. This was to substantially affect the TCC site. At one point there were grand designs to sell off the TCC site, which has a nice view and pleasant grounds. At the end of the study the main building closed for dust to gather over mounted stag's heads set high up on the walls, on the dark and heavy portraits of imposing elders and on the various engraved heraldic symbols.

The hospital has some 2500 admissions and discharges per annum. In context, the overall trend in Scotland, as in England, is for shorter admissions and increasing numbers of readmissions. The REH has a long-established tradition of rehabilitative work with long-stay patients. The situation of the hospital in the middle of Morningside, a desirable residential area, does not make it typical of Scotland's psychiatric hospitals.

There is, in addition, a system of hostels (5 units with 54 beds) away from but close to the main hospital sites. Two of the hostel units (13 beds) are intended as more independent hostels, referred to as transitional units. The other hostel beds are longer-term or permanent beds. One hostel is seen just as a long-stay resident hostel.

There is a filter whereby the long-stay service takes applications from the acute part; a clinical meeting decides whether to accept a referral and there is a waiting list for the service. There is also movement between the long-stay wards in this part of the system as patients move for clinical and other reasons. The majority of patients who pass through this filter will have diagnoses of schizophrenia (72% of the under 65 population currently have this diagnosis), while only some 6 per cent have neurotic or personality disorder ICD-9 codes on the Lothian Psychiatric Case Register (LPCR).

The acute service of the hospital has lengths of stay measured usually in weeks. In contrast, the long-stay population, largely resident at the TCC site, have lengths of stay ranging from a few months to very long stays: one patient was admitted just before the Wall Street crash. The majority of this group are seen as patients who have been unable to benefit from resettlement. Age is a key factor in placing patients at various sites at the TCC and the hostels. The sites which are considered as more active rehabilitation sites have younger patients on average.

The move for the patient into the medium-term/longer-stay section is a significant one. The person is moving to a separate part of the hospital with a different set of expectations, a different focus and a different pace.

Some 262 long-stay patients were identified in 1986 and 259 were identified for the current study from the LPCR (patients in hospital for 9 months plus, aged over 18, excluding dementia diagnoses). Of this latter group, 138 were under 65. The long-stay population has an average age of 60 but it would be wrong to assume that this elderly population at the TCC site is synonymous with the term 'old long-stay' patients. Of the 121 patients, with functional diagnoses over 65 years, 60 per cent were first admitted as elderly patients (i.e. >60 years) and only 20 per cent of those currently aged over 65 were admitted under 40 years of age. There are 81 patients who have been in for 10 years or more.

The hospital has a lower prevalence of old long-stay than the Scotland average: 36 per 100,000 compared with 59 per 100,000; and a lower average length of stay: 26 per cent over 30 years compared with 54 per cent nationally. REH is increasingly dealing with admissions of elderly patients with other than functional diagnoses, as is the case nationally.

BACKGROUND

Policy differences between Scotland and England have been described by Hunter and Wistow (1987) and Titterton (1991).

The Team for The Assessment of Psychiatric Services (TAPS 1989) report refers to government policy encouraging hospital closure and/or run-down and the reprovision of services. There can be no clearer demarcation line between England and Scotland than the fact that there has so far been no hospital closure or run-down programme in Scotland comparable to that in England.

In England and Wales the hospital run-down programme (at various stages of completion) has been playing to mixed reviews. While major studies (conducted by TAPS and others) are largely positive about run-down (recognising that so far the policy has been conducted with 'creamed-off' patients), others (for example, SANE and the NSF) see the policy as disastrous, claiming that the hospital provision is disappearing and that patients are dumped on a community unable or unwilling to cope. (See Hatch and Nissel 1989 and Goodwin 1990 for further discussion.)

With this background in mind, the REH TCC working group (later called 'Comcare') was set up to oversee the closure of two wards at the REH and the development of alternative packages of care for 30 patients. Thus a 'natural experiment', ripe for research, appeared to be taking place and one which, certainly at the time of its first inception (discussions began in the mid-1980s) was at the forefront of practice in Scotland. The Social Work Research Centre at Stirling University became involved and various researchers bravely wrestled with a complex local situation and a difficult research brief.

A variety of factors, partly outlined in the full research report, combined to delay both the study and the closure plan (Simic, O'Donnell and Gilfillan 1991). The study was redirected to examining patients leaving hospital through the normal rehabilitation procedures rather than through the package of care arranged by Comcare. In fact, the joint planning exercise, involving the health board, the social work department and voluntary agencies, after years of discussion ultimately came to nothing, to be replaced by a bilateral agreement between one voluntary agency and the Mental Health Unit. The acrimonious failure of this joint planning enterprise was documented by another researcher (Wilson 1990).

Quality of Life

The REH study used, as a conceptual framework, the notion of 'Quality of Life' (QOL). QOL is the key concept in rehabilitation and in the rhetoric behind community care but there continues to be a debate about the best way of assessing it. There is also a debate about who is the best judge of the outcome – the patient or the professional. It has been said (Leff 1990) that the most important factor is the patient's subjective sense of well-being. Other authorities have placed the emphasis on professional judgement of the patient's well-being (Rescher 1982). This study has accepted that the patient's subjective view is an important element, but only an element in QOL evaluation.

QOL can be defined as 'goodness' of life, which may be assessed using both objective and subjective indicators (Rescher 1982). The QOL of the patient, it should be noted, is not the only issue: the person's impact on those around them is equally important in accurately examining QOL.

There is also an issue to do with the notion of directly comparing 'hospital' care and 'community' care. There is no straightforward picture of which is 'better', should they be starkly juxtaposed as competing models (Jones, Robinson and Golightly 1986). It has been said that the clarity of boundary is more semantic than real and the term 'community care', questioned by Titmuss almost a quarter a century ago as an accurate label, has been seen to be of limited value but of such common currency that it has no practicable alternative (House of Commons Social Services Committee 1985, Dyer 1991). Where are the boundaries between hospital and community? It is recognised that 'institutional' practices are not exclusive to hospital nor even to what might be termed 'institutions', e.g. larger homes for older people (Allen *et al.* 1989). Community care for many has been called 'trans-institutionalisation' in practice, where the patient moves from one sort of institutional living to another (see also Chapter 4).

This study focused on describing outcomes for the patients in terms of destination, their networks and activities, and other descriptive information; on psychiatric assessment of mental state; on professional judgements of patient functioning; and on patient reports and assessments of their own experiences. All this information was intended to provide a comprehensive picture of the subjects' QOL over time. It should be noted that even a year is a short time in the context of chronic conditions.

Description of Method

A more complete description of the method and the measures employed is in the full report; no more than a brief outline will be given here (Simic *et al.* 1991).

Those people leaving hospital over a thirteen month period were 'matched' with patients staying in over the period to derive a comparison group, and outcomes for both groups were compared over time and with each other. To this end patients were interviewed; where possible, family or professional supporters were also interviewed. Patients were interviewed in hospital before discharge, a month after discharge and at nine months' follow-up by the author and by a research psychiatrist. The author also interviewed professional and other third-party informants (with subjects' permission) to coincide with these interviews. Service use was monitored by an additional standardised questionnaire and by interviewing an informant (again with the subject's permission) at one month after discharge, four months after and at nine months' follow-up.

The patient interview developed for this study was based primarily on the work of Lehman in the USA (Lehman 1983a,b, 1988, Lehman, Possideute and Hawker 1986). The interview was semi-structured and covered areas central to QOL assessment: contacts with professionals, daily activities and routines, living situation, family contacts, other significant relationships, mental health and attitude to medication, finances, physical health, safety and attitude to leaving hospital. Objective questions were asked in each topic area or domain, that is, questions calling for basic factual information on circumstances. Patients' subjective judgements were solicited and, in addition to open discussion, they were asked to rate their satisfaction with each particular area of their life and a measure of morale was completed by the researcher.

Those offering care or support, usually professionals, were interviewed and functioning and mental state measures completed. The principal measures used were the MRSS or Morningside Rehabilitation Status Scale (Affleck and McGuire 1984); the SBS or Social Behaviour Schedule (Sturt and Wykes 1986), the standard version of the MRC Social Performance Schedule, an itemised behaviour checklist; and the ABS, a shortened version of the Adaptive Behaviour Schedule (Margolius 1986). The use of both the MRSS and the SBS was considered particularly important to allow comparisons within Scotland and with major English studies.

Some of the findings from the measures will be described here; readers are referred to the full REH report for the rest (Simic *et al.* 1991).

The Sample

This is a brief description of the sample studied and some key findings about them and their stay in hospital.

Half of the 24 discharged patients or 'leavers' were male and half were female. Only one person had a partner. The ages ranged, with an even distribution, from 20 to 64 years. Two-thirds had a diagnosis of schizophrenia. They were mainly 'revolving-door' patients, with just three who would generally be referred to as traditional long-stay residents – those who had 'grown old in care'. This was consistent with previous years and it was found that just six patients with lengths of stay between 5 years and 10 years were discharged in the period 1980–1990, according to the Lothian Psychiatric Case Register. Of the leavers, most (18) had had under 3 years' stay. The shortest stay was 10 months and the longest was 16 years.

While their current lengths of stay were short relative to the traditional long-stay groups, their overall contact with services was by no means recent or brief. They had an average of 6 previous admissions (ranging between 1 and 17) and had spent, as a group, half their time in and half out of hospital since first admissions to the REH. Thus, the discharged group had a history of mixed care (i.e. periods of in-patient care of varying lengths, day care at times, follow-up at out-patient departments at other times, and out of contact for periods) in the context of a long-term chronic illness. Almost half (11) of the discharged group had been in contact with the psychiatric services for 10 years or more.

Most of the leavers came from the long- or medium-stay wards and only four came from acute wards, although this was more than expected. Patients were discharged from a number of sites at the hospital, not primarily through the hostels system; this was also a surprising finding. The most common site to be discharged to was supported accommodation of one sort or another, primarily to flat or house shares with non-resident support. Only one of the cases had previously been discharged to such accommodation. Thus it was a new experience of care for the group as a whole. There were very few carers involved and in only one case was there a discharge to a relative and this an unplanned one from an acute ward. Absence of a family carer may be a defining feature in long-term admission.

There was a clear difference between those discharged and those staying in hospital on mental state and functioning measures used. The key differentiating feature was the increased level of symptomatology found in the matches. This is, perhaps, the simplest and most striking difference indicated both by the measures and supported by clinical judgement. Other important differences between the groups were to do with increased behaviour problems and lower self-care and domestic skills in the stayers group. It is not by any means the case that the subject group were without symptoms or related secondary handicaps, but rather that the comparison group were markedly more ill and/or disturbed.

Patient attitude was a major feature in the discharge process, including the important factor of the motivation to leave. This was a motivation exhibited keenly by many of the discharged subjects. Thus, the rehabilitation system selected some, and the more able volunteered themselves, for inclusion in a discharge programme or to leave anyway without such support. Patients can, according to whether they have been compulsorily or informally admitted, take their own leave regardless of whether any of the professionals involved consider they are being rehabilitated. 'Rehabilitation' as an activity and as a concept is discussed in the main report (Simic *et al.* 1991).

INTO THE COMMUNITY – OUTCOMES

A relatively small number of people left different wards at the REH, with differing lengths of stay, but most having had a long history of contact with the psychiatric services. Some had undergone formal rehabilitation and some had not. Almost all went to supported accommodation, mostly run by one or two voluntary associations. This section describes how they were followed up and how they fared. Leavers were interviewed within a month of leaving, briefly a couple of months later, and had a full follow-up interview no earlier than nine months after discharge. Those concerned with their care were also interviewed with the leaver's permission.

'What the patients say' and patient judgements about what happens to them is still not often given a sufficiently high profile in follow-up studies. This is largely because longitudinal studies involving interviewing patients are difficult (Jones *et al.* 1986). In this study patients, as part of an interview, rated their satisfaction with a set number of life domains using a Likert-type scale (see Figure 5.1); they were also asked to complete a short rating scale intended as a measure of general morale.

Worst			Mixed			Best
1	2	3	4	5	6	7

Figure 5.1. *The Satisfaction Rating Scale (Representation)*

I'd like to ask you how you've been feeling lately. In the last month, how often have you felt…			
	Never	**Sometimes**	**Often**
bored	2	1	0
that things were going your way	0	1	2
very lonely	2	1	0
restless	2	1	0
particularly excited or interested in something	0	1	2
upset	2	1	0

Figure 5.2. The Morale Scale (Specimen Questions)

Figure 5.2 is a specimen (the first six scale items) of the morale measure completed by the patients.

Table 5.1 Satisfaction Scores by Domain. Median Scores (n=8)

Life Domains	Time 1	Time 3
(Satisfaction with):		
Life in general	4.0	5.0
Activity	4.0	5.5
Living situation	3.5	5.0
Partner	*	*
Parents	*	*
Children	*	*
Siblings	*	*
Professional support	4.5	5.5
Friendships	5.5	5.5
Money	4.5	5.5
Medication	4.5	4.5
State of mind	4.0	4.0
Physical health	6.0	6.0
Safety (indoors)	5.5	6.0
Safety (outside)	6.0	5.5
Prospect of leaving	5.0	n/a
Advice re leaving	3.5	4.5
Morale	53.0	63.5

* = too few observations

It was disappointing that only 8 of the 24 cases had complete sets of ratings over time from the patient interview – six cases would not and 8 could not complete, and these two 'defaulting' categories accounted for most of the missing ratings. This was taken as an indicator of the level of disability of this group and reinforces the difficulty of engaging such patients over a length of time. The result for the study was that, while judgements directly from leavers will be reported on, the main study analysis was based largely on third-party reports.

There were, however, some tentative but interesting conclusions to be drawn from even the limited information given directly by the leavers.

Briefly, no negative changes were indicated over time with scores remaining constant or improving. The only exceptions were the ratings of satisfaction with safety within the immediate living environment (indoors) which improved and with safety with the surrounding environment (neighbourhood) which worsened over time.

The overall morale score shows some improvement over time.

Four categories produced a dearth of information: answers to questions in domains covering partner, parents, children and siblings were largely blank indicating a level of social isolation and a constricted set of social roles.

The most marked changes were increased satisfaction with living situation and with day to day activity. Assessments of satisfaction with professional support, with money, with personal safety and with medication all show some improvement. Satisfaction ratings tend to cluster around scores of 5 on the 1–7 point scale, that is, one step into the positive side of the scale. Only two scores are below the scale mid-point (and thus on the negative side of the scale); these are to do with the patients' living situation and activities when in hospital. Overall, patients' ratings would indicate no dramatic change with some increased satisfaction.

Can we generalise to the whole group from such small numbers? There were no significant differences found on functioning and mental state measures between those able to complete ratings and those not able or unwilling, giving some support to a generalisation.

Third Party Ratings/Judgements

Table 5.2 Comparison Over Time. Median Scores (n=19)

	Time 1		Time 3	
	SBS	MRSS	SBS	MRSS
Discharged	2.5	11.0	2.0	11.0
Matches	7.0	18.5	7.5	19.0

Crucial outcome measures in the judgement of QOL are measures indicating levels of and change in mental state and functioning over time. Comparisons are made on the 19 matched-pairs who had information available at final visit.

A general level of stability in both the discharged group and those matched cases remaining in hospital is indicated by the measures. The discharged group, however, did show some deterioration in the MRSS item relating to effects of current symptoms. While matches show a trend in the same direction with the same item, 7 discharged subjects had scores indicating minor worsening of symptoms since hospital, and no cases showed improvement. As can be seen from Table 5.2, the significant differentiation shown between subjects and matches when in hospital was retained at final visit with much the same levels of differentiation indicated. Thus, both relative and absolute stability of both the discharged subjects group and their matches, overall, would appear to be the general conclusion to be drawn about their functioning over the period of follow-up.

In addition to use of standardised measures, information was collated on the circumstances of the leavers in relation to key areas of their lives. The next section describes this.

INTO THE COMMUNITY – SERVICE PROVISION

Accommodation

Most people discharged (15/24) went initially to supported accommodation (11) or to a staffed hostel (4). Two others went to other hostels: ex-serviceman's (1) and residential home (1). None of the patients (4) from the acute wards went to similar provision (three went to private addresses and one to sheltered accommodation). This leaves just three discharged subjects from the long-stay and medium-term wards who did not go to some form of supported provision with staff in daily contact.

In all, then, for 18 of the 24 cases the bulk of service follow-up came from the bricks and mortar of specifically provided accommodation – supported, sheltered and staffed – and from the staff support 'built-in' to these sites, whether non-resident support workers or resident care staff. In the main, the services were provided by voluntary agencies.

Difficulties with coordinating services have been documented and the problems of achieving 'consumer choice' given the acute shortage of services in Scotland have been raised (Huxley 1990, COSLA 1990). Where specific housing provision is an ill-planned aspect of care in the community, there may be major problems. A survey of psychiatric patients discharged into Westminster found that although core health and social work services were available, there was much unmet need, particularly for those wanting some specialised support, as well as a considerable gap in provision for constructive occupation (Hatch and Nissel 1989). The biggest gap, however, was in basic housing needs.

Professional Contact

GP At least 12 discharged subjects reported having had some contact with their health centre or GP after discharge during the follow-up period, but direct contact was minimal. Those who reported having visited GP surgeries or health centres tended to be going for repeat prescriptions or to see a CPN for injection rather than to see the GP directly. There was no case of a discharged subject who reported going to see the GP for reasons directly related to their psychiatric problems.

Psychiatrist Indications, from patient reports and from LPCR records, are that 7 discharged subjects had contact with a psychiatrist at some point(s) over the follow-up period. This was via out-patient follow-up (5 cases) and at the day hospital (1 case) and one case of a home visit for an assessment under the mental health act. There was, other than this last case, only one other case of a psychiatrist home visit recorded on the case register for the follow-up period.

CPNs 12 discharged subjects had some contact with CPNs over the period in a variety of settings: home visit, at the REH Continuing Care clinic, at day centres, at health centres, or at place of occupation (e.g. SAMH's kitchen). The nature of the contact was very variable and usually brief, the most common single reason for contact being described by patients as for administration of injection.

Nurses There was some limited follow-up of patients from ward nurses, reported in just two cases (follow-up home visits). This was usually much appreciated by patients and by community workers but contact was brief.

Social worker One case from the acute ward (readmitted and still in at the study's end) had some post-discharge contact at a couple of crisis points with an area social worker ('he's a rather low priority case for us'). One other case at the local authority hostel had some brief contact with the hospital social worker just after discharge regarding practical matters. Otherwise there was no input from social work departments. 'Mental health social work has a low priority generally in SWDs', said one hospital social worker who had little experience of being able to pass on long-term cases to area offices. Few area social workers were reported as having had any specialist training.

Psychologist One person from an acute ward stayed in contact with a psychologist by visiting him at hospital. One case had brief contact with a private psychologist.

Other One person had regular contact with a council homeless project worker over a period of six months. A number of people had very variable levels of contact with drop-in centres and other projects run by voluntary organisations or by the health board. One person, from the acute ward, returned to the ward for a weekly support group.

Support workers The professionals whom the discharged patients had most contact with were the support workers at the supported accommodation sites and the staff at the hostels. Both of the supported accommodation agencies had non-resident support staff present for some period of each day although the level of input was very different between the agencies. One agency had someone present for a period of half an hour or thereabouts (it was flexible) each day plus a weekly house meeting, the other agency had someone present for a substantial period of each day.

Both agencies had out-of-hours emergency numbers for contact which were relatively little used. Staff were most commonly called out over the period of the follow-up because the smoke detectors tended to overreact to the cookers. In general, patients were very positive about the support workers and there were few criticisms.

The most obvious difference contrasting care staff attitudes and working practices in supported accommodation sites and care staff in hospital is the comparison between working in new, relatively small and developing agencies like the voluntary associations, and working in what seemed like the 'House of Usher' – the crumbling and closing REH TCC site.

Activity

Activity levels (in terms of daytime occupation and other social contacts) remained much the same over the post-discharge period. Thus, the level of activity people had at the time of leaving hospital – and this varied greatly – remained largely unchanged. One leaver stopped going to a regular day occupation (this case was discharged from the hospital hostel to a staffed hostel initially giving up the day placement at SAMH's kitchen and, latterly, leaving the hostel place).

Any attempt to make a direct link between activity levels or occupation and successful outcome are dogged by problems of definition and by a great variation in patients' preferences. For example, two cases, one who worked five days per week in open employment and one who preferred to stay around the house and did not want any sort of occupation, had almost exactly the same subjective satisfaction scores with this area of their lives.

For those people moving to supported accommodation and hostel places there was a financial disincentive to open employment as the earnings disregard for those in receipt of income support was just £15.00 per week. After that, for every pound earned income support is reduced by the same amount.

The need for 'sheltered' occupation has been recognised for the population studied but there is little such employment offered. Options are either attendance at a day hospital or day centre or, as a non-medical alternative, Employment Training (ET) schemes (e.g. SAMH's kitchen). These are time-limited (usually for one year) and increasingly under pressure to deal with training for open employment, rather than being sheltered employment by another name. When one of the discharged subjects first went to SAMH's kitchen it was reported by staff that some 2 per cent of 'trainees' eventually got open employment. Currently, the externally set target is 20 per cent. This is bound to result in a change in the nature of the candidates accepted for a place in favour of those most likely to be employable, in order to retain funding. One new venture involving one of the discharged cases is a sandwich/fast food enterprise run as a private company. The person who moved from SAMH's kitchen to this venture was one of those for whom some structured occupation was seen by all concerned as crucial to his well-being and who was lucky enough to get this job.

Activity levels showing an increase in satisfaction ratings were likely to be associated with factors other than just having a formal occupation. It is likely that it reflects a general increase in satisfaction with what might be described as 'sociable' activity, partly because of the nature of the accommodation affording easier access to general facilities and partly to do with staff support. Support staff, unlike hospital staff, had time available to support the residents in social activities and daily would be either engaging in practical activities around the house or helping the tenants go shopping or some other trip out.

Living Situation

The most marked change for the discharged subjects as a group was the experience of moving to their new accommodation. As mentioned above, the vast majority of subjects went to a supported 'package' of care based on either supported accommodation itself or some other supported living situation or a hostel. Only one of the cases moving to supported accommodation or hostel had been in a similar sort of provision before. Thus, the lengthy stay in hospital represented something of a watershed in their lives. While there was not unequivocal praise from subjects for the new living situation nor universal criticism of life in hospital, subjects were generally happier in their new surroundings. The most common significant change reported was increased freedom and greater choice. Being away from intrusive or threatening people was the next most common positive change reported. Few negative changes were mentioned and when they were it was to do with having to do household chores, or suffering from others not pulling their weight around the house.

A very important point to recognise is that staff–patient ratios are different when comparing hospital wards with supported accommodation and to community hostels, and this is bound to have an effect on the levels of support and kinds of activities engaged in (or not). Ward staff–patient ratios tend to be in the region of 3 nursing staff to 17–20+ patients at the hospital, with trained staff often being moved to cover other wards, while 3 support workers to 8–12 residents is common practice for one of the voluntary organisations' supported accommodation and 2.5 staff to 8 residents in another voluntary organisation's staffed hostel.

Staff interviewed at supported accommodation sites and at the hostels saw the level of handicap experienced by the patients they were now receiving as higher than earlier 'intakes'.

Four people moved on from their initial hostel or supported accommodation sites just after their final visit follow-up, just one of these moving to another place that was supported. One other went on to B & B (by choice), and the other two drifted into Grassmarket hostels, e.g. Salvation Army, having lost their places at hostel and supported accommodation, respectively.

SIGNIFICANT OTHERS

Family

While the majority of subjects had living relatives, those with active contact were very few. It is of note that no subject had dependants themselves.

One of the great concerns of community care critics has been the level of burden on relatives attendant upon the loss of hospital places. Of course, in Scotland there has been no hospital run-down or closure programme to compare with England and Wales. Burden on relatives is well-documented and has an extensive literature (Fadden et al. 1987, Atkinson 1986, Simic 1989, Wallace 1987). However, there is little evidence to date of burden produced as a direct result of discharge of long-stay patients from hospital. The burden is extensive but is unrelated directly and immediately to hospital discharges. Thus, there is no evidence that patients are going back to the care of relatives from long-stay places. The picture may be very different for short-term patients who get admitted to acute wards but long-stay patients exhibit a degree of alienation from close relatives when, that is, they are there at all. Major studies in England of the closure of Freiern and Claybury hospitals and of Cane Hill hospital, for example, have shown that they have very low levels of relative involvement in their discharge plans. It may be that presence of a caring relative, in fact, acts as a prophylactic to long-stay admission.

There was little evidence of any direct involvement of hospital staff with what few families there were of the long-stay patients in the study and little evidence of involvement of community staff with them either. The study did, however, have some cases of carer involvement to report on. One leaver was discharged with a high level of support but was resistant to accepting help from anyone other than relatives (a sister and brother-in-law) who visited virtually every other day for the year or so he was out of hospital, helping him with the most basic of self-care tasks and providing virtually all his social support. They themselves were older. The care of older sufferers from mental illness by carers themselves who are elderly is also well-documented (Hicks 1988). Another leaver, in a staffed hostel, spent one overnight stay per week with his mother, a widow. The relationship was a rather strained one for both parties. She herself was unable to see the care staff as in any way some source of help for her and was antagonistic towards them.

The nature and the levels of burden experiences by the few carers identified was very similar to that experienced by carers reported on in a previous study conducted by the author (Simic 1989). This found an extensive burden with some evidence of a rift between the carer and support services.

Friendships

There was wide variation amongst the subject group but, generally, the number of those with close alliances involving a number of people was small: 15 of the discharged cases had networks of from nought to two or three people (often known through the hospital). Just six cases had reasonably extensive networks of contacts outside agency staff and for these cases the networks were, in different ways, crucial to their survival. In only one of these cases was there a readmission, and this a brief one. These networks were long-established and the subjects were well-recognised as socially competent.

There was a range of expectations displayed by leavers, from those who would have wanted better relationships with other people to those who definitely did not want that sort of intimacy. As with occupation, satisfaction scores on this domain are unrelated to network size.

Money

This was an area of surprisingly few complaints. This must be, at least in some way, associated with expectations which are adjusted downwards. Patients in hospital had in the region of £9 to live on and those in supported accommodation had little more. Clothing grants and other funds offered by supported accommodation provision increased disposable incomes by, in relative terms, substantial amounts of money. About half of the discharged subjects smoked and many reported smoking a sufficient quantity to use up a large proportion of, and in many cases more than, their reported weekly income. Where there was wider family in some contact they often were called upon to 'sub' the subject's income, especially for cigarettes.

Confusion over benefits, debt problems, problems of survival on subsistence level income have all been well-documented in this client group (Stewart 1988). Those who moved on to supported accommodation experienced their problems relating to money being buffered by staff support, by extra income (e.g. clothing allowances paid by supported accommodation agencies on top of the resident's weekly income support figure) and by the voluntary association bearing arrears of rent for periods that private agencies would be unlikely to tolerate. One person had great difficulty adjusting to paying over his rent, and particularly in understanding that the money received from the DSS (in excess of £150 pw) was not all his to spend. He would have most probably been evicted from his accommodation with a less tolerant attitude and, in the event, rent direct arrangements had to be made despite it being against the agency's philosophy of resident responsibility for rent payment.

Medication

In general, most subjects were either positive about their medication or ambivalent about it. If ambivalent, they nonetheless perceived medication as having some positive influence which, at worst, they saw as a necessary evil. Attitude to medication may be a differentiating factor between the group discharged and those remaining. This is difficult to gauge because hospital practices tend to enforce compliance while there is more choice (for good or ill) for the patient when away from hospital. At the supported accommodation sites and hostels people are expected to be responsible for their own medication and/or comply with arrangements for depot injection. There was a range of sites from which patients obtained their medication (from the GP directly, from the CPNs at health centre, day centre, employment training centre, from the visiting CPN, at the Continuing Care clinic, from the nurse at day hospital, or returning to the ward for the nurse to administer). Most patients did not seem to show much knowledge about their medication and rarely any apparent curiosity. 'It's to keep me calm', 'It's to control my nerves', 'It's to keep me on an even keel', 'I don't know' were the most common responses to questioning about what they perceived medication to be doing.

Mental State

People's views of their own mental state were very variable between individuals but constant over time. Almost all those interviewed had seen themselves as worse in the past than at the time of interview.

Questions about the role of admission and the role of the hospital in relation to the patients' mental state again evidenced wide variation in attitude. While most had something of a negative attitude to the hospital, and for many this would be an understatement, this did not necessarily represent a rejection of the role of admission in the patients' life.

Physical Health

The group as a whole was relatively young and it was the case that overall physical health presented few problems. There was one amputee (with diabetes), one person with a gastric problem, two with severe asthmatic problems (one of these also with angina), one with a broken and distorted spine, and another with a permanent limp (the latter two injuries both from past suicide attempts), and one wheelchair-bound case with multiple sclerosis.

Safety

Perceptions of personal safety both indoors and outside improved over the period. While, for some patients, hospital was seen as a place of security it would be naive to equate the hospital with safety and 'community' placements with increased risk. There were from many patients complaints about the intrusiveness and threatening nature of other patients at the hospital (usually those patients who were most disturbed), one or two patients made guarded (historical) references to alleged ill-treatment by staff, particularly those patients with memories of being in the state hospital or who had required to be taken to one of the locked wards at REH. None (as far as is known) of the discharged subjects experienced any threat over the period and none was in trouble with the police.

There are one or two other points relating to issues of safety that should be mentioned. It is of note that none of the community facilities reported any problems associated with fire risk over a period of some two years. This is a relatively commonly identified problem for patients on the long-stay wards, especially those with older patients. Thus, either those who are severe fire-risks do not get discharged or this risk is an institutional 'myth'. All the supported accommodation sites and hostels had fire detectors. None of the voluntary organisation staff reported any substantial call on their out-of-hours emergency system. The need for 24 hour care is also commonly cited as crucial for long-stay hospital patients.

Prospect of Leaving

Sixteen of the discharged cases, at the time they were first interviewed, rated themselves as having a strong desire to leave while just three did not wish to go. Of those interviewed, nobody thought at the end of the follow-up period that they had made the wrong decision. The prospect of leaving was associated with some anxiety but often with some optimism although it must be remembered that almost all of the cases were going to provision they had not experienced before.

Advice on Leaving

In the main, this seemed to be rather limited although it was not an area of much dissatisfaction. Patients, in the main, were offered supported accommodation or hostel placements and, in the main, either having been steered in that direction or having moved in that direction under their own steam, they accepted it if it was offered to them. There was not a notable degree of choice in what was on offer.

THROUGH THE 'NET' AND OTHER PROBLEMS

There are certain outcomes for patients in QOL studies which are cited as a priori 'failures', for example, drifting into a vagrant lifestyle or becoming homeless, becoming a burden to family, going to prison, or gross deterioration in physical and mental health and self-care (Wallace 1987, Knapp et al. 1990). On the other hand there are, in contrast to these 'failures', some positive features that go together to make up the overall QOL picture. These include: the extent to which a patient is actually more integrated into the community rather than just catered for in a mini-institution, client attitudes to their new circumstances, subjective well-being, the degree of choice they are able to exercise, social and professional networks, activity levels, symptoms and mental state, behavioural problems (Malin 1987, Brown 1988).

There is no evidence in this study that long-stay patients leaving the REH were 'dumped' or were destitute (this accords with other study findings, e.g. TAPS 1989). There were some problematical cases that became more evident over time which deserve highlighting. There is no evidence of any person in the study completely losing touch with psychiatric or support services, although for some this might be an extremely tenuous level of contact.

One leaver came from and returned to a vagrant lifestyle, amid much debate about the presence of a mental illness and the appropriateness of his admission in the first place. He initially was discharged to an ex-serviceman's hostel but within a short space of time was sleeping rough again and was last seen in an arcade entrance under a blanket.

Another lived in very poor conditions supported by a partner and by a CPN but was on the brink of being sectioned on occasions because of his 'appalling' living conditions. This subject, discharged from the hospital hostels, was extremely resistant to being readmitted despite his living conditions – he hated hospital. For some years he had been a half-time patient at the hospital having his own house outside. His circumstances were singular in that he not only had a chronic 'treatment-resistant' illness but also was profoundly deaf.

Three leavers moved on from their initial supported accommodation/hostel places. Some minimal contact, however, was retained with psychiatric services: one moved on to lodgings, a private boarding house with a landlady who 'specialised' in lodgers with mental illness, and still kept in sporadic contact with the OT day unit and the Continuing Care Clinic; the two others moved on to Salvation Army hostels, retaining some limited CPN contact.

One further leaver moved on from a local authority hostel to a supported accommodation place again just after final visit, just one more move in a peripatetic lifestyle.

One leaver from the acute wards disappeared from Edinburgh at the point of discharge (returning to Glasgow), requesting but being refused readmission because of longstanding non-compliance with treatment. There was no further information on this person.

Readmissions

Readmission, particularly a short one, is by no means a failure. Admission should not be seen as a negative event and controlled admission and treatment may represent good management (including self-management) of a longstanding condition. Lengthy readmissions, though, would be of concern and those that occurred are examined here. These sorts of readmissions might give pointers to inherent problems in particular models of care, shortcomings that might need to be addressed.

There were three cases that were readmitted during the course of the follow-up period and remained in-patients at the end of that period. One could say, on the one hand, that this is merely three cases and, thus, of little or no worry, or one could say that it represents more than 12 per cent of discharged cases either being unreprovidable for, given current service levels, or having some special features of which services would have to take note – a statistic of greater concern. TAPS are currently reporting some 9 per cent being readmitted on a long-term basis (reported in the *British Medical Journal* 24 October, 1992).

There was some evidence in the study that 'problematical' outcomes – one of which is lengthy readmission – may be predictable from a combination of functioning and daily living skills scores. Further work would need to be done to claim that this a predictive tool. Those cases below the group median on an adapted daily living skills scale used in the study and those in the lowest band of MRSS score are the cases associated with greatest risk of readmission and/or experiencing severe problems in the community. It is also clear that there are cases that either instrument alone might not immediately identify as being at risk.

SUMMARY OF MAIN FINDINGS

- Quality of life (QOL) is a central issue in the debate about the services for people with a chronic mental illness. In the REH study formal measures were combined with descriptive information, and with patient judgements and with a range of professional opinions, to form an overall picture of QOL over time.

- Leavers are mainly going to supported accommodation of one sort or another. This is mainly run by voluntary organisations and a transfer of care appears to be taking place, from hospital to voluntary association.

- Many leavers have severe and chronic handicaps.

- A change of immediate environment is the biggest change for patients moving from hospital wards to small-scale housing or small-scale hostels.

- Patients were more satisfied with their living situation, and their general satisfaction and morale were indicated as stable or improved over time. Some settings have better staff ratios than hospital.

- It is difficult for those leaving hospital to get occupation of some sort and especially difficult to get some sheltered working environment. This lack of occupation is a major feature of the discharged group's experience of post-hospital care.

- It is hard for professionals to develop 'packages of care' around independent accommodation; thus the emphasis is on a bricks and mortar solution plus support staff who may or may not be resident.

- Most of those leaving hospital had a limited social network, although some of the patients recognised as more sociable had bigger networks which were important to their survival.

- The most common professional contact with the patients is from supported accommodation non-resident support workers or from hostel staff. Other professional follow-up is negligible. The main medical follow-up is from CPNs.

- Long-stay psychiatric cases are a low priority for social workers and virtually no social worker follow-up was recorded. Direct contact with GPs was negligible.

- Mental state and functioning measures indicated stability over time. The proportion of 'problematical' cases was of some concern, particularly the evidence that it was not until the end of the follow-up period that some problems began to show.

- It would seem to be the case that voluntary agencies are receiving 'creamed off' (the more able) patients and some perceive that this will change the nature of the service leaving the local authority and, ultimately, the hospital to perform the function of provider of 'last resort'.

- The biggest change shown in satisfaction ratings between hospital life and life away from the REH was in satisfaction with living situation and with professional support. The only negative change was with safety outside on the streets.

- There were few carers in the study and just one resident carer. No resident carer was involved with subjects from the long-stay wards. There were two non-resident carers identified.

- The physical health of the group was relatively good although it is of note that two cases with marked problems from old injuries were cases who had received those injuries through deliberate self-harm.

- Most cases were shown to be very keen to be leaving hospital and, while there was some ambivalence in a few cases, almost all at final visit still preferred life outside hospital. Many recognised the beneficial effects of a hospital admission or, at least, its necessity. None of those interviewed wanted to return.

CONCLUSION

This has provided findings of a study of a largely 'revolving-door' group of patients who left the REH over a period after having had a lengthy stay. Most, but not all, left from the long-term wards. Most were very keen to leave. Most stayed out and a number exhibited a static or somewhat improved picture of 'quality of life'. Some also exhibited severe mental state or behavioural problems resulting in major disruption to their lives, especially towards the end of the follow-up period.

There is a sort of dance of chronic illness sufferers with service-providers. It is somewhat circular, old partners regularly experiencing *déjà vu* as they meet up again and follow well-rehearsed steps. This is evident in the present study group's long, mixed and repeated contact with psychiatric services. Many of the patients themselves referred to the Edinburgh 'circuit' of day centres and units, seeing it as something they go around. Now a kind of social experiment is under way. This is the introduction of supported accommodation and the burgeoning of voluntary agency involvement in the care of this client group. As one form of care is seen graphically to be waning – the TCC, a gargantuan and Gothic reminder of an earlier age – a new one is developing: small-scale supported accommodation run on a non-medical model. The success of this new form of care will depend on its impact, long-term, on the quality of life of the chronic sufferers who use it. It is a markedly different model to hospital and the move from relatively large, relatively anonymous living in hospital wards to the relative intimacy of the hostels and group homes covered by this study must be a culture shock to many.

There are problems in trying to break out of old moulds and there was evidence in the study that a more independent model of support, providing help in the setting of more integrated living, is difficult to organise and difficult to finance: different agencies tend not to work well together and finance for provision comes with the bricks and mortar of the accommodation.

Over the lifetime of this study, most patients were happier with the overall improvement to their quality of life in the move away from a Victorian provision which was a crumbling edifice anyway – and most fared well or at least adequately. There was a more than slight discordant note from a number of patients whose illness and problems prevented them from settling in a new style of living and had to move on again back into Salvation Army hostels or the street or back into hospital. Last – but not least – a distant rumble of concern may be heard from care staff in hospitals and social service hostels who increasingly see themselves as providers of last resort.

REFERENCES

Affleck, J.W. and McGuire, R.J. (1984) The measurement of psychiatric rehabilitation status: a review of the needs and a new scale. *British Journal of Psychiatry, 145*, 517–525.

Allen, C.I. *et al.* (1989) A comparison of practices, attitudes and interactions in 2 established units for people with a psychiatric disorder. *Psychological Medicine, 19*, 459–467.

Atkinson, J.M. (1986) *Schizophrenia at Home.* Beckenham: Croom Helm.

Brown, R.I. (ed) (1988) *Quality of Life for Handicapped People.* Beckenham: Croom Helm.

Convention of Scottish Local Authorities (1990) *Caring for People: Community Care in the Next Decade and Beyond – The Convention's Response.* Discussion Paper, January.

Dyer, J.A.T. (1991) Rehabilitation and Community Care. In *Companion to Psychiatric Studies, 5th Edition.* Edinburgh: Livingstone.

Fadden, G. *et al.* (1987) The burden of care. *British Journal of Psychiatry, 150,* 285–292.

Goodwin, S. (1990) *Community Care and the Future of Mental Health Provision.* Aldershot: Gower.

Hatch, S. and Nissel, C. (1989) *Is Community Care Working?* Westminster: Westminster Association for Mental Health.

Hicks, C. (1988) *Who Cares.* London: Virago.

House of Commons Social Services Committee (1985) *Community Care with Special Reference to Adult Mentally Ill and Mentally Handicapped people.* London: HMSO.

Hunter, D. and Wistow, G. (1987) *Community Care in Britain: Variations on a Theme.* London: King Edward's Hospital Fund.

Huxley, P. (1990) The organisation of services. Paper for the *5th European symposium on Social Psychiatry, Manchester.*

Jones, K., Robinson, M. and Golightly, M. (1986) Long-term psychiatric patients in the community. *British Journal of Psychiatry, 149,* 537–540.

Knapp, M. *et al.* (1990) Care in the Community. *PSSRU Newsletter,* May.

Leff, J. (1990) Response to conference question. In *TAPS (1990) Annual Conference Report.* Freiern Hospital.

Lehman, A.F. (1983a) The effects of psychiatric symptoms on quality of life assessments among the chronically mentally ill. *Evaluation and Program Planning, 6*, 2, 143–151.

Lehman, A.F. (1983b) The well-being of chronic mental patients. Assessing their quality of life. *Archives of General Psychiatry, 40*, 369–373.

Lehman, A.F., Possidente, S. and Hawker, F. (1986) The quality of life of chronic patients in a state hospital and in community residences. *Hospital and Community Psychiatry, 37*, 9, 901–907.

Lehman, A.F. (1988) A quality of life interview for the chronically mentally ill. *Evaluation and Program Planning, 11*, 1, 51–62.

Malin, N. (ed) (1987) *Reassessing Community Care*. Beckenham: Croom Helm.

Margolius, O. (1986) *Adaptive Behaviour Scale*. Mimeo, Team for the Assessment of Psychiatric Services, Friern Hospital.

Rescher (1982) quoted in Huxley, P. Quality of life measurement in mental health services. *Good Practices in Mental Health*.

Simic, P. (1989) Aspects of Burden. Unpublished *MSc Thesis*, Department of Psychiatry, Manchester University.

Simic, P., O'Donnell, O. and Gilfillan S. (1991) *A study of the Rehabilitation to the Community of Long-term Psychiatric Patients at the Royal Edinburgh Hospital*. Stirling University: Social Work Research Centre.

Stewart, G. (1988) Maintaining people with a mental disability in the community. *SPRU Research Seminar Paper, March*.

Sturt, E. and Wykes T. (1986) The measurement of social behaviour in psychiatric patients: an assessment of the reliability and validity of the SBS schedule. *British Journal of Psychiatry, 148*, 1–11.

TAPS (1989) Moving long-stay psychiatric patients into the community. *Annual Conference Report*. Friern Hospital.

Titterton, M. (1991) 'Caring for mentally disabled people in Scotland'. *Social Policy and Administration, 25*, 2, 136–148.

Wallace, M. (1987) The forgotten illness. *The Times*, May.

Wilson, D. (1990) Comcare – a report on an Edinburgh Care Initiative. *Unpublished Report*. Stirling: Stirling University.

CHAPTER 6

'The Best Move I've Made'
The Role of Housing for Those with Mental Health Problems

Alison Petch

I remember the housing scheme
where we both stayed.
The same houses, different homes,
where the choices were made.

Liz Lochhead

The community care debate must inevitably focus much attention on the mechanics of caring – who is to do it, with the support of which mechanisms, at what financial or personal costs. None of this can take place however unless the fundamental provision of a roof over the head is in place. Only then can the symbolic transformation of house into home begin to take place. As the Eleventh Report of the House of Commons Social Services Committee (1990) highlighted, 'having somewhere to call home is the cornerstone of effective community care' (para 112).

Although the key role of housing has been argued for some time (Kay and Legg 1986, NFHA/MIND 1987, Braisby, Echlin, Hill and Smith 1988), its status is very much secondary to that of health and social care in the recent legislation. In *Caring for People* (DHSS 1989), for example, housing merits but four paragraphs whereas entire chapters are devoted to the roles and responsibilities of social services authorities and of the health service. In terms of joint working, a permissive rather than a directive approach is adopted:

> Social Service authorities will need to work closely with housing authorities, housing associations and other providers of housing of all types in developing plans for a full and flexible range of housing. Where necessary, housing needs should form part of the assessment of care needs and the occupational therapist may have a key role here. (para 3.5.4)

Earlier, however, in his report *Community Care: Agenda for Action*, Griffiths (1988) had recommended that the role of housing agencies be much more closely defined as the provider of stock:

> The responsibility of public housing authorities (local authority hous-ing authorities, Housing Corporation etc.) should be limited to arrang-ing and sometimes financing and managing the 'bricks and mortar' of housing needed for community care purposes. (para 6.10)

In the *National Health Service and Community Care Act* itself (1990), the only statutory requirement with regard to housing is that there be consultation with providing agencies in the preparation of the community care plans.

In Scotland the series of guidance papers from the Scottish Office on the implementation of the community care arrangements has included a Circular from the Environment Department on *Housing and Community Care* (Scottish Office 1991). The essential nature of the housing contribution is recognised:

> Housing has a particular and crucial role to play in the success of community care. The availability of a range of suitable housing for those who need community care is essential if their needs are to be properly met. (para 1.4.1)

The strategies proposed in order to ensure this contribution include partici-pation by housing authorities in the community care planning process, con-sideration of community care needs in the preparation of the housing plan together with participation in the assessment of the needs of individuals, and attention to the use of both their own stock and through their enabling role of that of other agencies in the meeting of identified need (para 1.4.2). The importance of consultation during the planning process with Scottish Homes, housing associations and other specialist providers is also highlighted. Per-haps the most radical recommendation of the Circular, moving well beyond the 'bricks and mortar' role of Griffiths, is that housing staff should be available to contribute to the social work-led assessment of care needs. Further:

> Housing authorities should also decide on and implement their own contributions to packages of care, in close collaboration with social work authorities. (para 1.6.2)

Although the exhortations to the various bodies on community care needs are welcome, some skilful juggling will be necessary if the different statutory plans are to interrelate. Community care plans are to be three year rolling documents and are produced at regional level. Housing plans cover a five year period but with the crucial financial allocations on an annual cycle – and in all but the unitary authorities this is of course a district function. Housing associations produce annual business plans which now feed into the annual plans which Scottish Homes produce for each of their districts. Health boards also are expected to produce an account of their community care policies and the steps they intend in order to achieve them. As the Care in the Community Scottish Working Group (1990) has highlighted:

There are, therefore, at least five different, relatively separate, bodies involved in community care planning, all of which have a role to play in the provision and funding of community care. It is essential that a co-ordinating structure is put in place which permits the planning and funding of future provision of the accommodation and support requirements of community care to be delivered. (para 4.1)

The decision in seven regions to produce joint health board and social work department community care plans has to be welcomed; their integration with the intentions of the housing agencies (as in Lothian) would be a further advance.

SPECIAL NEEDS HOUSING

The housing requirements of those with community care needs differ of course not only according to the special needs group but also according to the specific needs and preferences of the individuals. In addition to the four groups traditionally identified – elderly people, people with physical disabilities, individuals with mental health problems and those with learning difficulties – housing authorities are urged to pay attention to identifying and meeting the housing needs of individuals with dementia, those who have AIDS or are HIV positive, individuals with profound or multiple handicaps and those who misuse drugs or alcohol. Notwithstanding the individual nature of any one person's needs, there are nonetheless certain requirements likely to attach to the housing needs of certain of the special needs groups. Most obvious are the access requirements of those with physical disabilities and to a lesser extent the elderly. For many however, and this has perhaps been where it has been more difficult to secure housing provision in the past, the requirements in terms of the fabric are no different than for any other individual or housing group. The special requirements are in terms of the support package that needs to be present in addition to the housing provision *per se*. Availability, however, whether of land for new-build, of property for conversion, or of stock for allocation, can very often be a central concern.

   This contribution will focus on one of the special needs groups, individuals with mental health problems, and will illustrate from a study of a number of special housing provisions the catalytic role of such projects in the promotion of community care. Recent years have seen the development of a number of projects which provide an intensity of support higher than the traditional group home (detailed for example by Pritlove 1985). Such developments have shifted the boundaries in terms of the identity of those who may be maintained within the community.

HOUSING FOR MENTAL HEALTH NEEDS

As with any special needs group, the majority of individuals with mental health problems live across a range of tenures throughout the community, dependent to a greater or lesser extent on formal and informal care and carer mechanisms. For a number of individuals, however, the provision of some form of supported accommodation allows a move outwith the psychiatric hospital or prevents potential admission from the community when independent living has become difficult. Provision to meet such needs can take a variety of forms, ranged across a spectrum according to the intensity of support. At the lower support level may be the independent local authority or housing association tenancy in which the tenant receives an occasional visit from a support worker. At the upper end may be a nursing type facility where there is intensive twenty-four hour cover, and at various stages in between may be variants of the individual or small group living model where there is a fair degree of support available in the form of staff cover.

The residential care allowance has supported much of the recent growth in accommodation of this type, the intensity of support that could be provided in such a provision often appearing appropriate both for individuals who might not otherwise have been discharged from hospital and for those, perhaps caught in a pattern of 'revolving door' admissions, for whom independent living has proved problematic. Within the last five years there has been considerable growth in Scotland in the number of supported accommodation projects for those with mental health problems, although from a very low base. By far the majority of such projects have been developed through the impetus of the voluntary sector, although both health boards and local authorities have contributed by way of supplementary funding or through the provision of housing stock.

An important distinction, not always appreciated in the earlier stages of development, is whether a provision is primarily perceived as a long-term facility, a potentially permanent base for an individual, or whether there is expectation of movement. A transitional project assumes a model of rehabilitation whereby, after some pre-defined or flexible period of support, an individual is expected to move to either some independent situation or to a less intensively supported facility.

While such a path may be appropriate for some, the great strength of many recently developed projects would appear to lie in their acceptance of the need for permanently supported alternatives to institutional care. A number of the first projects of this type received among their first tenants individuals who had pursued a depressing path on the variant of hospital to limited stay hostel to tenancy to bed and breakfast to hospital. The creation of a permanent alternative allowed a chock to be inserted in the revolving door.

PROJECT EVALUATION

Eleven supported accommodation projects across Scotland provided the basis for an evaluation carried out at the Social Work Research Centre during 1988–89 (Petch 1990, 1992). Of these provisions at least six placed no immediate constraints on the length of stay, with the potential for a 'permanent' placement. All but one were outwith the statutory sector, including two developed by specialist housing associations, and all but two were financed for revenue costs through the residential care allowance. Several of the projects were the first developments for agencies which have subsequently established a number of provisions of this type. Initial negotiations had often been protracted, with a number of the projects resulting from some form of joint planning mechanism. Health boards and local authorities had contributed in a number of instances to capital costs, underwriting for example initial staffing costs and voids or making available surplus property. In addition a number of authorities have enhanced the revenue funding through the provision of supplementation.

The availability of property is, not surprisingly, a major hurdle in the development of projects of this type. If local authority stock is sought, availability varies widely between different areas, influenced in part of course by the policies which determine the allocation of a diminishing stock. Acquisition through open purchase is often not an option for developments of this type, and while surplus property from, for example, a health board may appear an attractive proposition it is often not of a type or in a location that facilitates policies of normalisation. Even when appropriate property has been secured, there may ensue lengthy wrangles with planning, building control or other departments depending upon the liberality of their interpretation of different regulations, for example on change of use. One of the projects in this study, where extensive renovation of district council housing stock took place, was driven to presenting the ultimatum of three people actually moving in with their suitcases in order to secure, after several postponements, minimum standards for completion such as the removal of boarding from windows.

Such stories are familiar, however, to those involved in the development process. The focus of this evaluation was on the experience of the individuals living within the projects. Each project was visited at three six-monthly intervals in order to answer three key research questions:

- Can individuals with a considerable history of mental health problems and hospital admission live in supported accommodation?
- What are the effects on the individual's quality of life?
- What are the effects in terms of psychiatric symptomatology and social functioning of a move outside hospital?

All individuals who were willing were interviewed on each occasion, resulting across the three data collection points in 255 detailed interviews with 145 individuals (52 female and 93 male). In the main movement accounted for the instances where only one or two interviews were achieved (71 and 38 individuals respectively). Additionally, project staff completed measures of social functioning and rehabilitation status in respect of those who were interviewed. The interviews provide a rich source of data which allows some sense to be made of the responses of those who whether by choice or circumstance experience a supported accommodation project.

Half of those who were interviewed in this study had moved to their project from psychiatric hospital and a further fifth, confirming the argument presented above, from another supported (but generally time-limited) provision. Fourteen per cent had previously been living with family and seven per cent had given up a tenancy. The remainder had moved from a range of unsatisfactory digs, bed and breakfast or homelessness. Of particular importance is the indication that for two-thirds of the sample no alternative to their current provision was considered at the time of referral. And indeed for a further 27 per cent the only potential alternative was another supported provision. Only for a handful of people was either a tenancy or residence with friend or family an option, indicative of the need for high levels of ongoing support attached to the housing function. The large majority had been referred to projects through some professional route, although just under one in five had arrived as a result of self or family referral.

There are obviously important differences between projects even when the broad target and funding pattern is similar. Some had been developed with close links to a specific hospital and were committed to taking at least the initial placements from that source. In these instances there were often people who had spent lengthy periods in hospital – eleven in the study had been hospitalised for over twenty years. A couple of the projects were targeted at younger people, while in others a majority of those interviewed had experienced a succession of short term admissions, often to both hospital and other temporary placements. Overall 14 per cent had been in hospital for over ten years, 31 per cent between one and ten years and 27 per cent less than a year. The experience of the remaining 28 per cent accords with the 'revolving door' description.

Many of those who were interviewed wrestle with serious mental health problems. Fifty-six per cent carried a diagnosis of schizophrenia, ten per cent a depressive disorder and six per cent an affective psychosis. Eight per cent were considered to have a personality or behavioural problem and for five per cent the major problem was drug or alcohol abuse. A variety of other problems had been experienced by the remaining individuals (15%), of which seven per cent had a diagnosis varying over time. Eighty-eight per cent were in receipt of regular medication.

FIRST IMPRESSIONS

> I think it was the only decision I could make. I just couldn't take any more bedsits. I had been in bedsits for about four years and I have been moving from place to place most of my life and I need somewhere permanent to settle down.

Moving to a new housing situation is stressful for all. For those who may be making a move after many years in hospital, or who from the community are acknowledging their need for a higher level of support, anxiety levels are likely to be accentuated. Oft repeated assertions from professionals and indeed from some individuals within institutions that there is no desire for change or movement should therefore be treated with some caution. The status quo is often a preferable short-term expedient. The experience of those within this study confirms this picture. Prior to moving to the project it was only a minority who were positively looking forward to moving in. Over a third were apprehensive, unwilling or would have preferred to go elsewhere; others described a complex of emotions ranging from disinterest to over-excitement. Only a third would have said they were positively looking forward to the change. Yet by the time of the first interview with respondents, over three-quarters preferred living in the project to where they had been before. Amongst the small numbers (7% of the total) who expressed a preference for their previous location and those (16%) who were ambivalent were individuals who for various reasons had had to leave family or friends where for choice they would have stayed. Initial anxiety therefore appears rapidly to dissipate. The preference, moreover, is sustained over time.

The uncertainty over the initial move is accentuated by a general feeling of being ill-informed. Asked what they knew about the project before they came, forty per cent could offer nothing beyond perhaps the fact that it was for people with mental health problems and could not cite an informant that they had been able to question. Others were able to cite rather more in the way of details that they had gleaned, but only some of those in hospital-linked projects who had been involved to some extent in the development of the project felt any familiarity prior to arrival.

> They took us to the showroom place and shop in G – curtain material, hand towels, bath towels, face cloth – we get them all the same colour.

BRICKS AND MORTAR

> I just feel it's part of my life because I've never had a home – it's just like a home to you.

Amongst the eleven projects were a variety of housing types and arrangements. They included converted older property, new-build complexes with flats of various sizes and, a reflection of policies of normalisation, an increasing number of 'ordinary' houses or flats in 'ordinary' streets. Locations ranged from city centre to suburb to small rural town. Certain locations, particularly the periphery, were distinctly less popular, and there was a clear preference for single rooms, for space, and for maximisation of facilities and comforts. For many, however, the actual fabric of the house or the specific location was less important than the fact that it provided, often for the first time in a long while, a source of security and privacy.

Lengthy debates have taken place over the optimum size for supported projects. Recent trends have led away from the larger hostels of the past and contemporary discussion is much more often around the definition of 'small', whether developments should be for two, for three, for four or more. An important consideration is the potential length of stay in a project. Individuals may be willing to tolerate shorter, time-limited arrangements which would be unacceptable on a permanent basis. Of similar importance is the extent to which any sharing arrangements are mutually arranged, perhaps by individuals moving together from hospital. Ironically, many domestic dwellings are suited to a grouping of three, a communal area and a room each, yet it is the dynamics of three which most often gives rise to comment. Certainly there were a number of complaints from individuals in this position, particularly in new schemes where space constraints added to the tensions:

> It does smoulder away. It's not a really happy environment to live. They never interfere but you hear tittle tattle and you are frightened at times to say anything because it's three people with different mental illnesses. You can't get away from that and if you say the wrong thing there is a sort of austerism creeps in and they don't speak.

On the other hand, particularly where groupings were not *ad hoc* and subject to change, there were some projects where houses of three functioned without difficulty.

A further design issue arises in terms of communal space, particularly in projects which group a number of individual units, either in a core and cluster model or in some other configuration. Within the study there were two projects which comprised a number of flats. Both these projects were new build, with the specialist provision for mental health a part of a larger complex. Both of the projects had included a communal area as part of the development and in one of the projects this was a major asset for at least some of the tenants:

> I am more in the common room than I am in the flat. I could sit there for maybe four hours at a time.

This area was close to the entrance to the complex, was comfortably furnished with games and refreshment facilities, and opened onto a patio-type area. By contrast, in the project where the facility might be considered more essential as all the flats were single tenancies, the bleak and inaccessible nature of the room had rendered it useless. Requiring a key for entry and with no facilities to encourage anyone to drop in, tenants were effectively denied a potential source of support which for a number had been a crucial factor in offsetting fears of isolation in moving to a project of individual flats.

LIVING WITH OTHERS

> There is a provision for you to be private if you want to be or come out of your room and mix with any people, so you have options.

The provision of some form of supported accommodation implies, save for the single tenancy, some artificial manipulation of living arrangements. Individuals who may have nothing more in common with their co-residents than the experience of mental health problems are asked to coexist, preferably peacefully, under the same roof. The philosophy of an individual project may determine to what extent individuals are expected to engage in joint arrangements, be they domestic or more fundamentally supportive. Certain projects place a value on sharing, say in communal eating, or facilitate two or three individuals going together to some external activity. In other projects an individual could, if preferred, pursue a fairly solitary existence. The extent to which individual preferences match up with the reality depends of course on a subtle interplay between expectation and outcome. A number spoke of an advantage in the slightly larger unit, four or five rather than two or three, in that it provided a certain degree of privacy and protection against the potential intensity of group living:

> A unit of people small enough to get on individually but large enough to provide quite a bit of company.

> Sometimes I think I'd prefer more because it would not be so personal, not so noticeable if you're not down.

Significantly, one of the most respected providers in the field speaks of providing 'space within which people are free of pressure to be other than themselves'. Such space can of course be both physical and psychological.

The tolerance of individuals however should not be underestimated. Only a quarter of those interviewed were prepared to say they got on well with their fellow residents. Half felt the situation was 'OK' while the remaining quarter had more mixed feelings. Nonetheless the majority were prepared to accept the necessity of living alongside others in order to obtain the other benefits of support. Three out of every five were content with the number with whom they lived, while one in five would have preferred fewer.

THE SUPPORT ELEMENT

> You can discuss what you want in here but you have also got staff throughout the day who are friendly and helpful. They will help you with meals, whatever. It just depends how much you need yourself. I don't think I need that much but it's good to talk to people that haven't been ill. I can get on with the support workers quite a lot.

The task of the support workers attached to projects is crucial; indeed it is their presence which is the essential component of the provision. The pattern of staffing varies between projects. An increasing proportion of longer term provisions maintain twenty-four hour cover not through the direct presence of sleep-in staff but by contact through some form of paging system. For the projects in the study it tended to be those with the more frequent resident turnover, younger and perhaps more likely to experience acute crisis, where a constant staff presence was maintained. Thus, the staff to resident ratio ranged from .1 to .78 with a grouping in the region of .35.

Support workers vary as to their background. Some projects like to employ individuals from nursing or social work backgrounds; others rely more upon personal qualities and the ability to integrate individuals into the community around them. The support function can demand a range of inputs, from the practical and domestic to the counselling and therapeutic. As the key facet of such projects, it carries not surprisingly a number of dilemmas. At the centre is the balance between support and independence, offering the necessary backup but not obliterating the movement towards greater autonomy. Another is the extent to which workers present options and leave the action to the individual or alternatively get involved themselves in the activity alongside the person:

> I thought there would be more help, more communication. I think there should be more participation with the staff. More encouragement. Not encouragement because they give you that but more, I don't know, involvement. Them doing it as well.

The choice may depend in part on the perception of the role of the facility in providing an active rehabilitative function as opposed to more relaxed ongoing support. A similar dilemma is the degree to which workers feel they must maintain a certain distance: indeed one of the projects in the study had a practice-based philosophy perhaps loosely characterised as 'therapeutic neglect'. The motivation of workers is not always however understood or at least appreciated by individuals. Reluctance for example to fulfil a friendship role can seem hard when, as will be shown below, the social network is already minimal.

The level of contact with outside professional support tends, as with other focused resources, not to be great. Long-term mental health problems have not the same appeal as the acute crisis for the majority of psychiatrists: accordingly less than half had had contact with a psychiatrist since moving to the project. Just over half had been seen by a social worker but this was most often in connection with the move to the provision. Only a handful received regular support unless there was a statutory requirement for contact. Routine depot and other medication was most often supplied by general practitioner or community nurse; again such contact tended to be seen as routine with little evidence of more substantive input.

FRIENDS AND FAMILY

> When I was ill I lost, probably, all contact with friends. Friends no longer were friends and things like that. It was just that I changed and probably they changed towards me over a period of years.

Norms for the level and content of social contact can be difficult to determine. The researcher can ask about the numbers of friends and the substance of contact, but responses are plagued by the vagaries of definition. In particular there may be a reluctance by some to reveal just how thin is the veneer of social interaction. At first interview just under a quarter reported having no friends. A further third referred only to individuals within the project or were non-committal. The poverty of friendship is indicated by the following response to the questions in this area:

> Some of the nurses that were friends did come to see me on Sunday and they were nice friends – came with some of my clothes and stayed about fifteen minutes. I let them see my room, all round the kitchen, everything like that.

Under half (44%) specifically identified individual friendships, half of these citing one or two people, the other half three or more. The mistake must not be made however of attributing the lack of social contact to the supported accommodation itself. Most often it is the legacy of periods of illness, of broken networks, and perhaps of enforced isolation. Indeed there was encouraging evidence that the proportion reporting increased friendships since they had moved to the project rose from 10 per cent to 28 per cent, encouraging in that at least half of those interviewed expressed a desire for more and closer friendships. The quality of a friendship was thought to be particularly important – 'I've got lots of buddies rather than real friends'.

The extent to which family contacts were live varied between those projects with predominantly younger members and those which individuals had entered after long periods in hospital:

> They don't want to see me, so I don't want to see them, I say tough. They're ashamed of me – let them be like that. There is nothing I can do about it but I think more should be brought out about this mentally ill and all this.

Of those in their thirties for example only a quarter were in touch with most of their immediate family, compared with seven out of ten of those in their twenties. While 58 per cent were content with the amount of contact they had, 39 per cent would have liked more. Even when the contact is there, the quality of the contact may fall short of what is desired – 'now what do you mean by contact, just seeing them or having some sort of a real relationship?'

PASSING THE TIME

> They seem to want you to get involved with the community. I think they would like it if I was out seeing friends, going to the theatre and having meals, eating out, probably buying clothes with my clothing allowance. Always doing something during the day. Going for walks in the evening, getting fresh air so I can sleep better, but that doesn't work with me. I would say their ideas are quite good but I am depressed at the moment. I just can't live up to it and I feel I am being asked too much. Too much is expected of me.

Access to supported accommodation for an individual is a major achievement. Nonetheless it cannot be an end in itself. Whether it be perceived as a relatively short placement or as a lifetime option, consideration has to be given to the best way for any individual of filling their time. Moreover there must be careful consideration in response to individual needs of the optimum balance between freedom of choice and the benefits of coercion.

Even where it might be an option, the financial structure of the residential care allowance current at the time of writing virtually precludes employment on the open market. The alternatives in terms of regular activity are therefore some form of ET or hospital-based employment, some variant of occupational therapy or day centre or a more innovative form of day provision. At initial interview 35 per cent were involved in activity in one of these forms, half for more than three days a week, although there was considerable variation between different projects. A quarter were primarily project based without structured activity while one of the projects had its own programme of activities. Others had more informal activities which took them outwith the house – walking, visiting friends or pubs, voluntary work.

In terms of searching for the balance appropriate for each individual, half had suggestions for other things they would like to do, with for some a strong motivation to move outwith the psychiatric net. For some this involved sports, hobbies or study but for others there was the desire for work – 'if you do nothing all day the quality of life is not that good – a job would improve the quality of life for me'. Many however are restricted by the debilitating nature of their illness – 'because of the increased medication the lethargy has increased proportionately', 'I would like to do more but I find it difficult to get the impetus to do it'.

There is, nonetheless, some evidence from the study of increasing activity levels over time. Comparing those who have been in projects for less than three months with those resident for nine months or more, the proportion without any form of outside activity (including clubs and groups) falls from over half (55%) to under a third (32%). There can be a danger of assuming that once individuals are within supported accommodation the need for social contact has been met. Significantly, when asked if they were involved with activities with others in the project, 39 per cent were not, and a further 9 per cent only in the context of an organised project group.

PAYING THE BILLS

Barely enough to sole your shoes with.

The involvement of individuals in both social networks and outside activities cannot be divorced from the limited financial resources available to facilitate such participation. At the time of the study the majority were in receipt of a weekly allowance of £10.05, a princely sum to gain entry to the community. Although those who managed the food element had a larger sum with which to juggle, increased activity could only be gained at the cost of a poor diet. In such a context benefits such as concessionary travel, subsidised entry fees or a clothing grant can be of a value far beyond their cost. Nonetheless a policy which speaks of integration and normalisation rings pretty hollow if the only doors that can be entered are those without entrance fees.

OVERVIEW

It is not the purpose of this contribution to present detailed research findings, rather to use the study of these projects as a focus for the more general discussion of the housing context. Nonetheless it is important to record that the three original research questions were all answered in the affirmative. It is now without question that supported accommodation provides a viable alternative. In terms of quality of life, respondents in the study scored ten specific dimensions on a seven-point 'delighted–terrible' scale. The higher levels of satisfaction were with the house, area and the support available within the projects; at the lower end of the scale were the personal finance, the family and social contact, and the participation in activity. On a more general assessment, asked to compare their current life with several years previous, almost three-quarters considered it to have improved (26% 'somewhat better' and 47% 'much better'). For those in projects more than nine months, only 7 per cent make a negative comparison while the great majority, 81 per cent, make a positive comparison. Finally, in terms of social functioning and psychiatric symptomatology, on the various measures employed in the study, stability is maintained with no evidence of any deterioration.

LOOKING TO THE FUTURE

The effectiveness of supported accommodation of this type is now without question. Indeed the dimensions receiving highest approval in this study rather neatly encapsulate the dual functions of the housing and support roles. As with any development which has passed the innovatory stage, the challenge for the future is to maintain the quality of each provision, to extend the range of provision in order to implement choice, and to ensure that there is ongoing re-evaluation and adjustment to individual needs. An excellent handbook which highlights the principles which should drive the development of supported accommodation within ordinary housing stock has been prepared by the Scottish Ordinary Housing Working Group (1991). At a broader planning level, the slow rate of progress ensures unfortunately that the guidance of Britain, Currie and Philipson (1986) on the detail of joint initiatives between welfare and housing agencies is by no means outdated.

A number of more fundamental issues however need to be addressed. The first can only be highlighted: the uncertainty engendered by the transfer to local authorities of funding responsibility to replace the residential care allowance in April 1993. Although current placements are protected, the potential for further expansion will depend upon the priorities that are adopted locally. Moreover the necessity of raising the level of financial resources available to the individual must be constantly reiterated. Concern over this specific funding arrangement is of course but one item on an agenda which screams for greater attention to both the capital and revenue sources necessary to fund a range of community initiatives. It will be interesting to see, for example, to what extent the Special Needs Allowance now implemented by Scottish Homes is more enabling than the hostel deficit grant.

A second major consideration epitomises the interrelated nature of the housing and support roles. As detailed above, there has been a flurry of projects developed where the model established a housing base with support attached into which individuals moved. The danger always attached to such a model is that the response to the individual becomes service led rather than needs led. There are already however some examples of projects developing support around the individual within their own home. As further developments of this nature evolve it will be important to discover how intensive are the packages of care that can be arranged and what extent of disability they can sustain. The theory of the care management role holds much promise in this area; the reality must await the detail of implementation.

The extent of disability which can be sustained within some variant of supported accommodation is the third major item on the future agenda. Reference is often made to studies in Scotland (McCreadie and McCannell 1989, Livingston and Bryson 1989, McCreadie, Stewart, Robertson and Dingwall 1991) which have estimated that at least one-third of current long-stay patients under the age of sixty-five could, with appropriate support, live outwith hospital. Given the rapidly evolving nature of the support that is available (and at least south of the Border the substantial shift in policy with the commitment to the closure of the majority of psychiatric hospitals) it is probably time to rework such estimates. In particular the characteristics of those who can be maintained within the community is continually subject to renegotiation as mechanisms are devised for meeting more intensive support needs within a small scale rather than an institutional setting.

The argument presented here has focused in the main on the contribution of supported accommodation to the achievement of community care. Of equal importance for housing authorities however is consideration of, for example, access to mainstream provision in the guise of allocation policies. Is there to be special consideration for those moving from supported provisions or from the support of informal carers (as in certain district councils)? Likewise, what is to be the provision for crisis or for respite schemes which can provide the safety mechanism for the maintenance of community placement?

Fundamental to more wholescale progress therefore must be a rejection of any narrow conception of the housing function such as that posited by Griffiths. It must be replaced by a recognition that, despite the poor history of inter-agency cooperation (Kohls 1989), such collaboration is essential to the achievement of the marriage of the housing and support function which lies at the very heart of effective community care.

REFERENCES

Braisby, D., Echlin, R., Hill, S. and Smith, H. (1988) *Changing Futures: Housing and Support Services for People Discharged from Psychiatric Hospitals.* King's Fund Project Paper 76. London: King's Fund Institute.

Britain, A., Currie, H. and Philipson, F. (1986) *Joint Initiatives, A Guide to Special Projects Between Welfare and Housing Agencies.* Edinburgh: Scottish Council for Single Homeless.

Care in the Community Scottish Working Group (1990) *Community Care: Housing and Support Issues in Scotland.* Edinburgh: Scottish Council for Single Homeless.

DHSS (1989) *Caring for People, Community Care in the Next Decade and Beyond.* London: HMSO.

Griffiths, R. (1988) *Community Care: Agenda for Action.* London: HMSO

House of Commons Social Services Committee (1990) *Community Care: Services for People with a Mental Handicap and People with a Mental Illness.* Eleventh Report. London: HMSO.

Kay, A. and Legg, C. (1986) *Discharged to the Community, A Review of Housing and Support in London for People Leaving Psychiatric Care.* Good Practices in Mental Health. London: Housing Research Group, City University.

Kohls, M. (1989) *Stop... Start... Stutter. A Research Report on Joint Planning Between Health Boards, Local Authorities and Voluntary Organisations in Scotland.* Care in the Community Scottish Working Group. Edinburgh: Scottish Council for Single Homeless.

Livingston, M.G. and Bryson, A. (1989) The Glasgow rehabilitation survey. *British Journal of Psychiatry 154,* 620–624.

McCreadie, R.G. and McCannell, E. (1989) The Scottish survey of new chronics: five-year follow-up. *British Journal of Psychiatry 155,* 348–351.

McCreadie, R.G., Stewart, M., Robertson, L. and Dingwall, J.M. (1991) The Scottish survey of old long-stay in-patients. *British Journal of Psychiatry 158,* 398–402.

NFHA/MIND (1987) *Housing: the Foundation of Community Care.* London: NFHA/MIND.

Petch, A. (1990) *'Heaven Compared to a Hospital Ward': An Evaluation of Eleven Supported Accommodation Projects for those with Mental Health Problems.* Stirling: University of Stirling Social Work Research Centre.

Petch, A. (1992) *At Home in the Community.* Aldershot: Avebury.

Pritlove, J. (1985) *Group Homes: An Inside Story.* Sheffield: University of Sheffield. Joint Unit for Social Services Research, University of Sheffield.

Scottish Office (1991) *Community Care in Scotland: Housing and Community Care.* Scottish Office circular.

Scottish Ordinary Housing Working Group (1991) *Ordinary Housing: From Principles to Practice.* Glasgow: Integrate.

CHAPTER 7

Case Management
A Review of UK Developments and Issues

David Challis

INTRODUCTION

Despite the immense diversity of patterns of organisation, structure and funding it is possible to identify some broadly similar trends in community-based services for vulnerable people. For example, in their study of emerging patterns of change in services for older people in three European countries, Kraan *et al.* (1991) noted a move away from institution-based care, the enhancement of home-based care and the development of mechanisms of coordination and case management. In the care of older people in many other countries such as the USA, Australia and elsewhere a similar trend can be observed (Challis 1992a, b). In the development of community mental health services, often conceived of as an alternative to institutional care, similar trends have also been observed (Huxley, Hagan, Hennelly and Hunt 1990). Long-term care policy for other client groups has also taken not dissimilar forms, with the desire to develop community services being stressed (DHSS 1983, Secretaries of State for Health and Social Security, Wales and Scotland 1989). In the USA for people with mental handicap or learning disabilities discharge from hospital and developing continuity of care have been key themes, with case management made mandatory to improve coordination of care after discharge (Intagliata 1982). Underlying this is a major debate about the extent to which community services complement or substitute for institutional care. Thus, in the UK as elsewhere, case management has become a central component in policies developing community care, through the provision of more intensive coordinated home-based care and thereby potentially impacting upon utilisation of institutional care.

CASE OR CARE MANAGEMENT

The origins of case management lie in the recognition of the need for coordination of services which are fragmented either due to the presence of multiple agencies or multiple providers within an agency as in the United Kingdom. In the United States, multiple funding of programmes of care makes the fragmentation even more complex (Rubin 1987). Recognition of this need for coordination generally seems to have arisen from changes in the balance of long-term care provision from institutional care to home-based care (Intagliata 1982, DCS 1986, Griffiths 1988) although some of the same arguments have been applied to good practice within other settings. Examples of this include the role of the key worker within residential care homes or multi-disciplinary teams. However, there are important differences between these key worker approaches, which aim to coordinate a single service or team more appropriately to individual needs often on a short-term basis, and case management, which aims to coordinate multiple services and providers, usually on a long-term basis. Miller (1983) quotes the conclusion of the US Presidential Commission on Mental Health for case management:

> Strategies focused solely on organisations are not enough. A human link is required. A case manager can provide this link and assist in assuring continuity of care and a coordinated program of services. (Miller 1983, p.5–6)

In general, therefore, the origins of case management lie in the 'need to coordinate delivery of long-term care services to individual clients' (Austin 1983, p.16). Thus the objectives of case management can be seen as very similar to those identified for community mental health services in the USA and the UK: comprehensiveness, coordination, access, acceptability, efficiency, effectiveness and accountability (Huxley *et al.* 1990).

The origins of case management, then, lie in the need for coordination of home-based care, albeit with a broader range of objectives including client-centred care and effective use of resources (Challis 1992b). How may case management be best defined? Definitions of case management usually revolve around the statement of functions, specification of core tasks, delineation of the recipients of the service and identification of the context within which it takes place. Each of these would seem to be an important component of its definition.

1. In overall functional terms, Austin (1983) defines case management as '...a mechanism for linking and coordinating segments of a service delivery system...to ensure the most comprehensive programme for meeting an individual's needs for care' (p.16). This involves continuity of involvement and is based upon comprehensive assessment of the individual's needs (Kane 1990).

2. A second common feature of definition is that case management involves the performance of a series of core tasks in long-term care (Steinberg and Carter 1983, DOH 1991). While there is some variation in the precise description of these, for example the Department of Health has included 'Publishing Information', which elsewhere might be considered as part of case-finding, there would seem to be across the literature a broad general consensus. These core tasks are case finding and screening, assessment, care planning, implementing and monitoring the care plan. As such these core tasks may usefully be differentiated from more short-term activities of care providers (Challis *et al.* 1990). However, case management is more than a set of processes in long-term care since in undertaking

these tasks it also involves advocacy and integrating formal and informal care (Capitman, Haskins and Bernstein 1986).

3. Another key element is that case management is concerned with meeting the needs of people with long-term care problems (Steinberg and Carter 1983). The definition of this group is not easy. Davies and Challis (1986) characterise long-term care populations as: those using a high proportion of health and social care expenditure, individuals with multiple and varied needs, recipients of multiple and inflexible services of which social care is the largest component. Ballew and Mink (1986) describe case management as concerned with people experiencing multiple problems that require multiple sources of help, and who experience difficulty in utilising that help. The role of case management is thus seen as combining brokerage with interpersonal skills since it is focused both '… on the network of services needed by multi-problem clients and the interaction between members of the network' (p.8). Therefore case management is concerned with providing services to a specific target group and need not be seen as the mechanism for providing all forms of care for those who need assistance in coping with everyday living (Kane 1990). This specificity is evident in the application of case management to community care developments in a number of countries (Challis 1992a, b).

4. Thus, the definition includes comprehensive assessment, continuity, coordination, the performance of the core tasks of case management and the meeting of needs for long-term care population and hence providing services to a specific target group. A final but crucial contextual element is identified by Miller (1983) who notes that a focus on client level activities is insufficient since it does not address the idea of a case management system. Kane (1990) links case management practice with system level activities through the use of comprehensive assessments to provide aggregated information for needs-based planning by agencies. In short, case management is designed not just to influence care at the individual client level but also at the system level through the aggregate of a myriad of care decisions at the individual client level which exert pressure for change upon patterns of provision themselves. An underlying objective is to render those patterns of services more relevant to individual needs (Austin 1983).

Let us now examine some of the UK experience of case management and related activities. Ideally, studies should provide information about the model of case management, operational and clinical process, outcomes and costs. Since much of the work is relatively new it is not possible to use such stringent criteria; nonetheless they should be borne in mind when considering the available information about different studies. The evidence is discussed in relation to different client groups but it should be remembered that each of these has a tradition of service and practice developments which, although of general relevance, influence the underlying assumptions of the case management programmes for particular groups. Examples include the influence upon programmes for older persons of intensive home care services and the associated move towards targeting, the role of independent living for those with physical disabilities and normalisation for the learning disability field.

Case Management for Older People

The Kent and Gateshead Schemes The model of case management that was developed in these schemes was designed to ensure that improved performance of the core tasks of case management could contribute towards more effective and efficient long-term care (Challis and Davies 1985, 1986, Challis *et al.* 1990, Davies and Challis 1986). The devolution of control of resources, within an overall cost framework, to individual social workers, acting as case managers, was designed to permit more flexible responses to needs and the integration of fragmented services into a planned pattern of care to provide a realistic alternative to institutional care.

These studies of case management in social care settings were conducted in a retirement area of South East England (Thanet, Kent) (Challis and Davies 1980, 1985, 1986, Davies and Challis 1986) and an urban industrial area of North East England (Gateshead) (Challis *et al.* 1988, 1990, 1992). The evidence of these studies in different areas was that social workers with greater budgetary flexibility, acting as case managers, were able to respond more effectively than is usually the case. The care provided reflected more closely the assessed needs of clients and, through control of a budget, assessments became more wide ranging and problem focused and were no longer, as often before, focused on the narrow concerns of service eligibility. The budget was also used to provide help not available from existing services. It was found that many problems frequently associated with the breakdown of community care, such as severe stress on carers, confusional states and risk of falling were more effectively managed at home than is usually the case. It was found that this approach significantly reduced the need for institutional care of vulnerable elderly people. Over 60 per cent of those receiving the case management schemes remained at home over one year compared with far fewer of the control groups who were receiving the usual range of services. There were marked improvements in the levels of satisfaction and well-being of elderly people and their carers and these were achieved at no greater cost than is normally expended in the care of such individuals.

Within the case management service in Gateshead a pilot health and social care scheme was developed around primary care. Additional funds were made available to add to the existing team of social workers, a part-time doctor, a full-time nurse and a part-time physiotherapist, with a flexible budget split equally between health and social services (Challis *et al.* 1990, 1992). This case management service was designed to focus upon very frail people on the margin of institutional care and based around a large group practice. In this pilot scheme the only outcome data available was upon destination for two small samples of cases (28). After twelve months 62 per cent of those receiving the case management service remained at home compared with only 21 per cent receiving the usual services, a similar result to the earlier findings. There was thus a marked reduction on admissions to institutional care and furthermore those people who died were able to do so within their own homes. As in the social care scheme there was no significant difference in costs for the case management approach compared with the existing provision of services to similar cases for the National Health Service, the Social Services Department or society as a whole.

The Darlington Project A similar approach to case management was tested in a multi-disciplinary scheme based upon geriatric care (Challis *et al.* 1989, 1991a, b) funded under the Care in the Community Initiative (DHSS 1983). Here case managers employed by the social care agency were members of a geriatric multi-disciplinary team, most of the rest of whose members were health service employees. The case managers in this service not only deployed a flexible budget, but also were able to allocate the time of multi-purpose care workers who spanned the role of home help, nursing aide and paramedical aide. This scheme was devised to provide an alternative for elderly people who would otherwise have received long-stay hospital care. The case managers' prime function was, in consultation with the multi-disciplinary team, to participate in and coordinate assessments, to develop, coordinate and regularly review a package of care, linking together all the necessary resources from a range of different providers. Each case manager was responsible for between fifteen and twenty elderly people and was also responsible for a team of approximately eighteen home care assistants. Much of the budget was allocated to home care assistant time but resources were also spent on paying for additional services from members of the community to permit more flexible care as in the social care schemes. Improvements in the well-being of elderly people and a lower level of carer stress were observed for those receiving this new service compared with patients in long-stay hospital care. These gains were achieved at a lower cost than was normally expended upon such patients (Challis *et al.* 1989, 1991a, b), reflecting the higher institutional cost of hospital care. There appeared to be considerable opportunity for locating case management services in a secondary health care setting particularly where that service had a community orientation.

The EPIC Project Another example of a case management scheme developed for vulnerable elderly people is the EPIC (Elderly People in the Community) project in Stirling (Bland, Hudson and Dobson 1992) and is discussed in Chapter 8. In this study a multi-disciplinary case management team with four case managers from different backgrounds, social work, health visitor, community psychiatric nursing and occupational therapy, were established with a team leader from the social work department. The team was located in a general hospital and the service was targeted upon elderly people whose needs placed them at risk of placement in institutional care. The team had a modest devolved budget and costed the services both from the devolved budget and other sources to an overall limit of two-thirds of the cost of a place in institutional care. Whether this was two-thirds of the cost of a place in a residential care home or a hospital setting was dependent on the assessment of the needs of the individual concerned. The team also employed its own home carers from its budget. Although the final report is still awaited there were some interesting developments in this study. It was one of the few case management schemes to develop a standardised method of referral and screening (Lutz 1989) and also developed its own computerised database. Like many case management schemes newly established within an existing service system, it experienced difficulties in case finding in its early stages and the experience of the evaluation suggests the importance of considering not just case management at a practice level but also the managerial implications and infrastructure necessary for effective case management. Another question that this scheme raised was that about the suitable organisational locus for case management, for example whether a hospital-based service should be a separate unit or should be linked to a multidisciplinary team.

The Gloucester Project Another study principally a health authority initiative was the Gloucester project (Dant, Carley, Gearing and Johnson 1991) This study attempted to base care coordinators for frail elderly people in three primary health care teams. It was targeted on elderly people seen as at risk within those practices. The definition of 'at risk' was necessarily vague and had to be revised during the project, inevitably raising questions about targeting. The care coordinators were not employed by either Health or Social Services and did not have any formal influence over the allocation of resources although they controlled a very small budget provided by the health authority to cover minor purchases. Given the structure of services, of course, it would not be realistic to have expected the health authority to pay for what amounted to substitute social care. The study did not provide comparative data on outcomes or significant cost information although there was indication that the presence of coordinators led to further needs being met and some degree of satisfaction from elderly people themselves. However, equally important was the observation that the care coordinators had an organisationally unclear role, not being based in either key agency. The lack of control of resources meant that 'all they had were their own skills of negotiation and persuasion...' (p.131). This necessarily limited their ability to act as case managers which of course would be the more accentuated under the new community care arrangements. Another important observation was that despite their unclear role, the coordinators had to undertake more than straightforward brokerage. Their assessments necessarily required a degree of human relationship skills that might not have been apparent in the initial establishment of the scheme. For example, in dealing with clients who were reluctant to receive help, 'they explored the reasons behind the refusal – perhaps to do with personal experience in the past or a particular experience with a service' (p.54). These observations about organisation, degree of influence on the service system and the nature of the worker's role echo the experience of other studies.

The Home Support Scheme for Dementia sufferers The aim of this scheme was to provide enhanced home support to dementia sufferers partly through the provision of additional paid carers to fill gaps in care not met by other agencies. Case management was not seen as one of the components. However, it was hoped that the scheme would promote more individualised care to this group, bridging gaps in care where existing provision was non-existent, collaborate with existing services to avoid overlap or competition and where necessary to coordinate services to ensure a suitable package of care was provided. Hence even brokerage and coordination were not seen as mainstream tasks, rather the main focus was upon 'gap-filling' and upon liaison with other services (Askham and Thompson 1990, p.41).

The service was organised by development officers employed by Age Concern who were to recruit and organise the paid carers. In practice the extent to which the development officers were responsible for directly supporting clients and for ongoing monitoring was not foreseen (Askham and Thompson 1990, p.41). There was considerable duplication of effort with existing staff such as social workers, part of which must be attributable in part to the lack of expectation that any one person was to take over the coordinatory function. This responsibility was not an expectation of their role although on occasions they will have undertaken it by default. Being in an external agency, lacking influence over decisions over mainstream resources and without a clear remit for coordination, it is unsurprising that the development officers were reluctant to play the role of case manager, seeing this as the role of other agencies (Askham and Thompson 1990, p.45).

There were problems in the evaluation concerning sample size and adequacy which made the analysis of the impact of the scheme difficult to discern. There were no evident overall effects upon institutionalisation although some elderly people living alone with no informal carer were supported who otherwise would probably have entered an institutional setting. There did not seem to be any evident gain for carers (Askham and Thompson 1990).

Case Management for People with Learning Disability

The Andover Case Management Project A joint health and social services initiative in Andover (NDT 1991) provided 1.5 case managers to provide for 20 clients with further resources for brokerage of services. The case managers were supposed to deal with people with substantial needs, an unclear definition of targeting which was deliberate in this study. The role of case managers was to assess, design care plans and negotiate services. The perception was that existing services were inflexible and at an early stage case managers were given a budget to influence services. The early experience of this study was that case management was seen as a more complex activity than had been supposed in early planning. Three major issues were identified in the early stages of the project. Firstly there was the importance of management linkages to case management since otherwise a focus upon client level activities would produce no changes in the system itself. Secondly the requirement for greater clarity about targeting, which related to a need for knowledge not only about the role of case management and what it was expected and designed to achieve but also about those who were eligible for this kind of service. A third area of concern was that of assessment and the difficulties of shifting towards more client-centred approaches away from a service focused approach. In the evaluation it was concluded that several major changes were required for effective implementation of case management. First there was a need for information about service costs, secondly a need for case managers to have direct access to a devolved budget, thirdly the need for case managers to be able to contract at the level of the individual client as well as agencies undertaking block contracts and fourthly a need for effective and usable management information systems containing data on client characteristics, community resources, costs and budgeting.

The Wakefield Case Management Project Another attempt to develop case management in this field was the Wakefield case management project. This was a scheme designed to move people with moderate to severe learning difficulties from long-stay hospital settings into the community. Two case managers and a project coordinator were appointed by the district health authority. The remit of the case managers was to act as key worker with an advocacy role on behalf of individual people both in planning, coordination of services, organising and following up their discharge. The project coordinator acted as budget manager with approximately £160,000 of which £60,000 was salaries and the rest pump-priming funds. The expectation was that these pump-priming funds were not for revenue expenditure but were for more long-term capital-based items. In addition each person had £9500 dowry (later a revenue transfer) plus the social security benefits to which they would be entitled on discharge. This was an interesting model since it attempted to internalise within a team the relationship between advocacy and resource constraints whereby case managers advocated on behalf of their client and patterns of expenditure were determined by the team manager. It therefore offers a model of a partially devolved budget to team manager level (Richardson and Higgins 1990). Unfortunately there is no evidence how this mechanism worked in practice.

The project appeared to have had highly problematic expectations and a lack of congruence between structure and goals. These were related to case management as a revenue-based service with predominantly coordinatory functions and the primacy of capital goods for people leaving hospital whose first need was shelter and accommodation. There were clearly conflicts for a revenue-based service in setting up care packages which required substantial capital expenditure and few people were discharged from hospital. Although the nature of the client group itself meant that the case management process took longer for these individuals than for others, the major reason for the slowness of the project in achieving substantial goals was the sheer time process of organising transitions, particularly in the absence of commitment by the key agencies who were resource providers. Suitable housing was needed for discharge but was not available and setting up suitable sources of care after housing took even further time in the absence of suitable services. It appeared that the local authorities' prime concern was patients already living in their own homes and patients being discharged from hospital were a lower priority. Important points which emerge in the study are, firstly, the need for clear and realistic expectations of what is desired to be achieved through the introduction of case management and, secondly, the need for case management to be seen not just as a client level service but also for the management of case management to be addressed. Particularly in such a project, requiring inter-agency commitment and involvement for any realistic achievements, management commitment to its goals was central (Richardson and Higgins 1992).

The Maidstone Community Care Project A third approach to case management for this client group was the Maidstone Community Care Project. Funded under the Care in the Community Initiative (DHSS 1983) it was one of 28 pilot projects to discharge people from inappropriate hospital care to more appropriate settings (Renshaw *et al.* 1988). The aim was to discharge 50 people from a long-stay hospital to a range of facilities, private housing and the rented sector. Case managers were provided with budgets of up to two-thirds of the cost of hospital care, and had restricted caseloads of about 20 people. In providing support weekly contracts were developed between case managers, care staff and users (Cambridge 1992, Knapp *et al.* 1992). There is relatively little material available on the operation of the service. However the available evidence suggests that for most people most aspects of quality of life were improved and no adverse effects on families were evident. The average costs appeared to be some 13 per cent higher than the hospital alternative (Haycox and Brand 1991).

Case Management for People with Physical Handicaps and Disabilities

The CHOICE Project This was one of three coordinated care schemes for disabled people funded by the King's Fund Centre. The others were concerned with providing coordinated care after head injury (Morris *et al.* 1988) and with rehabilitation after the onset of disability (Nichols 1988). The CHOICE service (Anderson *et al.* 1988, Pilling 1988) was established for people with physical disabilities. Two case managers were established in an independent agency, one full-time and one part-time, both having a social worker background. The service covered the Camden and Islington areas of north London, and was based on the proposition that a specialised service with detailed knowledge of services and disability was required to effectively meet the needs of those with disabilities. This was not a controlled evaluation of case management but involved interviews with clients and interviews with clients of services but not receiving case management. The nature of this service being provided by an independent agency raises some particularly interesting features. In the evaluation, a significant number of clients (27 per cent) would have liked the case management service to have had more authority and resources although it was quite clear that they valued the sympathetic response and speed of action above all else. It is noteworthy that these latter points are common features of an effective and efficient service whoever the provider and these were valued more than independence from statutory authorities. However the advocacy role was valued by service providers in other agencies due to the independence of the case managers although there was some degree of role duplication. The extent to which this agency undertook direct work or counselling was considered carefully and a limited model evolved where counselling was a legitimate role where it was involved in helping clients understand their needs and to accept services but where it was a long-term requirement it would be undertaken by another provider.

The Resource Worker Project Another example in this area was the Resource Worker Project. This was an attempt to develop a service for families coping with severely disabled children (Glendinning 1984, 1986). The aim was to overcome the fragmentation of services for disabled children and their families and to alleviate their isolation. Specialist social workers or 'Resource Workers' were employed to provide information, advice, practical help and support to families with a severely handicapped child. These were part-time workers not based in a statutory or voluntary agency although they received information and bi-monthly consultation from Barnado's fulltime staff.

Their main activities involved regular contact with families, providing information and advice, counselling, liaison between the formal and informal networks of care, coordinating delivery of services and acting as advocates. There were clear advantages and disadvantages to their independent status. On the one hand there was a lack of authority, influence and credibility: 'Working on an independent intervention meant that Resource Workers had neither the access to material resources nor the authority and established credibility of an employing welfare agency' (Glendinning 1986, p.66). This also meant that they were somewhat isolated and lacked support, not being part of the day to day practice of an agency. Furthermore they lacked any control of resources beyond their capacity to persuade. On the other hand workers felt that they had been more 'imaginative and persistent' than if they had been part of the established service system (Glendinning 1986, p.67).

The evidence indicated that there were real improvements in the level and type of services received and of the well-being of families who received the Resource Workers compared with other families with disabled children. When asked about the relative merits of a supportive service or a cash grant 89 per cent of families identified the service as more suitable to their needs (Glendinning 1986).

Case Management in Mental Health

In the UK settings there is as yet little published material on the role of case management in supporting the chronically mentally ill. There is useful discussion of the potential role of case management in this area by Clifford and Craig (1988) and some of the problems of implementation in Onyett (1992). Currently, major studies are being undertaken to test the feasibility of different case management systems for the long-term mentally ill in several parts of the UK (Ryan, Ford and Clifford 1991). Although there are many examples of key worker approaches adopted in multi-disciplinary teams it would not be appropriate to describe these within a discussion of case management although at times such individuals may take on a long-term care role.

There is, however, considerable work from which we can learn in other countries. Perhaps the most well known and rigorously evaluated is the work of Stein and Test (1980, 1985), from their work in Dane County, Wisconsin. The service which was developed was targeted upon chronically impaired patients, those who had often failed to gain any benefits from more community-based services that had been introduced as a substitute for in-patient care. The principles underlying this approach to support of patients with schizophrenia were clear. In organisational terms for every catchment area there should be one central planning agency which controls all the funds for the service. All patients are assigned to a case manager or to a core service team that undertakes case management functions. Case management was thus perceived as both an individual role and, with the most difficult and demanding patients, as a team responsibility. Associated with the organisational principles were a set of core clinical principles. These included assertive outreach, individually tailored programmes of care, ongoing monitoring, titration of levels of support according to needs, training and support in patients' familiar environments ('in vivo'), building upon patients' strengths, treating them as responsible citizens and provision of crisis intervention (Stein, Diamond and Factor 1989). This involved teaching crucial daily living skills to patients, assertive outreach to reduce non-compliance with treatment regimes, provision of careful support to families and carers and avoidance of hospitalisation. The linkage of organisational principles, clinical principles and the norms and incentives of day to day practice is very evident in this service. Instead of separate Mental Health budgets for in-patient and community services, there is one budget, held by the County Mental Health Board, consisting of all the funds provided from County, State and Federal sources. The County contracts with a range of suppliers for community-based services and patterns of practice determine budget allocations:

> The dollar literally follows the patient: If an indigent patient is hospitalised, in any hospital, including the State hospital, the County pays the bill. If hospitalisation can be avoided, the county keeps the money that was saved and uses it to further enrich community programs. In addition, Dane County plans budgets for inpatient costs on the basis of the previous year's usage. If inpatient costs exceed the budgeted amount, then community program budgets for the following year must be cut to pay for the higher inpatient costs (Stein *et al.* 1989 p.31)

The authors suggest that the logical link between practice goals (community-based treatment), practice style, clinical principles, organisational principles and patterns of funding has permitted the development of a more effective service. It is noted that whereas for most of the USA in-patient care consumes some 70 per cent of the Mental Health Budget and Community services 30 per cent, in Wisconsin in-patient care receives 17 per cent and community services 83 per cent (Stein 1987, 1989, Stein *et al.* 1989). The original evaluation of this approach indicated that it led to a reduction in hospitalisation, improvements in social functioning and patient satisfaction, at no greater burden upon families and lower costs than traditional hospital-oriented services (Stein and Test 1980, Test and Stein 1980, Weisbrod, Test and Stein 1980).

The Madison approach is the most rigorously evaluated model of case management in mental health. It has been transferred to Australia where evaluation indicated similar outcomes although the service appeared less costly and relatives preferred the community-based service (Hoult *et al.* 1983, Reynolds and Hoult 1984). Related to it and more specifically focused upon case management are a number of different approaches. Rapp and his colleagues developed the 'Strengths' approach to case management for people with chronic mental health problems (Rapp and Chamberlain 1985). This model was based on the proposition that individuals with chronic mental impairments have the capacity to learn, grow and change and that intervention should focus upon strengths, that is retained skills. The approach is predominately supportive with a focus upon consumer self-determination and the primacy of the nature of the relationship between consumer and case manager, although like the Madison approach assertive outreach is employed. The authors argue that their model leads to a greater degree of community tenure, higher levels of goal attainment, improved vocational and independent living status and a high level of consumer satisfaction. However, many of the personnel used as case managers in this model are relatively inexperienced and untrained. Often they are trainees in social work and similar disciplines.

An alternative approach has been offered by Kanter (1987) who argues for a greater degree of professionalisation of case management based upon the need for knowledge and the fact that case management is more than a brokerage response involving the exercise of judgement, skill, counselling and other activities. Kanter (1989) proceeds to describe a persuasive model of clinical case management which manages to effectively span the continuum of brokerage at one end and highly therapeutic case management at the other. The approach can be seen as relevant for other client groups. He argues that case management is a specialised role in mental health settings and cannot be seen as merely an administrative system for coordinating resources. It requires that case management be located within the clinical team and not separate from it. Principles of the model include: continuity of care, both to permit the development of a relationship and to enhance the case manager's knowledge of an individual so as to permit effective exercise of judgement; use of the case management relationship – permitting improved intervention through time to prevent crises when clinical or external circumstances change; titration of support – exercising clinical judgement about levels of support, pace of intervention or increased independence; flexibility of response; facilitating patient resourcefulness – enhancing individual skills and strengths. Kanter (1989) argues that this represents a model of clinical case management requiring a professional level of skill and competence. This is seen as different from, although encompassing both, service brokerage and the more supportive model of case management (Rapp and Chamberlain 1985).

Building upon similar arguments about professional roles a highly therapeutically focused form of case management is emphatically demonstrated by Harris and Bergman (1987) who argue that case management is not only a brokerage model providing coordination of care but is itself a mode of treatment. It is in effect an intervention in its own right. They argue that the nature of the case management process itself is therapeutic in four ways. It is integrative, putting together that which was previously fragmented; based on planning it is rational; because it is based on prognostic judgment it is proactive; and by its very nature it is individualised. They argue that the case manager/client relationship is one that used appropriately produces the therapeutic objective of the internalisation of stable and integrative functioning. These debates about the degree of professionalisation, whether case management is brokerage or more than brokerage and so whether or not there is a clinical component of the job can be seen to emerge in other contexts also.

IMPLEMENTATION PROBLEMS IN CASE MANAGEMENT

From this brief overview of UK developments and some related work elsewhere there would seem to be a number of crucial factors related to the effective implementation and operation of case management. These are discussed below.

Targeting

Defining which people are appropriate for case management has been a concern of all the schemes discussed, since not all users of care services within the designated client groups require the overhead cost of a case manager. Two different aspects of targeting have been discussed, case-finding and screening (Challis and Davies 1986, Davies and Challis 1986). Nearly all the services were concerned with screening since they were focused upon high-need individuals. More effective case-finding and outreach were also noted in several developments.

Screening is crucial to policies for achieving a degree of substitution of institutional care by home care. Thus the Kent, Gateshead and Darlington case management services for elderly people were carefully targeted, focused upon people with considerable needs and a high probability of entry to institutional care, and yet, although the results indicate that they achieved greater efficiency than existing services (greater improvements in welfare at similar cost), only the Darlington study showed significant cost savings, reflecting the high cost of long-stay hospital care. If a similar case management approach were provided for individuals with a slightly lower level of need, for whom the opportunity for substitution of institutional by community care is less, then there is a possibility of rising average costs from higher levels of home care provision. While this might be justifiable in welfare terms it would not contribute to a policy of 'downward substitution' from higher cost to lower cost settings. Indeed, it is precisely the management of this dilemma between meeting broader welfare needs on the one hand and careful targeting of case management services on the other that would seem to account for the inability of some large-scale case management schemes elsewhere to achieve the desired downward substitution despite demonstrating welfare gains amongst those receiving the service (Hennessy and Hennessy 1990). Similarly, in reviewing 14 US case management programmes for the chronically mentally ill, Huxley (1991) has noted that a narrow target group definition is associated with reduced institutional care and positive outcomes.

However, the implementation of acceptable procedures for ensuring eligibility is complex. It will be important to ensure that those who receive case management are those for whom the service is designed. The apparent equity and ease of implementation of the relatively simple screening schedule have to be balanced against the complexity of the factors that make coping in the community problematic. In practice this means balancing objective and apparently equitable criteria with a degree of discretion which reflects the complexity of life situations. In the care of elderly people some American states use equivalent criteria to assess eligibility for the case management programme as they use for nursing homes (McDowell, Barniskis and Wright 1990). The attraction of such a system is that where case management is seen as providing an alternative option of home care to nursing home care it is clear that equivalent criteria are being utilised. Other American states with broader eligibility criteria use a range of activities of daily living indicators. Certainly it is clear that whatever indicators are used it will be necessary to ensure that adequate estimates are made of the population in need and the reliability of such indicators in identifying those individuals. The experience in the USA suggests that even well validated indicators tend to be quite variable when used in non-experimental and less controlled environments (Liu and Cornelius 1991, Luehrs and Ramthun 1991).

An alternative targeting approach was adopted in the several of the case management schemes described. Guidelines of varying degrees of specificity were agreed with potential referral sources but, recognising the complexity of circumstances which lead to need for institutional care, no rigid threshold of dependency was specified. In short accountability for targeting was held after a person had been accepted rather than at pre-entry using rigid criteria. Clearly such an approach has the advantage of permitting discretion but requires careful monitoring and is potentially subject to dispute. The development of mechanisms for achieving effective targeting is thus likely to be a continuing preoccupation of managers.

The Location of Case Management

Case management has been located in a variety of different settings, including Social Service Departments, Geriatric and Psychiatric multi-disciplinary teams, Primary care, Independent Agencies and even as independent actors. Clearly one facet of the implementation of case management is to identify appropriate settings to provide case management for individuals with different kinds of needs. Examination of how the core tasks may be best performed is one helpful way of analysing the relative advantages of different settings for providing case management. Thus the new General Practice Contract requires GPs to assess people over the age of 75 on an annual basis. Often these may require the provision of better social care rather than particular forms of health care treatment. Thus, case finding in a more widely acceptable setting may be particularly attractive for the provision of case management for elderly people. Such a setting may improve accessibility, and enable case managers to undertake broader based assessment by involving other members of the primary health care team and to form close links with other key providers of home support services such as community nursing. Conversely, services for those suffering from long-term problems of schizophrenia may be better provided as part of the community mental health environment with case managers being part of a psychiatric service. Similar arguments apply to the role of community mental handicap teams. There may also be a case for arguing that people whose needs are relatively rare within the catchment area of one local authority may have their needs better met by a service perhaps located in a non-profit agency covering several local authorities. All such debates raise important questions about the role of the multi-purpose generic social services team which was particularly common following the Seebohm reform of services. Patterns of change prior to the new community care legislation, which are likely to be reinforced, indicate a general trend away from the provision of services in generic teams towards various specialised settings (Challis and Ferlie 1987a, 1987b).

The Purchaser/Provider Separation

The separation of purchaser and provider is seen as an important part of the development of services in the UK with case management seen as a purchaser role (DoH 1990 para 4.5). As such its role is designed to influence the pattern of provision in more appropriate ways. Although there are few examples at the time of writing of a full purchaser arrangement with an internal market, close developments exist (Tyrell 1989). Of particular interest is that the different examples reveal significant variation in the degree of influence over resource allocation. This ranges from pure advocacy and negotiation in the CHOICE project (Pilling 1988), small 'top-up' budgets in the Gloucester Scheme (Dant *et al.* 1991), single service budgets (Askham *et al.* 1990) to more substantial budgets close to the full cost of community care (Challis and Davies 1985, 1986, Challis *et al.* 1988, 1989, 1990, 1991a, b). The Madison Scheme stressed most radically the concentration of all funding (Stein 1989, Stein *et al.* 1989). The distinction between purchaser/provider is seductively and deceptively simple and there are likely to be serious problems if it is treated as simply as it may appear. On the one hand there is macro-purchasing, the form of purchasing most commonly associated until the present time with health authorities contracting with particular providers to provide services for a district or an area. Such purchasing procedures may be developed by local authorities similarly; indeed, case management itself could be purchased on such a basis for particular client groups or for particular areas of the local authority. This process of managing an overall market and purchasing supply to meet the needs of a population within an area should be distinguished from the micro-purchasing role whereby case managers individually disperse their budgets (DoH 1991 para 1.18). The evidence suggests that some of the most client-sensitive responses to needs have been made by the individualised and often idiosyncratic purchases made by case managers on behalf of their clients.

However, the separation of purchaser and provider roles at the micro level raises more problems than at the macro level and there are dangers in the pursuit of too rigid a separation. Some roles and activities span the purchaser/provider divide and blur an apparently clear distinction. An obvious example is that of counselling; at one level it would be possible to define any forms of supportive counselling given as a provider function, namely that counselling is being provided. And yet, many practitioners would quite reasonably describe much of this process – engaging a person, forming a relationship with them and comprehending the depth of their problems so as to establish the right mix of support and services which they need – a purchaser function. It would seem that in many case management settings the provision of support and advice, save in very special circumstances, is in fact a purchaser rather than a provider role. Indeed, to make such an activity an exclusive provider function would make the nature of case management more an administrative role as we shall discuss later.

Hence the needs of effective practice do not always lead to organisationally neat solutions. In the care of a cognitively impaired elderly person, a hands-on carer (provider) might be used to contribute to assessment and other core tasks such as monitoring well-being, routine, diet or medication intake because of their proximity to the elderly person over a considerable period of time, albeit closely supported by a case manager. Again a rigid separation implies that individual components being purchased are homogeneous and yet in the care of vulnerable people good practice dictates consideration of the matching of hands-on carer with the cared-for person. Thus effective case management may often necessitate close links between those formally designated as providers and those formally designated as purchasers. This was recognised in a US Congress Report on the care of people with dementia which recommends: 'Agencies that provide services can provide Comprehensive Case Management... case managers in agencies that provide services can be effectively insulated from financial pressures to refer clients to services of their own agencies rather than more appropriate service of other agencies (OTA 1990 p.55).

The nature of these relationships between provider and purchaser need therefore to be explored carefully so that the process of separation does not lead to new problems of inappropriate care. One helpful way of viewing the separation is to be clear about the roles of service management and case management rather than those of purchaser and provider.

The Characteristics of the Case Management Process

One debate about the style of case management may be characterised as between 'administrative' and 'clinical' case management approaches (Kanter 1989, Harris and Bachrach 1988). Some agencies looking at the core tasks of case management appear to see them rather more as administrative activities, involving pure brokerage and service arranging, than requiring staff with human relations skills. Most of the examples of case management indicate that more than brokerage functions were required in practice, even if this were not made explicit in the initial planning (Askham and Thompson 1990, Dant *et al.* 1991). The studies undertaken in Kent, Darlington and Gateshead indicate that case management has been successful in performing the core tasks through combining practical care with the use of human relations skills, including counselling and support, not only to carers and users but also to direct care staff. Such an approach might not be deemed integral to an administrative model of case management which might see such inputs as resources to be purchased separately where necessary. This problem is evident in discussions about the separation of assessment and provision or, as commonly termed, 'the purchaser/provider split'. Looking at a variety of case management programmes, it would seem to be a most dogmatic definition which treated the provision of human relations skills and emotional support as only a 'provider' role, and also quite inappropriate in good practice. In reviewing case management studies in the mental health field Chamberlain and Rapp (1991) note: 'Simplistic notions of case management as a mere brokering of service seems to have been abandoned... (most) studies are based on case management interventions which emphasise relationship, intensity of involvement, outreach mode of service delivery etc. which were not usually included in earlier descriptions of case management' (p.185). Although there is considerable debate about the roles required of case managers and the specific skills and training which they require it would seem that the availability of trained personnel to fulfil this function is at best scarce. Such scarcity of appropriate staff could well influence the style of case management that develops in the absence of deliberate planning. Hence a clinical model of case management would seem to be a helpful counter to the risk of bureaucratisation and insensitivity in the new care arrangements.

The Context of Case Management: Management and Environment

Much discussion of case management focuses upon the performance of the core tasks of case management in client level work and upon styles and types of fieldwork practice. Nonetheless, the managerial, agency and funding environment within which such practice takes place will tend to determine what is perceived as possible and reasonable solutions to meeting need. The Madison Mental Health Service illustrates clearly how the practice environment and perceptions of what is possible are influenced by the context of funding (Stein *et al.* 1988). Hence, practice content is likely to be determined by the nature of the practice context and to focus upon practice content alone can only be a partial explanation of the forces at work. For example, a hypothetical case management scheme which provided relatively low budgets to case managers to support vulnerable elderly people, under the care arrangements prior to the transfer of social security funds, would be likely to offer an incentive for case managers not to support the most vulnerable, since these would consume a very large part of a small budget. Hence, a practice *context* variable (the size of the budget) will influence practice *content* variables (who is served with what mix of services and in what way) in a critical fashion. Similarly, other contextual factors such as degree of managerial support for the development, which agency employs the case managers, their span of budgetary control, where they are located and what choice of target population is made will again influence the content of what case managers see as realistic and viable choices. These will be critical features in developing case management systems, as the experience of the Wakefield and Andover studies demonstrates. Again adequate structures were lacking for the generalisation of the Gloucester study while the CHOICE, Resource Worker and Home Support Project indicate some of the implications of being within or outside the key managing and providing agencies.

At the managerial level there will need development of approaches to quality assurance and supervision which differ from much current practice. The Department of Health guidance states that:

> Middle managers... will also have to develop new skills in the promotion of a more entrepreneurial approach by practitioners... important though cost consciousness will be it should be balanced by an appro-

priate concern for the quality of care that is being provided. (DoH 1991 para 3.29)

Thus careful monitoring should be applied to the case management process itself as well as to the services organised by case managers. This will require the development of record systems to monitor process, cost and outcomes. There are examples elsewhere of minimum standards both for staff knowledge and training and also for patterns of response which provide helpful guidelines (NICBLTC 1988, Seattle 1986).

CONCLUSION

In view of the kinds of changes in the pattern of community care that are desired, and policy-makers' expectations of the role of case management as one of the processes intended to achieve these changes, clarity about target populations, models of case management, degrees of freedom permitted to practitioners within these models, management of these services and how they fit into the broader system of care is essential. Such clarity demands that whatever case management model is implemented it requires a coherent logic which clarifies the relationship between structure, location, target group, practice model and likely day to day pressures and incentives and expected outcomes. In the absence of such clarity, investment in case management systems could risk being a more expensive response that fails to produce real gains in welfare or changes in the pattern of provision.

REFERENCES

Anderson, A., Scott-Parker, S., Banks, P., Kerr, V. and Pilling, D. (1988) Case manager project, Camden. In D. Hunter (ed) *Bridging the Gap: Case Management and Advocacy for People with Physical Handicaps*. London: King Edward's Hospital Fund.

Askham, J. and Thompson, C. (1990) *Dementia and Home Care: A Research Report on a Home Support Scheme for Dementia Sufferers, Research Paper No. 4*. Mitcham, Surrey: Age Concern Institute of Gerontology.

Austin, C. (1983) *Case management in long-term care: options and opportunities. Health and Social Work, 8*, 1, 16–30.

Ballew, J. and Mink, G. (1986) *Case Management in the Human Services*. Springfield Ill: Charles C. Thomas.

Bland, R., Hudson, H. and Dobson, B. (1992) *The EPIC Evaluation: Interim Report*. University of Stirling, Scotland.

Cambridge, P. (1992) Questions for case management II. In S. Onyett and P. Cambridge (eds) *Case Management: Issues in Practice*. Canterbury: University of Kent.

Capitman, J.A., Haskins, B. and Bernstein, J. (1986) Case management approaches in community-oriented long-term care demonstrations, *Gerontologist, 26*, 398–404.

Challis, D. (1992a) The care of the elderly in Europe. New directions – social care. *European Journal of Gerontology*.

Challis, D. (1992b) Community care of elderly people: bringing together scarcity and choice, needs and costs. *Financial Accountability and Management, 8*, 77–95.

Challis, D., Darton, R., Johnson, L., Stone, M., Traske, K. and Wall, B. (1989) *Supporting Frail Elderly People at Home: The Darlington Community Care Project.* University of Kent at Canterbury: Personal Social Services Research Unit, University of Kent at Canterbury.

Challis, D., Darton, R., Johnson, L., Stone, M. and Traske, K. (1991a) An evaluation of an alternative to long-stay hospital care for frail elderly patients: Part I The model of care. *Age and Ageing 20*, 236–244.

Challis, D., Darton, R., Johnson, L., Stone, M. and Traske, K. (1991b) An evaluation of an alternative to long-stay hospital care for the frail elderly: Part II Costs and outcomes. *Age and Ageing 20*, 245–254.

Challis, D. and Davies, B. (1985) Long term care for the elderly: the community care scheme. *British Journal of Social Work 15*, 563–579.

Challis, D. and Davies, B. (1986) *Case Management in Community Care.* Aldershot: Gower.

Challis, D., Chessum, R., Chesterman, J., Luckett, R. and Traske, K. (1992) Case management in health and social care. In F. Lackzo and C. Victor (eds) *Social Policy and Elderly People.* Aldershot: Gower.

Challis, D., Chessum, R., Chesterman, J., Luckett, R. and Woods, B. (1988) Community Care for the frail elderly: an urban experiment. *British Journal of Social Work 18* (Supplement), 43–54.

Challis, D., Chessum, R., Chesterman, J., Luckett, R. and Traske, K. (1990) *Case Management in Social and Health Care.* Canterbury: University of Kent, Personal Social Services Research Unit.

Challis, D. and Ferlie, E. (1987a) Changing patterns of fieldwork organisation: II The team leaders view. *British Journal of Social Work, 17*, 147–167.

Challis, D. and Ferlie, E. (1987b) The myth of generic practice: Specialisation in social work. *Journal of Social Policy, 17*, 1–22.

Chamberlain, R. and Rapp, C.A. (1991) A decade of case management: A methodological review of outcome research. *Community Mental Journal, 27*, 171–188.

Clifford, P. and Craig, T. (1988) *Case Management Systems for the Long-term Mentally Ill.* London: National Unit for Psychiatric Research and Development.

Dant, T., Carley, M., Gearing, B. and Johnson, M. (1989) *Coordinating Care: Final Report of the Care for Elderly People at Home Project.* Milton Keynes and London: Open University/Policy Studies Institute.

Davies, B. and Challis, D. (1986) *Matching Resources to Needs in Community Care.* Aldershot: Gower.

Department of Community Services (DCS) (1986) *Nursing Homes and Hostels Review.* Canberra, Australia: Australian Government Publishing Service.

Department of Health (DoH) (1990) *Caring for People: Community Care in the Next Decade and Beyond.* Policy Guidance, Department of Health. London: HMSO.

Department of Health (DoH) (1991) *Care Management and Assessment: Managers Guide.* London: HMSO.

DHSS (1983) *Care in the Community.* HC(83)6, LAC(83)5. London: HMSO.

Fisher, M. (1991) Defining the practice content of case management. *Social Work and Social Science Review* 2, 204–230.

Glendinning, C. (1984) The Resource Worker Project: evaluating a specialist social work service for severely disabled children and their families. *The British Journal of Social Work 14*, 103–116.

Glendinning, C. (1986) *A Single Door: Social Work with Families of Severely Disabled Children*. London: Allen and Unwin.

Griffiths, R. (1988) *Community Care: Agenda for Action*. London: HMSO.

Harris, M. and Bachrach, L. (eds) (1988) *Clinical Case Management, New Directions for Mental Health Services No 40*. San Francisco: Jossey-Bass.

Harris, M. and Bergman, H. (1987) Case management with the chronically mentally ill: a clinical perspective. *American Journal of Orthopsychiatry, 57*, 296–302.

Haycox, A. and Brand, D. (1991) *Evaluating Community Care: A Case Study of Maidstone Community Care Project*. Manchester and London: North Western Regional Health Authority and Social Services Inspectorate.

Hennessy, C. and Hennessy, M. (1990) Community-based long term for the elderly: evaluation practice reconsidered. *Medical Care Review 47*, 221–259.

Hoult, J., Reynolds, I., Charbonneau-Powis, M., Weekes, P. and Briggs, J. (1983) Psychiatric hospital versus community treatment: the results of a randomised trial. *Australian and New Zealand Journal of Psychiatry 17*, 160–167.

Huxley, P., Hagan, T., Hennelly, R. and Hunt, J. (1990) *Effective Community Mental Health Services*. Aldershot: Gower.

Huxley, P. (1991) Effective case management for mentally ill people: the relevance of recent evidence from the USA for case management services in the United Kingdom. *Social Work and Social Science Review 2*, 192–203.

Intagliata, J. (1982) Improving the quality of community care for the chronically mentally disabled: the role of case management. *Schizophrenia Bulletin 8*, 655–674.

Kane, R. (1990) *What is Case Management Anyway?* University of Minnesota, Minneapolis: Long-term Care Decisions Resource Centre.

Kanter, J. (1987) Mental health case management: a professional domain? *Social Work 32*, 461–462.

Kanter, J. (1989) Clinical case management: definition, principles, components. *Hospital and Community Psychiatry 40*, 361–368.

Knapp, M., Cambridge, P., Thomason, C., Beecham, J., Allen, C. and Darton, R. (1992) *Care in the Community: Challenge and Demonstration*. Aldershot: Gower.

Kraan, R.J., Baldock, J., Davies, B., Evers, A., Johansson, L., Knapen, M., Thorslund, M. and Tunissen, C. (1991) *Care for the Elderly: Significant Innovations in Three European Countries*. Boulder, Colorado: Campus/Westview.

Liu, K. and Cornelius, E. (1991) Activities of daily living and eligibility for home care. In D. Rowland and B. Lyons (eds) *Financing Home Care: Improving Protection for Disabled Elderly People*. Baltimore, MD: Johns Hopkins University Press.

Luehrs, J. and Ramthun, R. (1991) State approaches to functional assessments for home care. In D. Rowland and B. Lyons (eds) *Financing Home Care: Improving*

Protection for Disabled Elderly People. Baltimore, MD: Johns Hopkins University Press.

Lutz, B. (1989) *Report of Development and Testing of Screening and Assessment Instruments, Paper No 12.* University of Stirling: Social Work Research Centre.

McDowell, D., Barniskis, L. and Wright, S. (1990) The Wisconsin Community Options Programme: planning and packaging long-term support for individuals. In A. Howe, E. Ozanne and C. Selby Smith (eds) *Community Care Policy and Practice: New Directions in Australia.* Victoria, Australia: Monash University Public Sector Management Institute.

Miller, G. (1983) Case management: the essential service. In C. Sanborn (ed) *Case Management in Mental Health Services.* New York: Haworth Press.

Morris, J., Greenwood, R., Murphy, L., Brooks, N. and Dunn G. (1988) Head Injuries Project, St Bartholomew's Hospital. In D. Hunter (ed) *Bridging the Gap: Case Management and Advocacy for People with Physical Handicaps.* London: King Edward's Hospital Fund.

Nichols, F. (1988) Disability team for Westminster and Chelsea. In D. Hunter (ed) *Bridging the Gap: Case Management and Advocacy for People with Physical Handicaps.* London: King Edward's Hospital Fund.

NDT (1991) *The Andover Case Management Project.* London: National Development Team.

National Institute on Community-Based Long Term Care (NICBLTC) (1988) *Care Management Standards: Guidelines for Practice.* Washington, DC: National Institute on Community-Based Long Term Care, National Institute on Aging.

Office of Technology Assessment (OTA) (1990) *Confused Minds, Burdened Families.* Washington, DC: Office of Technology Assessment, Congress of the United States.

Onyett, S. (1992) *Case Management in Mental Health.* London: Chapman and Hall.

Pilling, D. (1988) *The Case Manager Project: Report of the Evaluation.* City University, London: Rehabilitation Resource Centre.

Rapp, C.A. and Chamberlain, R. (1985) Case management services for the chronically mentally ill. *Social Work 30,* 417–422.

Renshaw, J., Hampson, R., Thomason, C., Darton, R., Judge, K. and Knapp, M. (1988) *Care in the Community: The First Steps.* Aldershot: Gower.

Reynolds, I. and Hoult, J. (1984) The relatives of the mentally ill: a comparative trial of community oriented and a hospital oriented psychiatric care. *Journal of Nervous and Mental Disease 172,* 480–489.

Richardson, A. and Higgins, R. (1990) *Case Management in Practice: Reflections on the Wakefield Case Management Project, Working Paper 1.* University of Leeds, Leeds: Nuffield Institute for Health Service Studies.

Richardson, A. and Higgins, R. (1992) *The Limits of Case Management: Lessons from the Wakefield Case Management Project, Working Paper 5.* University of Leeds, Leeds: The Nuffield Institute for Health Services Studies.

Rubin, A. (1987) Case management. *Social Work 28,* 49–54.

Ryan, P., Ford, R. and Clifford, P. (1991) *Case Management and Community Care.* London: Research and Development in Psychiatry.

Seattle (1986) *Case Management Program: Policies and Procedures Manual.* Seattle, Washington: Seattle-King County Division on Aging.

Secretaries of State for Health, Social Security, Wales and Scotland (1989) *Caring for People: Community Care in the Next Decade and Beyond.* London: HMSO.

Stein, L. (1987) Funding a system of care for schizophrenia. *Psychiatric Annals 17*, 592–598.

Stein, L. (1989) *Wisconsin's System of Mental Health Financing.* University of Wisconsin, Madison, WI: Mental Health Research Centre.

Stein, L.I. and Test, M.A. (1985) The evolution of the training in community living model. In L. Stein and M.A. Test (eds) The training in community living model: a decade of experience. *New Directions in Mental Health Service, No. 26.* San Francisco: Jossey-Bass.

Stein, L. and Test, M.A. (1980) Alternative to mental hospital treatment: I. conceptual model, treatment programme, and clinical evaluation. *Archives of General Psychiatry 37*, 392–397.

Stein, L., Diamond, R. and Factor, R. (1989) *A System Approach to the Care of Persons with Schizophrenia.* University of Wisconsin, Madison, WI: Mental Health Research Centre.

Steinberg, R.M. and Carter, G.W. (1983) *Case Management and the Elderly.* Lexington, MA: Heath.

Test, M.A. and Stein, L.I. (1980) Alternative to mental hospital treatment: III. social cost. *Archives of General Psychiatry 37*, 409–412.

Tyrell, P. (1989) *An Initial Evaluation of the Homebase Project.* Chester: Cheshire Social Services Department.

Weisbrod, B., Test, M.A. and Stein, L. (1980) Alternative to mental hospital treatment: II. economic benefit cost analysis. *Archives of General Psychiatry 37*, 400–405.

CHAPTER 8

EPIC – A Scottish
Case Management Experiment

Rosemary Bland

INTRODUCTION

Enormous changes and developments are being planned and put in place by social work departments in Scotland, like the rest of the United Kingdom, following the implementation of the NHS and Community Care Act 1990. Health Boards, too, have duties under the same legislation but the parallel approach to planning envisaged in the White Paper *Caring for People* (1989) combined with the lack of statutory obligation on the two agencies to prepare joint community care plans has resulted in many of them not doing so. How then can existing duplication and gaps in service provision be avoided? Can there be a real move of financial spending from institutional to domiciliary based care and support? After so many uncertainties and delays, it will be a cruel disappointment if this opportunity to provide better services to people with mental health problems, people with learning and physical disabilities and older people in our society was missed and only minor tinkering in the way services are planned and delivered takes place. It is now increasingly clear that 'more than fine tuning of the existing arrangements will be needed' (Audit Commission 1986 p.65).

After a brief look at the more recent history in the area, this chapter will discuss these forthcoming changes in the light of preliminary experience in one experimental project for older people and try to draw conclusions about important aspects of the way services are currently organised which need attention if community care is to succeed.

RECENT HISTORICAL BACKGROUND

It is, perhaps, ironic that it should be the massive rise in expenditure by the Department of Social Security on residential and nursing home fees for elderly people which finally caused the Government to take action to bring community care nearer to a credible reality than at any time previously. The Audit Commission's trenchant criticism of the mess that passed for community care (or inaction) (1986) made it politically difficult to ignore a worsening situation any longer. We also have to acknowledge the demographic trend towards an increasingly ageing population which meant that perverse financial incentives to institutionalise older people in large numbers could no longer be allowed to continue unchallenged and unremedied. Griffiths produced a blueprint for the Government to act on and over which it hesitated an unduly long time, the White Paper *Caring for People* (1989) being their eventual response. The postponement until 1993 of the implementation of the NHS and Community Care Act 1990 as far as most local authority responsibility for Community Care is concerned served to highlight two things: first, the belated recognition that good community care is not cheap to provide and that considerably greater financial resources will therefore be required to do so; and second, the anticipated resistance of community charge payers to funding community care through a higher rate of charge.

So far as frail older people are concerned, recent social policy changes and legislation are likely to affect them whether they remain at home or find themselves in some form of institutional care. For the overwhelming majority of older people, remaining in their own home if possible until death is paramount (see Salvage 1986). Yet as many writers have shown, community-based services to elderly people have lacked cohesion and have been a haphazard collection of discrete, uncoordinated services, rarely developed collaboratively by different agencies and restricted in their availability (Audit Commission 1986, Plank 1977). This is due to a number of factors: organisational planning failure, this group of people having a range of health and social care needs which are the responsibility of several agencies and the difficulties these agencies experience in collaborating in service provision.

For instance, the highly valued Home Help Service was not originally created to provide a supportive service to (predominantly) older women with a range of care and support needs, but temporary domestic help to young, married women having home confinements (Dexter and Harbert 1983). The main client group has changed greatly but the service has been slow to do so and it is still only available to the majority of clients for a few hours two or three days a week (Social Work Services Group 1990). Trenchant criticism of the Home Help Service's failure to target elderly people in greatest need (SSI 1987) highlighted the inappropriateness of offering a thin spread of service to large numbers of elderly people with very varying levels of frailty, previous research having failed to find a strong relationship between client need and service received (Gwynne and Fean 1978).

It is unfortunate that local authorities were forced to reduce spending in the late 1970s, making expansion and development of home help/care services very difficult. However, more significantly, the relative spending on residential care and domiciliary and day care for elderly people, where approximately twice as much was spent on residential care as on community-based services, remained virtually the same between 1973 and 1980 (Parker 1990).

Regrettably, the 'Care in the Community Initiative' funded by the Department of Health in England and Wales (DHSS 1983) was not extended to Scotland. Seven of the 28 demonstration projects set up under the initiative (and evaluated by the Personal Social Services Research Unit at Kent) were for elderly people, the majority being concerned with discharging already hospitalised mentally ill and mentally handicapped people back into the community rather than sustaining them at home. However, it could be argued that the more generous arrangements for joint funding between health and local authorities were some indication of an attempt on central government's part to encourage innovation and development in community care. Similar funding arrangements for joint provision of services by health and social work in Scotland have always been less generous and may partly account for the slow progress made here. Pressure for change in Scotland has been noticeably weaker (Hunter and Wistow 1987) and it has been suggested that professional, administrative and cultural legacies have also been influential in this (Titterton 1990).

SOCIAL WORK WITH OLDER PEOPLE

Up to now, older people have not been seen by social work/service departments as having the same range of social and emotional difficulties as other client groups. Their main problem is seen as that of being old in itself and its perceived concomitant frailty. They are one of the least popular client groups as far as social workers' preferences are concerned (Neill, Warburton and McGuinness 1976, Holme and Maizels 1978, Davies and Challis 1986). The ever greater attention given by social work/services departments to policy and practice in the field of child protection has overridden the demographic realities of an ageing population which might otherwise have given older people a chance to move up the list of social work priorities. Older people are not deemed to require the high level of skilled help available to families with young children, since their need is seen to be primarily 'for services' rather than social work *per se* (Stevenson & Parsloe 1978, Goldberg and Connelly 1982). Professionals seem unaware that 'even' services for elderly people are sometimes unavailable or inadequate but that when provided, they are generally much appreciated by clients (Goldberg & Warburton, 1979).

Most social work with older people is carried out by unqualified staff (Stevenson and Parsloe 1978, Howe 1980). Recently, it has been estimated that no more than one-third of social work staff time (mainly that of social work assistants) is spent on elderly people (Sinclair, Parker, Leat and Williams 1990, Connor and Tibbitt 1988). Although the elderly client as a consumer with preferences and choices to make about services and social work help is increasingly emphasised in policy documents (*Caring for People* 1990) this is still largely at the lip service stage in organisational terms.

Likewise, the needs and rights of carers of older people are also acknowledged in policy documents but are only slowly being taken into account in practice (Griffiths 1988, *Caring for People* 1990). Not until the General Household Survey included a special section on Informal Carers for the DHSS was the extent of informal caring throughout the country quantified (Green 1988), with 1.4 million adults giving at least twenty hours a week to caring for someone. Over half (54%) of the six million carers identified in the survey were caring for somebody over the age of 75, compared with the percentage of carers looking after somebody under the age of 45, which was only 11 per cent. This gives a very clear indication of just how large the group caring for older people is and potentially how much political muscle they possess. However, as if to pre-empt any exercise of such muscle, the Government made it quite clear in *Growing Older* (DHSS 1981) that community care of older people was to continue to be provided informally by families rather than become the responsibility of public agencies. Notwithstanding the more recent policy document exhortations to take the needs and wishes of elderly people and family members seriously when planning support, many services still tend to be inflexible, with assessment of elderly people being service rather than needs led.

CASE MANAGEMENT AS A STRATEGY

Now that case (or care) management is higher on the agenda thanks to the National Health Service and Community Care Act (1990), it is important to reflect on how this came to be. An attempt to address the shortcomings in social work with older people in England was the community care experiment conducted in the Thanet area of Kent (Davies and Challis 1981). This model of community care was devised at the same time as demonstration case management projects were being set up in the United States to develop long-term care for elderly people in the community. These projects, set up in ten states, under the National Long-term Care Channelling Demonstration Program, were designed to secure a better match between need and service provision. In order to provide community-based support services to elderly people, some federal and state restrictions on eligibility had to be waived and funds made available from both the Medicare and Medicaid insurance schemes. The impetus behind these initiatives in the United States was similar to Britain, namely the degree of fragmentation in service provision and the tendency (reinforced by the inflexible federal nursing home insurance funding) for a substantial minority of elderly people to be unnecessarily directed towards long-term care in nursing homes rather than be offered support in their own home.

The success of the English model of case management in retaining frail older people at home with an enhanced quality of life for them and their carers was demonstrated over a twelve month and, subsequently, four year period (Challis and Davies 1986). The model has been further developed and modified in projects in Gateshead and Darlington (Challis *et al.* 1990, Challis *et al.* 1989), as described in Chapter 7. This chapter is a preliminary reflection on the experience of setting up a multi-disciplinary case management project for elderly people in Scotland based on the Kent and Gateshead models. It discusses the philosophy and practice in the Scottish project and reflects on the challenges encountered in trying to make good community support for older people a reality.

THE ELDERLY PEOPLE IN THE COMMUNITY PROJECT (EPIC)

The Stirling EPIC project was set up jointly by Central Regional Social Work Department and Forth Valley Health Board in 1990 in collaboration with the University of Stirling, following two years of negotiations. It operated within the geographical boundary of the former Stirling Burgh and was managed by a Steering Group drawn from officers of both agencies and chaired by a University Research Fellow. The Steering Group met monthly to monitor activity, deal with problems which arose and to develop the innovative nature of the service being provided. The project, which finished in its present form in March 1992, was evaluated by the University of Stirling with a grant from the Nuffield Foundation. The evaluation is currently being written up.

Like the Kent model, this project aimed to support frail older people and those caring for them, in their own homes, since most older people wish to remain there if at all possible (Salvage 1986). A move to residential care is seen as the last resort, necessitated by extreme physical or mental frailty and/or lack of adequate family support. Like the Kent and Gateshead models, EPIC had a devolved budget and a cost basis for care packages of two-thirds of a residential home bed (currently £245 per week) or, in cases of great frailty, the same proportion of cost of a long-stay hospital bed (currently between £320 and £380 per week, depending on the hospital).

The EPIC case management project differed from the original Kent model in several ways. First, the project was financed and staffed jointly by health and social work agencies. In their critique of the original Kent Case Management (Davies and Challis 1981) model, Davies and Challis acknowledge that it would have been preferable to have had health as well as social work staff as case managers since frail elderly people have health and social needs which are almost always intertwined. The Gateshead project had various health personnel seconded to it from time to time but it was primarily set up, staffed and funded by the Social Services Department (Challis *et al.* 1990). In Stirling it was decided, therefore, that EPIC should have a multi-disciplinary team of case managers – from social work, community nursing, community psychiatric nursing and occupational therapy. The professional background of the team leader was not prescribed but in the event the postholder came from social work. A team clerk completed the staffing, half of which had either been seconded or specially employed for the project by one or other of the sponsoring agencies.

It was hoped that having a multi-disciplinary group of case managers would enhance the project in several ways:

1. Individual case managers would act as informal consultants and advisers to each other about aspects of cases in which they had greater knowledge or expertise.

2. As a result of 1, each case manager would acquire a greater depth of understanding and range of skills than they brought to the project from the training background of one discrete profession. This would not only assist the case managers and give them greater confidence in their work with individual clients but would also help to clarify future training needs, particularly if joint training for case management was to be developed in the future.

3. A visit to the Gateshead Case Management project had shown the value of having social work and health personnel in the team there. In particular, workers felt that the District Nurse case manager eased access to other health service personnel and services for her social

work colleagues. This was achieved through well established personal contacts with individuals and the trust and respect already accorded to the individual by her health colleagues. She was able to confirm the 'bona fides' so to speak, of social work case managers, with regard to confidentiality of information and reliability so far as service response and delivery were concerned. In other words, she was able to dispel or modify some of the negative attitudes towards social workers held by some health care professionals, such as that their 'concern with "soft data" and the uniqeness of personal experience [which can be mistaken for] a lack of intellectual rigour, indecisiveness, or even incompetence' (Dalley 1989). Similarly, the district nurse case manager felt that her social worker case manager colleagues helped her find her way through the organisational bureaucracy of the local authority and gain a better understanding of the way the social work department functioned. Given the well documented misunderstandings and misperceptions of role, task and function between social work and health agencies, these seemed advantages well worth securing, since the result would hopefully be obvious in greater efficiency and improved services to clients (Huntington 1981, Dalley 1989).

Use of Home Carers

The EPIC project employed three 'helpers' to perform a range of personal and domestic tasks for elderly people in their own homes. (By contrast, the Kent scheme employed 104 helpers for its ninety-two clients over one year.) The EPIC employees, known as 'home carers', were broadly the equivalent of the 'community care workers' suggested by the Audit Commission (1986) and endorsed by Griffiths (1988). Paid at the same rates as home helps, they were given specially devised training in health and social aspects of caring for frail elderly people at home and were able to carry out a wider range of tasks and at times when traditional services are not usually available. The Audit Commission suggested that the training model being adopted by the nursing profession in Project 2000 of a common foundation programme might be used in training for community care, with the basic general training being recognised by various professional bodies and accredited as a module for further training and qualification as desired. The issue of training in the development of community care is still being debated, with the initial decision in Kent being not to train; one reason given was that it might deter some potential 'helpers' by making their activity 'too much like a job' (Davies and Challis 1986). Other arguments against training include the fear of creating an elite of trained helpers and the potential loss of flexibility of role by professionalisation. The home carers in EPIC were paid out of the budget held by the project. This is in contrast to the 'helpers' initially recruited individually to carry out specific tasks for individual clients in the Kent scheme (Davies and Challis 1981). The implications of having a special group of workers employed for around twenty hours a week rather than recruiting individuals as and when needed for specific tasks and individual clients, are considerable. First, a large proportion of the project budget was already committed, lessening the possibilities for experimentation with other new methods of support for clients. Second, there was no element of extra financial reward for particularly difficult or unpleasant care tasks. Since home carers were paid by the hour, rather than for performing a particular task or set of tasks for a client, there was no particular incentive to be efficient in the use of time or to pursue client-centred goals.

Screening

EPIC used as its referral form a screening instrument specially developed by a research fellow in the Social Work Research Centre at Stirling (Lutz 1989). This screening form was originally piloted on 'at risk' clients of a range of social work and health care professionals and showed some association between screening scores and outcome for clients when a random sample of 54 cases was followed up four months later. The form is now being further tested for its usefulness as a screening instrument by a social services team in Hampshire and a group of general practitioners in the same area.

In EPIC, the scores assigned to older people referred to the project were not used to target those most at risk since, initially at least, referrals were slow in coming. The basis of decision-making tended to be more influenced by any additional information volunteered by some referrers on the back of the form than the scores gained on the form itself. Doubts therefore arose about the team's willingness to use the screening form score as an indicator of risk for clients or to acknowledge or test its usefulness to them in decision-making. Prior personal knowledge of the referrer appeared to have greater influence on whether an elderly person was accepted for assessment or rejected at the referral.

The project referral form asked referrers twelve questions about the older person and their carers (if any). These were whether the older person:

- lived alone
- was unable to go outdoors alone
- had a history or well founded fear of falls
- was forgetful about things
- put him/herself or others at risk due to forgetfulness
- had problems with incontinence
- neglected him/herself by failing to eat, keep warm, or maintain personal appearance
- needed more help at some time of day/night than was currently being provided
- had a carer who was under physical or emotional strain
- had lost someone close through death, removal or institutionalisation in the last two years
- had been in hospital themselves in the last two years
- had given up their home and moved in with family, friends or other (only asked of those not living alone).

The questions were derived from a range of previous research findings, which had revealed an association between certain health or social factors and the probability of an elderly person being at risk of his or her domestic situation breaking down, with consequent institutionalisation (see Taylor and Ford 1983, Bland and Bland 1985).

Assessment

The Project Assessment Forms, also developed by Lutz, were not previously piloted and were being used and evaluated for the first time by the case managers. Information was collected from the elderly persons themselves where possible, on their housing, financial, health and social circumstances. The form gave space for recording the client's view of what help was needed and the action subsequently agreed. Where substantial support was already being given by a relative or friend, this individual was also asked about their needs as a carer, not necessarily on the same visit. These two perceptions of need were often at variance with each other, as might be expected. Care plans were subsequently devised with the elderly client and their caring relative or friend, using the services of a home carer as part of the plan where this was seen as the most useful and appropriate way to meet the assessed need.

Interim findings suggest that the case managers were reluctant to take the assessment forms out with them on home visits to clients, preferring to complete them later in the office and using them as a checklist or prompt. On the other hand, there seemed to be less reluctance to use the Carer Assessment Form on domiciliary visits. The evaluation will seek to understand the reasons behind these differing attitudes. There is a universal dislike of the assessment document but a reluctant belief that it is a necessary tool in care planning. However, when packages of care are examined by individual case managers, some differences in use of resources are discernible, with heavy use of home carers by some managers and very little by others for clients with apparently similar characteristics and needs.

A comparison group of elderly people registered with three primary health care centres outside the project catchment area, but eligible for the same hospital and social work services as EPIC clients, has being followed for the duration of the project in their use of these services (which will also be costed). Comparisons in outcome will be made with the sample of EPIC clients and it is also hoped to interview a sample of elderly people and their main carers as case studies.

The project evaluation has included detailed case studies of nine EPIC clients which illustrate the nature and extent of the unpaid, family carer contribution to sustaining the elderly person at home. On the evidence so far, this is substantial in many cases. However, as far as the case managers are concerned, some carers are secondary to the elderly client, to the extent that not all carers have met the case manager involved with their elderly relative. The case studies have thrown more light on how this affects the carer's attitude to the help EPIC provided. Other writers have acknowledged that the continued support of family and other unpaid carers is crucial to the success of community care (Wenger 1984, Sinclair, Parker, Leat and Williams

1990) and one of EPIC's declared aims was to prevent such support breaking down.

Great stress has been laid by government on the process of assessing need and rightly so (*Caring for People* 1989). Who should do the assessing is less clear, with some authorities proposing that this should be done by staff who are not necessarily professionally trained to carry out detailed and complex assessments. Since good and accurate assessment of need is one of the most important, if not the most important, elements of care planning, we seem to be in danger of repeating past mistakes where access to scarce and costly resources is controlled by unqualified staff.

A real barrier to effective case management encountered in this project was the thorny issue of multiple assessments. Although case managers have carried out a full assessment of the older person's needs in EPIC, most services which were asked to contribute an element of the care package insisted on doing their own assessment before providing the service. (In EPIC, requests for respite and day care were an honourable exception.) This was justified in some cases by the argument that budgets must be safeguarded and used appropriately. The older person was therefore subjected to multiple assessments by a range of service providers, undermining the whole 'management' aspect of the case management process and sometimes causing unacceptable delay in providing the support required. The case manager was unable to 'manage' the care and remained dependent on the service provider's assessment of need. For the future, this highlights the fundamental necessity of either having comprehensive assessments of need such as were being done in EPIC accepted by service providers, or agreement that a core assessment could be used across and between agencies. If this issue is not tackled and resolved by departments, case management will be highly inefficient and costly, justifying the criticism levelled at the Stirling model in some quarters that it was a 'Rolls Royce' model. There is an urgent need for rationalisation of assessments within social work/service authorities, let alone across agency boundaries and if managers fail to overcome opposition to this, case management will fail and community care with it.

Whilst case managers managed to alter their focus in assessment from the 'need for service' to client need, they appeared reluctant either to use new services in other sectors, or to employ the freedom given them by their budget to create new, more imaginative packages of support for their elderly clients and their carers. This may have been due to lack of management encouragement to be innovative and a reluctance to embark on new and 'risky' methods of service procurement, such as contracting with independent sector agencies. The sole experiment in this direction was with the Crossroads Care Attendant Scheme which had trained its employees in the art of caring and whose coordinator assumed the responsibility and therefore the 'risk' for the client whilst providing their service. The EPIC team did not use their budget to buy existing statutory services in order to bypass the bureaucratic arguments used to justify refusal of their own assessment of client need. There was a strong tendency to use existing services, even when these were not particularly appreciated by their users. Here again, there are implications for the quality of service being provided to elderly recipients and for existing statutory services themselves. To what extent are services prepared to change the way they respond to consumers and are authorities prepared to phase out services which will not change or which no longer meet people's needs in the way they wish? The great danger is that too little will change and that case management will be yet another layer superimposed as a mechanism for coordinating services on to existing local systems, as EPIC was in danger of becoming. This is similar to the 'basic' American model of case management (Davies and Challis 1986).

WHO SHOULD BE CASE MANAGERS?

Griffiths' recommendation to the Government that the lead role in community care should fall to local authority social services/work departments was not seen as necessarily the logical or best solution by everyone (Maclean 1989, Butrym 1989). During the long delay between the submission of the Griffiths report and the Government response there was much speculation that the lead role might yet be given to the health service, and to GPs in particular. With the encouragement to become budgetholders for patients' health care procurement, GPs were seen by some commentators to be better placed than many to act as case managers. Although there has been ministerial confirmation that local authorities will be the lead agencies, a pilot project in Bradford is being run with a group of General Practitioners who have opted to be budgetholders for patients, also acting as case managers (Clode 1991). The White Paper on Community Care (*Caring for People* 1989) left the question open, merely commenting that case managers 'will often be employed by the social services authority, but this need not always be so.'

In some community care mental health projects, community psychiatric nurses are acting as case managers (Ryan, Ford and Clifford 1991) illustrating that experimentation is being undertaken by health services aware of the potential of case management as a new strategy in long-term support of patients in the community.

In other multi-disciplinary team models, different professionals assume discrete roles and work together to provide a comprehensive service for the particular client/patient group. In EPIC, the team consisted of a group of individuals who were all performing the same role, namely that of a case manager, albeit from a different professional stance and background. Whether this results in very differing approaches to the assessment and meeting of client need remains to be seen once the evaluation is completed. Previous research would lead one to surmise that this may well be so (see Runciman 1989).

ATTITUDES OF OTHER AGENCIES

Maybe of even greater importance than the training background of case managers, is the existing service context within which they are attempting to implement a new way of working. Case managers had considerable difficulty in convincing professional sceptics that case management is a new and worthwhile method of providing long-term care to elderly people at home.

An information and publicity leaflet produced by the steering group and distributed to possible referrers before the project started did not prevent misunderstandings and disagreements about what EPIC was in business to provide. This may be due to varying and sometimes erroneous understandings of the meaning and process of case management, exacerbated by the professional uncertainties surrounding the role of some community nursing staff in community care following implementation of the 1990 Act. The model employed by the EPIC team was much less radical and innovative than those used in Kent and Gateshead and scepticism that case management was really case coordination by another name was understandable.

Some social workers hoped that the project would take on referrals and assessments for residential care and its failure to do so caused some resentment. General practitioners who referred an elderly person for residential care sometimes resented subsequent referral to EPIC, the implication being that the medical assessment of need had been overridden. Some very frail people were referred to the project too late in their 'care career' for successful long-term care to be provided at home and case managers felt, rightly or wrongly, that the main aim of the referrer was to secure the services of a home carer for a hard pressed family as a short-term measure rather than have a system of long-term support at home established. This was an understandable attitude on the part of the referrer, keen to secure help where it may be found, since home carers were not otherwise available in the area. However, this resulted in disappointment and frustration for case managers when their care plans proved to be not sustainable over any great period of time.

One way of overcoming the fragmented nature of health and social service provision has been to combine these under one organisation. This model of care for older people has been developed in San Francisco in the On Lok Project (Zawadski 1983). All the health and social care needs of elderly people can be met within the project, thus avoiding conflicts and problems with other agencies. On Lok has attracted a great deal of interest from around the world and its model of integrated service provision has been the inspiration behind a new integrated care project recently set up in various parts of England. Experiments such as this will provide more evidence and experience about the ingredients for successful collaboration in supporting older people and their families.

THE EMERGING STYLE OF CASE MANAGEMENT

The style of case management adopted in EPIC was what might be termed 'conservative' as opposed to the more 'radical' model pioneered in Kent. Support to elderly people by the project was provided almost entirely by existing services and as already discussed, the organisational boundaries and territories made the model clumsy and difficult to organise. No new forms of service have been developed to date apart from the home carers which were part of the project from the outset. It is understandable if other professionals working in the area think that they are doing case management already themselves (as they frequently assert), since the home carer service is the only novelty they are able to observe. However, it is undoubtedly true that much of the work done by case managers is invisible, such as their sustained attempts to engage particularly hard to reach clients in their care planning. One very frail lady who had had frequent hospital admissions because of her failure to cooperate in her medical care was found, during her assessment by a case manager, to have a profound love of music and this was provided by the team leader playing the piano to her until a volunteer was found to do so. This broke the cycle of dysfunctional behaviour and the lady was able to remain at home as she wished, with support from EPIC, where, she died peacefully some weeks later. Nevertheless, the potential for greater creativity in meeting need afforded by the existence of the project budget was to some extent under used.

Why is innovation difficult to achieve in case management, even when budgetary control is included in the model, as it was in EPIC? Several reasons seem to be emerging:

1. Case managers were not used to working in a culture where innovation was encouraged. Innovation involves risk-taking and risk-taking needs to be carefully calculated and supported by agencies. Moreover, managers themselves need to encourage their staff to be innovative in their care planning and this encouragement seemed to be lacking. There was an air of complacency which implied that not much needed to be changed, or even a sense of resignation that not much could be changed. If staff do not feel that it is safe to take calculated risks in providing more client-centred services because they are not confident that in the event of trouble they will be supported by their agencies, the model will not develop but will remain restricted to what is known and 'safe'.

2. There was a reluctance to 'raise expectations' among EPIC clients and family carers about services. This was compounded by the knowledge that the project was time limited and that some case managers would in all probability return to their former posts in the respective sponsoring organisations and might even find themselves delivering services to former EPIC clients from a discrete service base once more. There was a sense that it was unrealistic to encourage elderly people and their carers to articulate too loudly how they would like services to be provided and what form these services should take, since it would not be possible to deliver them in this way once EPIC finished and services 'returned to normal'. It is difficult to know whether this attitude is engendered by pessimistic mutterings in departments about future levels of funding for community care or by anxiety at the difficulty organisations are having in deciding the extent, if any, to which they are willing or able to change their functioning. Either way, the effect on clients in EPIC was that they received a traditional model of service rather than experiencing new ways of being supported at home. The case managers themselves missed the opportunity to experiment and innovate within the context of what was an experimental project itself, where the chance to try out new ways of working provided rare opportunities for self-development.

3. Uncertainty persisted for many months about the desire of sponsoring agencies to continue their collaboration in the project after March 1992 and what form, if any, future collaboration would take. It is easy to underestimate the period of time needed to bring about change in organisations and in the people working within them and perhaps it was asking too much to expect great changes within the relatively short space of two years. The initial opprobrium that the project had to endure from social work and health colleagues alike had an understandable impact on the case managers and it was only in the last six months or so that some professionals began to make referrals. This situation is not unique to this project but reflects the need for the new to demonstrate its trustworthiness and effectiveness before other professionals will use it or entrust clients/patients to it.

Earlier, it was mentioned that the agencies behind the project hoped that the case managers would teach and learn from each other and thus acquire a greater body of knowledge in the field of work with older people at home than they brought with them from their various training backgrounds. This happened to a more limited extent than was hoped. As one agency representative put it, 'I hoped that participation in EPIC would result in a greater blurring of roles but instead an ever widening chasm seems to be opening up.' This comment arose after very lengthy debates about which case managers, if any, were competent to assess what assistance an elderly person might need to take a bath at home. The issue remained unresolved. The one case manager who did feel this was within her field of competence was not keen to be called in by her fellow case managers as a consultant in this area. Instead, in one case, the district nurse was asked to act in this capacity. This calls into question the usefulness or point of having a large body of knowledge and expertise within the team if it is not used across caseloads to benefit the maximum number of clients and to enhance the project's skills in carrying out assessment of complex need.

Another issue for case management within an organisation is the extent to which case managers are really free to act as advocates and brokers on behalf of clients. In residential care, this is supposed to be resolved by having arm's length inspection units, separate from the local authority department providing the service, and therefore able to enforce quality control of residential and other services. The separation of the purchaser/procurer and provider roles envisaged for community care seeks to enhance advocate and broker roles but where case managers are not given budgetary control, they will be inevitably constrained by the agency. This might seem like an argument for placing case managers outside departments, but a King's Fund project set up to function in this way to advocate for people with physical disabilities found that it was independent of the service providers but did not always have the organisational links or 'clout' needed to secure services for clients (Pilling 1989).

There is a danger that departments may see case or care management as one of a range of skills that social workers or other departmental staff already possess. If that is so, it will lend credence to the belief that case management is already being done and that only small organisational changes are needed to introduce it formally into departmental work. The evidence from EPIC so far is that training for case management is not an option but an essential if it is seriously intended to implement a needs-led approach not only to assessment but also to service organisation and delivery. Most generic social workers have had very little, if any, training in working with elderly people on their professional courses and little experience since qualifying. Post-qualifying training is now available but is costly and with staff needing to learn the implications of the new child care legislation, case management may find the pressure on training budgets relegates its importance.

THE CONSUMERS OF EPIC

At the time of writing, it is too early to be able to give a complete picture of how the project is perceived by the elderly people it has helped and their families. From the first set of interviews, it emerged that some users were unaware that they were receiving a service from a new project. Quite understandably, older people (and other age groups as well) are sometimes unclear about the provenance of the professional visiting them at home, unless they are a nurse in uniform performing a specific nursing task. On second interview, users knew about the EPIC project involvement but had no clear understanding about case management or its focus on user empowerment. Those who received the services of a home carer knew the individual's name rather than their title. Some of those EPIC clients who were already receiving home help and other services before referral to the project did not perceive any marked differences. This is not always the case with carers, however, some of whom have made it clear that without EPIC's help, they would not have been able to continue caring. This suggests that strenuous efforts will have to be made to engage the elderly client in planning their care with case managers as an exercise in partnership. It is a relationship neither side has experienced previously in the context of community support. Consumers have not been invited to make choices about the form their support should take but have been assessed by one or other service and then offered a service or not (Sinclair et al. 1990). EPIC clients did not perceive themselves as making choices about support.

CONCLUSION

The challenge of the next decade and beyond for social work/services and health agencies after 1993 is whether or not they prove themselves able to bring about fundamental change in the way they are organised and how they respond to the needs of older people and their families. Some commentators have spelt out just how radical these changes need to be (e.g. Sinclair et al. 1990). Having set the agenda, it is now incumbent on government to make community care financially possible.

Case management will only succeed if it is accepted as a means of improving community-based support by both health and social service agencies. This requires a degree of conviction that there are worthwhile improvements to be made. As the consumer voice about satisfaction with health and social services is only just beginning to be heard, service providers may not readily acknow-ledge the need to change – a painful process wherever it occurs. Part of the difficulty is that many of the services currently are provided by monopolistic organisations. The dissatisfied consumer has few, if any, alternatives to which they can turn. Is there a role for the independent sector here? Could they provide case managers able to plan packages of community support for older people and their families which are innovative, cost effective and reflective of the consumer's needs and wishes? Voluntary organisations have much less power in this respect because of their sources of funding. Research so far shows few signs that local authorities envisage a major role for the voluntary sector in assessment and/or case management (SSI 1991). Involvement of the private sector in the provision of community care services is even more restricted and geographically patchy. Nevertheless, this fits in with the White Paper exhortation to use the independent sector more widely. Whether the resistance to such ideas in social work can be overcome in Britain remains to be seen.

REFERENCES

Audit Commission (1986) *Making a Reality of Community Care*. London: HMSO.

Bland, R. and Bland, R.E. (1985) Contract and admission to old people's homes. *British Journal of Social Work*, 133–144.

Butrym, Z. (1989) Health care and social work – what kind of relationship? In R. Taylor and J. Ford (eds) *Social Work and Health Care, Research Highlights in Social Work 19*. London: Jessica Kingsley Publishers.

Challis, D. and Davies, B. (1986) *Case Management in Community Care*. Aldershot: Gower.

Challis, D., Darton, R., Johnson, L., Stone, M., Traske, K. and Wall, B. (1989) *Supporting Frail Elderly People at Home*. Canterbury: University of Kent, PSSRU.

Challis, D., Chessum, R., Chesterman, J., Luckett, R. and Traske, K. (1990) *Case Management in Social and Health Care*. Canterbury: University of Kent, PSSRU.

Clode, D. (1991) Another injection. *Insight*, 11 April.

Connor, A. and Tibbitt, J. (1988) *Social Workers and Health Care in Hospitals*. Edinburgh: HMSO.

Dalley, G. (1989) Professional ideology or organisational tribalism? The health service–social work divide. In R. Taylor and J. Ford (eds) *Social Work and Health Care, Research Highlights in Social Work 19*. London: Jessica Kingsley Publishers.

Davies, B.P. and Challis, D.J. (1981) A production relations evaluation of the meeting of needs in the community care projects. In E.M. Goldberg and N. Connelly (eds) *Evaluative Research in Social Care. London: Heinemann*.

Davies, B. and Challis, D. (1986) *Matching Resources to Needs in Community Care*. Aldershot: Gower.

Department of Health (1990) *Caring for People in the Next Decade and Beyond*. London: HMSO.

Department of Health and Social Security (1981) *Growing Older, cmnd 8173*. London: HMSO.

Department of Health and Social Security (1983) *Care in the Community*. Circular.

Dexter, M. and Harbert, W. (1983) *The Home Help Service*. London: Tavistock.

Green, H. (1988) *Informal Carers: A Study Carried out on Behalf of the Department of Health and Social Security as Part of the 1985 General Household Survey*. London: HMSO.

Griffiths, R. (1988) *Community Care: Agenda for Action*. London: HMSO.

Gwynne, D. and Fean, L. (1978) *The Home Help Service in Cumbria*. Cumbria Social Services Department.

Holme, A. and Maizels, J. (1978) *Social Workers and Volunteers*. London: British Association of Social Workers/George Allan and Unwin.

Howe, D. (1980) Divisions of labour in the area teams of social services departments. *Social Policy and Administration 14*.

Hunter, D.J. and Wistow, G. (1987) *Community Care in Britain: Variations on a Theme*. London: Kings Fund.

Huntington, J. (1981) *Social Work and General Medical Practice: Collaboration or Conflict*. London: George Allen and Unwin.

Lutz, B. (1989) *Report of Development and Testing of Screening and Assessment Instruments, Social Work Research Centre Working Paper*. University of Stirling.

Maclean, U. (1989) *Dependent Territories: The Frail Elderly and Community Care*. London: Nuffield Provincial Hospitals Trust.

Neill, J.E., Warburton, R.W. and McGuinness, B. (1976) Post Seebohm social services: the social worker's viewpoint. *Social Work Today* 1 November.

Parker, R. (1990) In Sinclair, I., Parker, R., Leat, D. and Williams, J. (1990) *The Kaleidoscope of Care: A Review of Research on Welfare Provision for Elderly People*. London: NISW/HMSO.

Pilling, D. (1989) *The Case Manager Project: Report of the Evaluation*. London: Rehabilitation Resource Centre, Department of Systems Science, City University.

Plank, D. (1977) *Caring for the Elderly: Report of a Study of Caring for Dependent Elderly People in Eight London Boroughs*. London: Greater London Council.

Runciman, P. (1989) Health assessment of the elderly: a multidisciplinary perspective. In R. Taylor and J. Ford (eds) *Social Work and Health Care, Research Highlights in Social Work 19*. London: Jessica Kingsley Publishers.

Ryan, P., Ford, R. and Clifford, P. (1991) *Case Management in Community Care*. London: Research and Development for Psychiatry.

Salvage A. (1986) *Attitudes of the Over 75s to Health and Social Services: Final Report*. Cardiff: University of Wales College of Medicine, Research Team for the Care of the Elderly.

Sinclair, I., Parker, R., Leat, D. and Williams, J. (1990) *The Kaleidoscope of Care*. London: NISW/HMSO.

Social Services Inspectorate (1987a) *From Home Help to Home Care: An Analysis of Policy Resourcing and Service Management*. London: SSI Department of Health and Social Security.

Social Services Inspectorate (1991) *Assessment Systems and Community Care*. London: HMSO.

Social Work Services Group (1990) *Statistical Bulletin on Home Care Services, Day Care Establishments and Day Care Services*. Edinburgh: Scottish Education Department.

Stevenson, O. and Parsloe, P. (eds) (1978) *Social Services Teams: the Practitioner's View*. London: HMSO.

Titterton, M. (1990) *Caring for People in Scotland – A Report on Community Care in Scotland and the Implications of the White Paper and the NHS and Community Care Bill*. Report submitted to House of Commons Social Services Committee.

Taylor, R. and Ford, G. (1983) Inequalities in old age: an examination of age, sex and class differences in a sample of community elderly. *Ageing and Society*, 3, 2, 183–191.

Wenger, G.C. (1984) *The Supportive Network*. London: Allen and Unwin.

Zawadski, R. (ed) (1983) Community based systems of long-term care. *Home Health Services Quarterly*, 4, Nos. 3/4, Fall/Winter.

CHAPTER 9

The Role of the Voluntary Sector in the New Community Care Arrangements

Anne Connor*

INTRODUCTION

For many years voluntary organisations have had a key role in developing and providing social care for people in the community care client groups. Indeed, voluntary organisations have been providing services for people who are vulnerable as a result of age, disability or illness for much longer than the present statutory health or social care services.

Today, many voluntary organisations are continuing this strong tradition. They are involved in innovative forms of service development, establishing the right to services of groups of people whose needs have not always been recognised or respected by existing service providers. They are developing new forms of care, thus extending the range of services available to those in need of support, often drawing on the skills and resources of people in surrounding areas as managers or volunteers – such as small-scale local responses based within communities. These new services may be breaking new ground in terms of service delivery or bringing a well-established model of service to locations where it was not yet available. Similarly, service models have been developed – for example, adapting to the needs of families from ethnic communities in inner cities and of people living in far flung rural communities.

Increasingly, such voluntary services have complemented and expanded the range of statutory services already available, by filling in gaps in service networks or acting as feeder or follow-on services to mainstream provision such as acute hospital care. In this, voluntary organisations have been able to provide care that is both more appropriate to the needs of users and more cost-effective than delivering specialised, more intensive care to those who do not need that form of support at the time.

*   Central Research Unit, The Scottish Office. Any views expressed are those of the author and may not reflect the view of Social Work Services Group or other parts of The Scottish Office.

Another important role of voluntary organisations in the last decade or so, however, has been to draw in additional resources to existing service networks. Because grants have been available from central government and other donors to support voluntary activities in situations when equivalent support to services by Health Boards and social work or services departments is not forthcoming, the development of voluntary projects can be a welcome way of extending support. Recent examples include the use of the Manpower Services Commission Community Programme, Urban Aid funding and special programmes funded directly by The Scottish Office and other government departments in England and Wales.

With the impetus of the White Paper *Caring for People* and the subsequent National Health Service and Community Care Act, we can expect to see a growth of developments of this type. Voluntary organisations will be expected to play an increasing role as providers of community-based services for elderly, disabled and other vulnerable people in ways which are well-suited to users' needs and are a cost-effective way of complementing local authority and Health Board provision. The reasons for extending the role of voluntary organisations in this way have been debated at some length. Whatever the justification, however, the most pertinent question now is how can this role be made to work effectively in practice.

To answer this, it is useful to consider the recent experience of community-based social care projects such as those developed in response to some of the special programmes noted above. One good example of this is the Care in the Community Initiative, which ran from 1985 to 1988 and was funded by the Social Work Services Group of The Scottish Office under section 10 of the Social Work (Scotland) Act 1968. This programme was specifically intended to encourage the development of community-based direct services by voluntary organisations to people from most of the community care client groups. The experience of these projects is not dissimilar to events occurring elsewhere and described in a variety of research and other accounts (Renshaw, Hampson, Thomason, Darton, Judge and Knapp 1988). These projects demonstrated that voluntary-run projects can succeed in delivering a high quality of care to dependent people. However, they also showed how the course of achieving this outcome is not necessarily a smooth one. This chapter looks at some experiences of this programme which are relevant to the likely role of voluntary organisations under the new community care arrangements. Other aspects – such as the use of short-term grants, the ability of groups to fund-raise and the projects' impact as innovative service developments – are not considered in any depth here, but have been discussed in the research report on this programme and related publications (Connor 1991a, b, c, 1993a, 1993b).

The next section discusses aspects of the direct care given to users. The following section considers the organisational aspects which enhanced or limited the level or quality of service provided, while the last section considers the implications of the experience of this programme for the coming development of similar projects elsewhere.

LEVEL OF CARE AND CHARACTERISTICS OF USERS

People Who Used the Projects

The 23 projects provided care to most of the groups of people who are likely to feature under the new community care arrangements. They included people with dementia, other elderly people, adults and children with a physical disability, adults and children with learning disabilities and adults with mental health problems. A further project identified a range of additional supports and heightened awareness of the need for services by people who were deaf/blind. These users lived throughout Scotland and are probably fairly typical of the kind of people who will need support in the community.

Around 2,000 people and their families received a direct service from the 23 projects, while another 800 or so users received help through support groups and other indirect services. As can be seen from Table 9.1, the two largest groups of people to benefit from these projects were dementia sufferers and people with mental health problems. The numbers of people using specific projects ranged from 10 to over 300, reflecting the different types of service, the scope for expansion and the needs of users. For example, some projects cared for a small group of people throughout the two or three years of SWSG funding, such as a small day centre for people with dementia where users were initially in the mild to moderate stage of the illness and were able to stay with the project as their health declined. At the other extreme, some projects had a high turnover of users where users' illness meant they were likely to need hospital care within a year or two of joining the project, or where people used the project for only a short period at any time. This latter situation included people using the residential respite care projects and people with mental health problems who dropped-in to the support services when under stress and made less frequent use when they were feeling relatively well.

Table 9.1 Use of Projects by Groups of Users

Group of users (including carers)	Number using services			
	Direct	Indirect	All	%
Adults with mental health problems	670*	345*	1015	36.5
Old people with dementia	601	145	746	26.8
Other older people	328		328	11.8
Adults with a learning disability	131	170*	301	10.8
Adults with a physical disability	158		158	5.7
Deaf–blind people		140*	140	5.0
Children with a learning disability	82		82	2.9
Children with a physical disability	12		12	0.4
All users	**1982**	**800**	**2782**	**100.0**

* Estimates from one or more projects in category: excludes people who used service very infrequently.

The projects making up the Initiative had been intended to complement existing informal support and other services for people who were already well-established in the community and to improve the quality of life for users and their informal carers. In practice, however, the projects had to take on a more significant role than was initially anticipated in supporting these users in the community. This was partly because many people were more dependent than had been expected by the original planners, and partly because the level of existing services within the community for these groups of users was at best minimal. For between one-third and one-half of people in most client groups, these projects made a substantial contribution to maintaining the person in the community. The most marked impact was for the older people with dementia, where four out of every five users would have been struggling to survive in the medium to longer term without these supports (see Figure 9.1). (A copy of the classification system used in the research is given in the Appendix.)

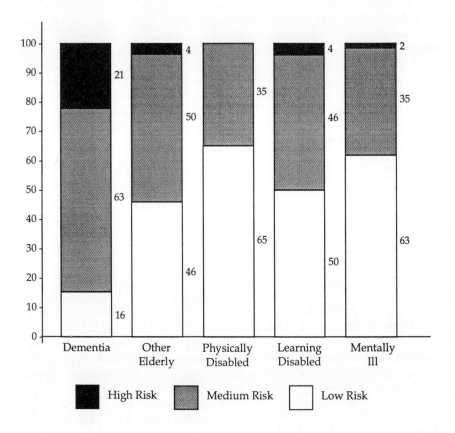

Figure 9.1 Levels of Risk of Main Groups of Clients

Two-thirds of the **older people with dementia** were just managing to cope and would have had difficulty remaining in the community if the new voluntary services were no longer there, while about a fifth were already having marked difficulties coping even with the support of the current service network. The main factors in this group being so dependent were the deterioration in the users' medical state and the strain which this imposed on their families. Another factor which often compounded these problems was the users' social isolation. Almost half the 600 direct users with dementia lived alone. Most were women (78%) and aged over 75 (70%): inevitably, they included many people who had recently been widowed and were in any case having problems adapting to unfamiliar tasks such as handling domestic finances and coping with grief and loneliness. About two-thirds of those who lived alone had family members or friends who provided informal care living nearby. There were still some 15 per cent of users who were known to have no family or other informal support, while for a further 21 per cent the support was available only on an irregular basis. The users who had little or no informal support were also *less* likely to be receiving help from the statutory services: these were mostly cases where the illness had only recently been diagnosed and this was the first main service offered to the person or where the person had consistently refused all offers of help in the past. The majority of users' families, neighbours and friends who were able to provide practical support and monitoring of the person's well-being managed to do so in a reliable, effective way. Inevitably, some of these informal care networks could not cope with the practical and emotional demands made by the person's deteriorating medical state.

The **other elderly people** who used this set of projects were generally coping better in the community and in this were perhaps more typical of the type of people whom these projects originally sought to support. Whereas the older people with dementia using the various types of service – specialised and general day centres and sitter services – made up a fairly homogeneous group, the elderly people who experienced ill health or who had other problems differed widely in their circumstances and so in the needs which they looked to these services – day care, home-based sitter services, residential respite care and practical support services – to meet. Most of this group were physically disabled as the result of sudden illness such as a stroke or a progressive illness such as multiple sclerosis. They were younger than the users with dementia and included a higher proportion of men: as a consequence a higher proportion – two-thirds rather than half – lived with a member of their family and this included more spouses, although both sets of older people relied heavily on adult sons and daughters and members of their extended family.

The people who were having more difficulty coping and who were at greater risk of coming to harm in the foreseeable future if the project was not available were typically those who lived alone, who were socially isolated as a consequence of their ill-health (for example, speech difficulties following a stroke or poor mobility), people who had suddenly become ill or disabled and had not had time to adjust or to build support networks, and individuals or families who had little or no support from extended informal or statutory networks.

These characteristics of loneliness and social and geographic isolation from family and other community support – often as a consequence of the person's illness – were shared by many of the **people with mental health problems**, even though at first glance this group was very different: younger (half aged under 40), mostly male (two-thirds), with fewer physical illnesses and in theory having access to a wider range of activities and facilities. This group of users were the least likely to be living with family members: a fifth were with family, three-fifths were living alone and a further fifth lived in shared accommodation, often with other people who had mental health problems. Sixty per cent of these users did however have relatives living nearby who were concerned about their welfare and whose roles as carers focused mainly on the monitoring and encouragement/support aspects rather than on practical or physical care. Many users had learned of the centre through the health service network and were either still receiving psychiatric care on an out-patient basis or had mental health problems which were chronic but now relatively stable or controlled. The factors associated with people in this group being assessed as likely to have problems coping in the community were the adoption of risky behaviour such as sleeping rough or alcohol abuse, when they slipped out of the informal and statutory service support and monitoring networks, and when other problems arose which put additional stress on that person, such as a bereavement or becoming homeless.

The way in which the type of services was linked to the characteristics of the user group is perhaps most clearly demonstrated by the circumstances of those **people with physical or learning disabilities** who used these projects. The majority were in contact with two large residential respite projects and their use of services was primarily to provide respite to their carers, with whom they lived. A smaller number of people benefited from two specialist re-housing and rehabilitation projects and they had very different characteristics: most were presently in hospital or another type of residential care and were aiming to live independently because they had no available family support or this would have been inappropriate. Users of a day centre for people with learning disabilities included people who were living at home and needed some additional support and those who were moving out of hospital: although the number of people using the project was small (no more than 20 users across two small centres at any given time) the wide range of needs which the project was having to meet posed some problems.

The factors associated with people from these two client groups being assessed as having or likely to have difficulty coping were: heavy dependence on immediate family members and often on a single person; the narrow range of services provided to support the family and the low likelihood of people living alone otherwise securing integrated packages of services; and other problems facing the family, especially where the user was a child with serious handicaps. In this, they were probably quite typical of other families with a disabled member, especially with a learning disability. The OPCS survey of informal carers showed that parents of adults with a learning disability were the least likely to have support from other sources, while Glendinning and

others have shown with great clarity the strains on families with a handicapped child (Glendinning 1983, 1986, Green 1988). The potential instability
of the care provided in the community for people with a learning difficulty
and the lower likelihood of such problems being identified quickly were often
emphasised by project staff, and this is reflected in the higher proportion
assessed as having difficulties coping in the longer term.

Delivery of Services

Few of the direct services in this programme developed as the organisations
themselves or SWSG as the funder/contracting partner had expected. The
main reason for this was the larger than expected numbers of referrals,
especially of very dependent people. The organisations' response to this was
to expand: for example, giving more places, providing additional care to
existing users, covering a larger physical area, or some combination of these.
Some projects planned this over the course of the first year or so, but others
introduced these changes very quickly as a response to the overwhelming
demand. A few projects were able to cope with these changes and higher
demands relatively easily but most encountered difficulties. There were three
main factors in this.

The most immediate was the **characteristics of the users**, especially when
their circumstances were not stable. Some projects were substantially user-
led, reacting to the needs of their users. When users were more ill, their carers
were feeling the strain more acutely or the support given by informal or other
service carers tended to vary, the demand placed on the project would
increase. Most projects could cope with a few users putting an expectedly high
demand on them at any given time. When a relatively high proportion of users
were living in crisis, however, the capacity of projects was often stretched. To
take an extreme – but not atypical – example, over a course of a single fortnight
a project providing support to people with dementia in their own homes had
users whose carers were themselves receiving hospital care, users who became violent or distressed and refused to let anyone other than the project
worker into their home, while one client's home became temporarily unsuitable as a result of a burst water pipe: all these situations required substantial
additional inputs from the project at a time when almost a quarter of the
project's staff and care workers were struggling to cope with a flu outbreak.

Another factor was the **type of provision**: for example, whether it was
possible to expand easily the number of care workers to accommodate new
referrals. Projects were more able to increase the number of users receiving
care when not hampered by physical constraints such as available space or
access to transport to bring users to the project. Thus the sitter services and
overnight respite service based on foster carers' homes were able to continue
to take on new clients while maintaining the care level given to existing users
more readily than could day centres or residential respite projects. The latter
projects could only offer care to new clients when the service to existing users
was reduced or when spaces became available as users went into long-term
care, moved away, made other arrangements or died. There were, however,
a few instances of projects securing more suitable premises and doubling the

level of service given within a few months even though the inputs of additional staff or volunteers were minimal.

The **cooperation of other professionals**, especially in making referrals and providing on-going support and advice, could then compound or alleviate other problems. All projects were better able to accommodate a steady flow of new referrals rather than sudden floods as referrers cleared their caseloads. They needed reliable information about clients and their wider circumstances, especially when the person was at risk, very dependent or there were other special circumstances: even a single such client could take up a great deal of time and resources if the project was ill-prepared and received little or no support from the statutory agency.

Overall, the pattern of service provision associated with good, efficient project development was in most instances also associated with improving the long-term quality and level of care provided to users. Where sudden changes were made to the level of service, even if triggered by the desire to help people, it was usually no more than a short-term advantage and, in the medium to longer term, the disruption to the service given to these and other users was not in their best interests.

Some projects also offered services designed specifically to meet the needs of carers – most frequently support groups. The reasons for this included concern for the needs and well-being of this group of people, and also finding some way of coping with referrals when the project could not hope to offer a direct service for some time. Most projects found the resources needed to do this properly were much more extensive than they had anticipated. Support for carers had usually been planned as the secondary strand to the main direct service provided by the project, or were introduced at a much later date as the need emerged. With hindsight, project coordinators were unanimous in their view that the level of demand for this form of support and the amount of time and different skills needed to provide it were such that this should have taken the form of a full, parallel service offered by the project or provided in some other way, financed and staffed appropriately, rather than just being tagged on.

The way in which these projects were managed had a major influence on both the level and quality of the service provided. For around a third of the projects more people could have received a service if problems related to the management of the project – such as staffing difficulties, volunteer recruitment, access to good quality training, inadequate information about client's needs and financial management – had been resolved. Typically, this could have resulted in increases of 50–100 per cent of the level of service given. For another third of projects the lack of sufficient additional income meant the level of care provided was kept below its full potential and the proportion of income taken up by inflexible overheads – such as the coordinator's salary and rent for an office or day centre – was higher than necessary. The quality of service given to users was also sometimes undermined. In seeking to maximise the numbers of people using these services, the steps taken sometimes had the unintended result of undermining the quality of care provided and even of putting individual users' well-being at risk.

Outcomes of Services

These projects were far from interchangeable, even when caring for the same client group, and emphasised the importance of planning provision around the needs of actual and potential users as far as possible. The extent to which individual people gained benefits was influenced by two factors: first, by their own circumstances and, second, by the type, level and quality of care provided by the project. For example, those elderly and other people who lived alone and had few contacts with family or friends found company, the opportunity to contribute to the well-being of other people and often gained a great deal of pleasure from events such as Christmas parties and the outings in the summer. Those people who lived with carers, however, often placed a great deal of emphasis on the value of the project in providing respite and thus enabling the carer to go on holiday, take on voluntary work or just have a break, and thus ease the relationship between the two people. The ways in which regular day care and irregular, but perhaps more intensive, home-based respite could contribute to these sorts of benefits were clearly quite different. For example, among the older people with dementia, the users themselves gained more benefits from the day care services, while their carers gained more benefits from the home-based respite and other supports.

Although the projects were all valued strongly by direct users and their carers, the factor which was emphasised most often by all users in their feedback was the reliability they could place in the service in both the short and longer-term. It was this reliability which meant that the benefits gained were not necessarily linked to the level of use – for example, carers were able to accept social, voluntary or employment commitments when they were confident that the project would be able to provide care for a few hours or overnight if necessary. Without this level of reliability many carers would not have undertaken these commitments at all – as indeed had happened to many families before these projects began delivering care. In this respect, however, the short-term funding of these projects caused anxieties and partly undermined the impact and value of the services.

Around 40 per cent of project users would most probably have been using hospital or long-term residential care if the project had not helped them to continue or begin to live in the community. This was most significant for the people with dementia, where around three-quarters of this group of users benefited in this way. In this regard, clearly the projects were of benefit not only to the direct users and their families but also in relieving or postponing demands on other resources. Generally, for other services there were two types of benefit: this relief on resources and the enabling of services to deliver a better quality of service to their existing users – for example, when the project became part of a package of care or was reinforcing the input of other professionals to an individual user.

ORGANISATION AND DEVELOPMENT OF COMMUNITY CARE PROJECTS

Whereas a great deal of attention has been given to the need for community-based services, issues of access, user involvement and equal opportunities and to the outputs and outcomes of these models of service, less has been given in the various writings on community care to the way services are managed. In the description above of the circumstances of users and the service that they received from this set of projects, it has already been noted that aspects of the management and organisation of the projects had an impact on the level and quality of the services given. In this, the experience of these projects was probably not atypical of many voluntary and statutory project-type services (Knight 1984).

The projects supported by the SWSG Care in the Community Initiative included a few examples of very good project structures – where services were well planned; the managers committed and involved; the coordinator, volunteer and paid care workers were well-trained and given on-going management support; and where there was sound financial planning and management, including fund-raising and the securing of long-term financial support. At the other extreme, a few projects had substantial difficulties throughout the period of the grant in all or most of these areas. The remainder of projects, which made up the great majority, had some difficulties at one point or another. What, then, were the types of problems that arose most frequently?

Management Committees

The starting point is probably the way in which projects are managed. Essentially, once a project has secured funding for the scheme or has been established within a statutory agency's own funding programme, managers have three main areas of on-going responsibility:

- recruiting the people who will organise and deliver direct care services

- overall responsibility for the scope and quality of the service offered to users

- overall financial management of the project, including fund-raising and identifying other sources of income if this is necessary and liaison with the main funders in respect of any grant support.

Within the Care in the Community Initiative, many managers assumed that once the project had received funding or the coordinator had been appointed their responsibilities had effectively been handed over. As the service got underway, however, the greater complexity of each of these three areas became more apparent.

This study identified a range of specific management tasks. There were many different ways of organising the projects, reflecting the different circumstances of the voluntary organisations. What was important was that all the key tasks were covered and that all the people concerned knew who was responsible for which tasks and were confident that they had the experience,

training and support necessary to fulfil the tasks for which they were responsible. Overall, projects had fewer problems and dealt with those that did arise
more readily when they had a simple management structure, because there
was less risk of tasks falling into an organisational gap between several
committees or people.

The most frequently occurring problems arose in relation to the supervision, training and on-going support given to the project coordinator, either
because no-one within the management committee had responsibility for this
or because the person nominally responsible did not have the necessary skills
or time to carry out the work in anything other than a fairly ad hoc way. These
same circumstances lay behind the situations in which there were problems
concerning financial management and fund-raising. However, a different set
of factors arose in the third main area of responsibility – the allocation of care
for the users. Most projects had been set up on the basis that the coordinator
would carry the main day to day responsibility for this, although a few project
management committees reserved the right to have the deciding say in
whether particular people began or continued to receive care. The most
common cause of problems here was when the referrers wished to exercise a
greater degree of control than the project staff and/or managers considered
appropriate, but the management committee did not have the skills or confidence to tackle this matter.

When the management of a project began to go wrong the effect could be
quite spectacular. For example, one coordinator paid a fuel bill by a personal
cheque, with her husband taking money from a savings account to cover the
sum, because the day care centre otherwise would have no heating for very
vulnerable older people in the middle of a severe winter: the management
committee had known of the problem for several months and the grant
income was sufficient to meet the sum, but no-one had taken responsibility
for ensuring the bill was paid. Another example was the situation of a
part-time coordinator at a day centre, with no formal training and limited
experience of this type of work, who managed and supported 20 volunteers
caring for very vulnerable, confused older people, working over 60 hours a
week herself and helping the volunteers visit clients at home. No-one in the
management committee thought they could offer appropriate management
and support to the coordinator and the volunteers, and committee members
were unwilling to step in to a long-standing disagreement between social
work and health care professionals about who should take lead responsibility
for assessing and supporting this user group.

Members of management committees usually came from a wide range of
backgrounds. Overall, there was a high level of continuity among the various
management committees, with most people remaining involved throughout
the duration of the project, especially when they were involved in a personal
rather than a professional capacity. For some projects this was a source of
strength as it enabled a group of very committed people to develop into a
team. However, this could also be the root of some of the management
problems, as the people who had been involved in setting up the projects and
securing funding were not necessarily the most appropriate to run the service,
as different skills and experience were required. Other issues were associated

with the involvement of professional staff in management committees. Again, there were examples of these links working in a way that was positive and beneficial for both the voluntary service and the appropriate statutory service provider. However, there were also examples of staff moving away to another post and suddenly leaving the management committee bereft of important knowledge and skills, of individuals being placed in a position of a conflict of loyalties and responsibilities when there was a dispute between the voluntary service and their employing department, and of 'information black holes' – where the other members of a committee simply assumed that because a social worker was on the committee there was no need for them to keep the Social Work Department informed of what they were planning, while the social worker assumed that someone else on the committee would be dealing with these matters in a more formal way.

As might be expected, very few people who became involved in the management committees had experience of all three of the main areas of project management. The view taken by many of the committees was that as long as someone associated with the project had relevant experience this would be sufficient but, as noted above, problems then arose when that person moved on and no replacement was available. These gaps in managers' experience could have been met to some extent by appropriate training and advice, but although training courses and other sources of information for project managers were available these were rarely taken up. Similarly, few projects were able to draw on outside expertise about management-related matters. To some extent this may have been a feature of these projects being run by voluntary organisations which were locally based, but those projects run by organisations which were part of a larger network, or which had a substantial level of sponsorship from a statutory agency, did not necessarily have as much advice and support from that source as might have been expected. Most members of project committees did not regard themselves as 'managers' and even those who did saw no need for any advice and training of this sort. On the few instances when managers did participate in training activities this was with a view to understanding the needs of the user group and/or to better understand what service their project was offering and the work of the staff and volunteers in providing care, rather than on issues related to project management.

Staff and Volunteers

The most important people in setting up these community care projects were the coordinators or project leaders. They had the main responsibility for bringing the service to life, seeing that it was run in an effective and efficient way and in a position to demonstrate its value and secure long-term funding by the time the SWSG grant was due to end.

Like many staff working in community-based care projects, the coordinators found themselves in posts associated with a considerable level of uncertainty as a consequence of the short-term nature of the funding. It is perhaps therefore no surprise that for one-third of the people appointed to these posts this was their first professional job, while for most of the others it represented a fairly major career change. Although the staff came from a wide range of professional and personal backgrounds their experience and knowledge in terms of the main elements of their jobs were quite similar. Two-thirds of the people appointed had little or no experience in one or other of the tasks which made up the greater part of their jobs: understanding the needs of this particular user group (25% being inexperienced) or carrying out the main areas of work associated with managing a service, such as supervising and training staff and volunteers and liaising with statutory and other voluntary organisations (56% inexperienced). In addition, four-fifths of those with responsibility for financial matters, such as day to day budget management, were taking on this task for the first time. All of the staff realised when they took up the post that there would be elements of the work which they would have to learn, and assumed that training would be provided. In practice, however, the training and on-going support and advice available to the staff mostly focused on aspects of caring for this user group – the feature about which they already knew most – and not on aspects of project management and development or financial management, about which they knew least.

Over time, project coordinators found their own sources of information and advice, often through informal networks involving other voluntary sector projects. For the less experienced staff, the form and ease of access to training and support had a direct impact on the way they spent their time and on the outcome of the tasks they performed. This, in turn, had a bearing on the service given to users and other aspects of project development. For over a third of these projects their pattern of development improved noticeably once the coordinators began to have access to appropriate advice and support on matters related to project management – for example, when an apparently intractable problem concerning volunteer recruitment was sorted out when a new approach was taken. It seems certain that had staff had access to relevant advice and training from the outset the level and quality of service given to clients in the early stages would have been improved.

One of the continuing debates concerned with the development of com- munity care projects is whether services are best provided by paid care workers, volunteers or a mixture of the two. Examples of all these approaches to service delivery were included in this set of projects. There was very strong agreement that the most difficult situation was when a project involved both paid staff and volunteers, and that if both groups of care workers were involved in a project it was best that they did a different type of work and that the two groups should be regarded as equally valuable, but clearly different. Otherwise, it was recognised that there were situations where paid workers were preferable to volunteers and vice versa: the factors associated with this included circumstances of the users, the type of service being provided, the personal circumstances of the people involved, including their other commit- ments, and the ethos and values of the organisations, which included the principle of payment being made for certain types of work and wish to involve volunteers and/or users or other people from the local community. Recruiting people as volunteers to projects which were not yet in existence, and to services caring for groups of users who do not have a particularly 'attractive' or well-understood image with the general public, posed some major chal- lenges to those services wishing to work with volunteers. However, the experience of these and other projects has shown that it is possible to deal successfully with these issues.

When the projects had the right type of care workers for their circumstances, those involving volunteers and paid care workers were equally successful. There was not found to be any difference among people working in a paid or voluntary capacity in their level of commitment to the service. There were also few differences in many aspects of project management, as the needs of the people doing the care work, the needs of their users and the ways in which coordinators provided supervision and support to the care workers had to be addressed irrespective of the employment status of the people concerned.

In addition to the volunteers recruited to work with clients, however, it has to be recognised that the users themselves fulfilled a valuable quasi-volunteer role. A few projects had intentionally developed this form of input. However, all the projects reported a higher than expected self-help element, including situations where users were extremely vulnerable and dependent. For example, in the day care centres for people with dementia, users in the early stages of the illness sometimes took on an active role, albeit under the encouragement and direction of the coordinator or other volunteers. Similarly, care workers in projects for people with learning disabilities commented on the valuable help given by users, and how the self-confidence and self-esteem the users gained from helping other people, rather than always being the recipients of help, was an important feature of the way people used and benefited from the service. The circumstances in which coordinators expressed concern about this type of situation were when the level of staffing or volunteering was so low that the project became dependent on this input and was then unable to make sufficient time to address the special needs of these particular users.

It also has to be recognised that caring for people who were very vulnerable and/or needed long-term support placed stresses on coordinators and care workers. These were exacerbated by concerns about the well-being of users should the project close when the SWSG grant ended, and by pressures on the project resulting from poor coordination with other services and/or a lack of support from other service providers – for example, when other agencies made inappropriate referrals, did not supply adequate background information about users or did not deliver the expected level of care to the users concerned.

Funding

These projects were funded under a specific short-term programme, receiving capital grant and/or revenue grant for up to three financial years. Projects therefore had to take steps to find steady income if they were to offer a secure service in the longer term. Not all the SWSG grants covered the full cost of projects, while some projects later made further expansions, so almost all projects had to maintain another grant or other source of funds from a statutory authority and/or were seeking funding from other sources.

To cover properly the issue of funding community care projects and the financial aspects of the role of the voluntary sector would require a book in its own right. It is sufficient to note that securing an adequate, reliable income was often far from easy. Factors which affected projects' ability to secure additional or continuation funding were:

- the insecurity of income levels on the part of the local authority and/or Health Board
- uncertainty about new funding arrangements
- a lack of public awareness or sympathy about the needs of the user group
- the way fund-raising and income-management were handled within the project: the most successful model was when accounts were kept by a specific member of the management committee and fund-raising was done by a separate 'friends of the project' group; the least successful was when these matters were left to project workers.

Other studies have also identified the type of service as a factor, with difficulties in raising funds for certain types of service, especially revenue funding for activities which are relatively 'invisible'. It is perhaps not surprising that raising money to buy a minibus or towards a building such as a day centre has generally been found to be easier than support for a respite care service based in users' or care givers' homes or for core overheads.

Within project expenditure, the cost per user decreased markedly over time as the initial start-up costs were absorbed in the increasing number of users. Generally, it took 12 to 18 months after the service had started for the unit costs to reach their natural long-term level. All this was much as expected. There were, however, fewer differences between the various types of service than had been expected. For example, once all relevant costs had been taken into consideration over the full period of the project, a day care centre using volunteers involved broadly the same cost as one using paid care workers. Similarly, the unit cost of a day care centre was similar to that for home-based services and other models of care. A more important factor in determining costs was the management of the project – when a service was slow to get off the ground or was beset by other problems which limited the level of care and/or pushed up costs, the unit cost of providing care was markedly higher than equivalent projects which had not experienced or had successfully tackled such problems. A contributing factor to some of the difficulties encountered by inexperienced staff and volunteers may have been projects' attempts to keep down salaries, expenses and training costs. Given the impact that this then had on the service given to users, it might be questioned how far the aim of achieving economy undermined the efficiency and effectiveness of the services secured.

Project Development

In terms of projects' development, the experience of the projects under this experimental programme highlights two key issues:

1. Setting up community-based care services takes longer than expected.
2. Planners and care providers should expect matters *not* to go smoothly.

From the point where the award of funding was notified to the project to the day when direct care was given to users, the quickest projects took four months and the longest took 19 months – i.e. just over half the total period when funding was available – while the average was eight months.

Factors which influenced this were:

- the type of service
- recruitment and training of the coordinator and care workers
- practical matters
- the ability of the organisation to tackle problems.

Generally, the more strands that needed to be in place before a service could begin, the longer the delay. It was possible to start a home-based respite care service for just a few users by recruiting one or two care workers and having a simple referral and assessment process, with more care workers and users joining the project over the coming months. Day care usually needed more elements to be in place – premises, transport, equipment and other practical arrangements; a group of staff or volunteers; assessment of a sufficient number of clients for a viable service. Residential care was more complex still, with additional requirements for registration and other checks. Projects then ran against such vagaries as unexpected building repairs, dependence on a single supplier, unreliable or unsuitable transport, difficulties in recruiting staff – and especially volunteers – to a service that did not yet exist and a reluctance on the part of other professionals to refer people to a service they had not been able to check out. In these circumstances, to have a good quality, reliable service being delivered to users in only eight months seems a remarkable achievement.

Once the projects were up and running different types of problems arose. Some projects had difficulty retaining staff or volunteers – a common experience among short-term funding schemes. As already noted, projects quickly encountered higher than expected levels of demand and demand from a more highly dependent group of people. As a result many projects expanded quickly. Here, the flexibility of the project and especially the skills of management committees and coordinators were extremely important. Interestingly, in this respect projects which were extensions of existing services fared rather less well than completely new services, perhaps because the people concerned in the better established projects were assuming that previous experience would still apply and were not ready for the new challenges.

By the end of the SWSG grant period, 16 of the 18 projects looking for revenue funding had received it, although not all new arrangements were of the same level as the Scottish Office funding or delivered promptly. The remaining two projects continued, but with considerable uncertainty. This meant that six projects had to make fairly radical changes to the service at the end of the initial grant period. All projects, staff and committees reported high levels of concern and debate and additional work, often over a year or more, as they sought on-going funding. Although projects tried to shield users from these worries, inevitably there was an impact on the level and/or quality of service given by most projects.

These projects approached a wide range of potential sources of funding, including Trusts, sponsorship, charging of fees and general fund raising. However, the only significant sources of funding that were ultimately secured were awards of grant from the Social Work Department and/or Health Board. The factors which determined the outcome of projects' search for funding, and therefore longer-term survival, appeared to be determined as much by the available sources and levels of funding and the handling of the grant allocation process by the voluntary organisation and potential funders, as by the quality and level of service provided by the project.

Patterns of Project Development

Standing back, it is possible to identify distinct phases in these projects' pattern of developments – a sort of 'project life-cycle'. These stages were:

- *Planning* This included the preliminary planning and development of an idea into a project, any feasibility studies or checking of the likely scale and type of demand, and securing funding.

- *Launching* This stage ran from appointing someone – usually the coordinator but sometimes a member of the management or steering committee – to organise the rest of the project, find premises, recruit staff or volunteers, set up the referral and assessment procedures and identify the first clients.

- *Service development* This stage ran from the first instances of service delivery to the point when the main pattern of service was established and the project had got over all the initial teething problems.

Projects then moved into one of three forms:

- *Consolidation* This involved little expansion beyond the established level of service – new clients were assessed as places were released or small increases in care were provided, for example recruiting a few extra care workers or delivering a few extra hours' care per week, while new volunteer or paid care workers were recruited and trained to replace people who left.

- *Expansion* This involved more marked increases in service, or care being delivered to a new client group – for example, adults as well as children with learning disabilities – or additional types of service, such as a befriending scheme as well as day care.

- *Winding Up* Where a service was reduced or withdrawn because the need was not as great as had been believed or because the project could not continue – for example, insufficient funding or the voluntary organisation deciding to withdraw.

For these projects, another stage was *finding and adjusting to new funding arrangements*. The timing of this stage, of course, coincided with some form of service delivery, and the outcome would decide whether the project continued as it was or moved into another phase, such as beginning to wind up, or moving from an expansion stage to one of consolidation, or vice versa if the new funder wanted the service extended into a new area, or perhaps even going back to the stage of planning and launching, etc., for a whole new scheme. Figure 9.2 shows how these various stages of project development can interact.

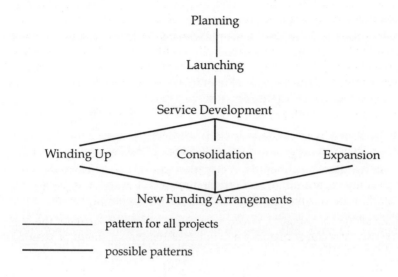

Planning

Launching

Service Development

Winding Up   Consolidation   Expansion

New Funding Arrangements

——————— pattern for all projects

——————— possible patterns

Figure 9.2 Stages of Project Development

From the experience of these projects, it would appear that the trick – or art – of successful project development is understanding what stage of the life-cycle a project is in, recognising when it is moving into a different phase, and in assessing whether the management arrangements concerning staff supervision and support, service planning and delivery and financial matters are still appropriate or need some adjustment. Steps then need to be taken to ensure that the transition is as smooth as possible, with the interests of the users being the main objective.

LESSONS FOR COMMUNITY CARE DEVELOPMENT

Circumstances of the Users and Potential Users

The experience of these community care projects highlights the need for assessment and development of services to be user-led, rather than service-led. The circumstances and needs of users in all the main groups of clients involved in these projects were complex and highly individual and, as such, the types of service and level and intensity of support they needed varied greatly. Overall, those projects which could manage greater flexibility were generally more successful in terms of the quality of care provided and impact for the greatest number of their users.

This also has implications for service planning, where flexibility and choice about types of service need to be accommodated. Providing a day care centre will meet some needs of some people with dementia, but on its own can never constitute an adequate, appropriate response to the support needs of all dementia sufferers and their families in an area.

By the same token, the kind of people who use a service will, to an extent, be shaped by the circumstances of the service. For this reason, basing plans for new services only on the needs of users of existing services will probably lead to distortions or further exclusion of those people whose circumstances presently put them outwith the formal service network.

Circumstances of Organisations Delivering Care

Not all voluntary organisations are in a position to deliver high quality care to all potential users and should not be expected to do so. The experience of these voluntary organisations and others throughout the country have demonstrated that many voluntary organisations are well able to provide certain types of care, or levels of service, or to work with users with a given level of need, but would have difficulties going beyond this. Some less experienced organisations, however, often have a great deal to offer in terms of enthusiasm, openness to new ideas and involvement of users and local people in a way to which traditional voluntary organisations are less accustomed. If voluntary organisations are going to extend the range of work which they do they will need to have access to advice, training and on-going support, all of which have resource implications for voluntary organisations and their referrers and/or funders, and will take time to have an impact.

In working with the voluntary sector, service planners and care managers will need to remember that not all voluntary organisations are the same and be aware of the strengths and limitations of services which specific voluntary organisations can provide.

Financial Management

Whatever the form of funding arrangements used, thought should be given by both funders and recipient voluntary organisations to the implications of the administrative and financial arrangements for the quality of service given to users, and care taken to avoid unintended, damaging consequences.

For the voluntary organisations participating in this Initiative the aim of providing a direct service in situations where potential – or more especially existing – users were at risk or experiencing a poorer quality of life sometimes led the organisation to enter into a funding arrangement which was not well-suited to the needs of that organisation or service. Specific issues which arose for the voluntary organisations were short-term arrangements and the associated difficulties in planning with any level of certainty; grants awarded for only part of the service expenditure necessitating higher levels of fund raising than the organisation could cope with readily; complex accounting arrangements to meet the requirements of several funding sources; and forms of tendering which limited the scope for changing the form of service in the way that managers thought would best meet the interests of users. For the funders there were inefficiencies in the use of funds and some distortion of the original objectives which underpinned support of specific projects and the overall Initiative.

Under the new community care arrangements Social Work and Social Services Departments and Health Boards are now able to draw on a wider range of funding arrangements with voluntary organisations, with greater use of contracts, service agreements and partnership arrangements as well as continued use of traditional grants. The experience of this Initiative suggests that the implications of a mismatch between the expectations of requirements of the voluntary organisation and funder may have far-reaching consequences for both agencies.

Whatever the type of financial relationship, however, projects need to be encouraged to keep the funder informed of progress and development at all appropriate organisational levels. Voluntary organisations may need advice on who should be the contact person within a funder for different aspects – such as day to day advice and information, planning about care to that client group and financial matters – and this should be kept up to date, for example, when these responsibilities are changing as a result of internal organisational developments. At the same time, many statutory organisations which are both funders and referrers for community care services will need to revise their internal communication in respect of the relationship with voluntary organisations.

Monitoring and Evaluation of Services

Much of the official material issued recently on monitoring and evaluating of community care has focused on the wider planning and development of services, rather than on the input of care to individual users or the provision and outcome of local services. The experience of the local projects comprising this programme suggests that this is an area which needs greater attention. Although most projects had record-keeping systems which met their own day to day needs, these proved insufficient for demands from potential funders for an overview of each project's impact and were often not detailed enough for case conferences and similar feedback on the current circumstances of and benefits gained by individual users. Project managers' abilities to plan effectively were also hampered by a lack of information.

It is possible that awareness of the need for more systematic, flexible reviews of individual clients' use of services and evaluations of overall service achievements has increased in the period since these projects were studied, but feedback from other service providers and funders suggests that many local voluntary organisations – and equivalent statutory services – still have difficulties in this area. In the case of the Section 10 Care in the Community projects these information gaps were met to an extent by feedback from the research data, but this resource is not available in other situations.

If voluntary organisations are to play the role expected of them in both the provision and wider development of community care services they will need to have appropriate forms of information gathering and the abilities to apply this data. For many organisations this will involve acquiring new skills and additional resources, such as administrative staff, advice and training. Parallel to this, service planners will need to consider how best to draw in feedback from a wide range of local projects and what their role should be in these new arrangements.

LOOKING AHEAD

What, then, is the future role of voluntary organisations in the provision of community care services likely to be?

At the extremes, two possible scenarios are suggested. One is an extension of the role of voluntary organisations, working in partnership with local authorities, Health Boards and Housing Associations to plan, develop and implement good quality care that is efficient in its delivery and effective in the outcomes for users. Within this, voluntary organisations can take on a key role in developing innovative forms of care as part of a diverse range of types and levels of service, including advice, counselling and advocacy inputs. This is then reflected in the range of financial arrangements between voluntary and statutory organisations. Users and those undertaking care management responsibilities on their behalf have greater choice and the scope for putting together packages of care well-suited to individual needs is enhanced.

The other extreme case is the reverse of this new golden age. Voluntary organisations become divided into those which are an integral part of the new arrangements and those which are excluded. Some enter into contracts with statutory service purchasers with the result of less independence, perhaps to the extent of struggling to maintain standards of care and influence on the form and focus of services against ever-tighter finance-led controls. Others operate at the margins of direct care, working in lower-priority – and therefore financially insecure – forms of care or limited to the extent of their own fund-raising, with little or no integration to the wider service network. Some voluntary organisations will not be able, or will not choose, to survive. Users have fewer real choices and are vulnerable to services they have come to know and trust being withdrawn.

The most likely course lies somewhere between these scenarios. When the new community care arrangements were first announced the fear of many people within the voluntary sector was that the second path was more likely. Since then, as the practical details have emerged and voluntary organisations themselves adapt to the new ideas and plans, there has been greater confidence that there will be positive opportunities.

Overall, the experience of the Scottish Office Care in the Community Initiative demonstrated that voluntary organisations do have the potential to make a major contribution to the provision and development of community-based care services for vulnerable people. However, this has more profound implications for both voluntary organisations and the statutory services with which they will be working than might be supposed. All the parties concerned can expect to need to re-think and adjust their methods of working if the most efficient and effective care is to be delivered to users.

The next few years will be an interesting time.

REFERENCES

Connor, A. (1991a) *Setting up Community Care Projects – A Practice Guide.* Edinburgh: The Scottish Office Central Research Unit.

Connor, A. (1991b) *Community Care Projects – Working Papers.* Edinburgh: The Scottish Office Central Research Unit.

Connor, A. (1991c) *Tell Them All About It.* Edinburgh: Age Concern Scotland.

Connor, A. (1993a) *Monitoring Ourselves.* London: Charities Evaluation Services.

Connor, A. (1993b) *Monitoring and Evaluation Made Easy: A Handbook for Voluntary Organisations.* London: HMSO.

Glendinning, C. (1983) *Unshared Care.* London: Routledge and Kegan Paul.

Glendinning, C. (1986) *A Single Door.* London: Allen and Unwin.

Green, H. (1988) *Informal Carers.* London: HMSO.

Knight, B. (ed) (1984) *Management in Voluntary Organisations, ARVAC Occasional Paper No.6.* London: ARVAC.

Renshaw, J. (1988) *Care in the Community: The First Steps.* Aldershot: Gower.

APPENDIX

Care in the Community Monitoring
Client Sample Overall Level of Coping and/or Risk

This framework for assessing users' levels of coping and risk was developed by the researchers towards the end of the study. Information about the circumstances and outcomes of services for a sample of users across every project had been gathered from project staff at six-monthly intervals to complement routine data on the scale of use. Assessments were made on those case details by the researchers to provide consistency. The validity of the schedule, particularly its application across different client groups, was checked by comparing scoring by two researchers and two experienced social workers. Further details of the development and application of the overall framework, which also considered the outcomes of service for users, and the findings are given in the Working Papers.

1. Not Coping/High Risk

Wholly dependent on services or carers, and would not cope with any reduction, even for short period.

> Physical well-being at risk.

> Carers under great pressure.

> Situation likely to break down.

Typical features:

- self neglect
- risk of abuse from others

- behaviour frequently putting person at risk (e.g. wandering, poor drug control, heavy drinking)
- not managing day to day affairs (e.g. paying bills)
- condition unstable or likely to deteriorate, needs constant monitoring
- existing levels of other services (i.e. if Community Care service withdraw) not sufficient to maintain person in community.

2. Barely Coping/Medium Risk

Carers coping at present, but unlikely to cope with an increased demand.

No risk to physical well-being yet, but possible in foreseeable future.

Typical features:

- managing with services and informal supports, but cannot cope with a reduction
- care demands very high and continuous
- client's physical and/or mental health deteriorating
- carer's ability to cope undermined or reduced
- possibility of some other backup services, but limited
- person needs other services but not accepting these
- risk-carrying behaviour occurring, but infrequent or monitored
- problems in managing affairs occurring, but infrequent or monitored.

3. Coping/Low Risk

Person and/or carers coping as well as expected in circumstances.

No risk to physical well-being.

Typical features:

- confused/frail/ill condition stable or controlled
- sufficiently alert and motivated to cope (or not worried about this and has informal support)
- good support from family and extended informal network and from services, with backups readily available
- coping on other aspects of day to day living, or has good support and advice.

CHAPTER 10

Evaluation and Consumers

Jacqueline M Atkinson and Lawrence Elliott

Evaluation has become one of the watchwords in health and social service research over the last ten years, partly in response to criticism that the personal social services were not taking research seriously (CCETSW/PSSC 1980, Reid and Hanrahan 1981, Thomas 1988). Although medicine has a stronger tradition of scientific research, research does not necessarily equate with evaluating services. In psychiatry, for example, a recent very good and much used book, *Research Methods in Psychiatry, A Beginner's Guide* (Freeman and Tryer 1989) does not include 'evaluation' as a word in any chapter heading nor does it appear in the index. This is not to say that evaluation as an issue is totally ignored, just that it can appear in other guises as, for example, medical audit or quality assurance monitoring (Fauman 1990).

The recent fashion for 'evaluative research' can blind us to the fact that we have always evaluated treatment and services, at least to some extent. In the past such judgements may have been crude, 'the patient got better' versus 'the patient died', but they were, nevertheless, descriptions of outcome and evaluations of treatment (Holland 1983). Measurement of outcome has always been the cornerstone for judging treatment, but evaluating services requires wider parameters. In the 1930s it was possible for researchers to conclude that all patients improved 'to a greater or lesser extent' (Tillotson 1939) and still get the article published in a reputable journal. Today we have become more sophisticated, developing more rigorous methodologies and making use of ever more refined statistical tests whilst seeking the elusive difference at a 'statistically significant' level. No-one would deny the need for rigour in research but it is all to easy to lose sight of the important, human questions in the search for sophisticated, statistical answers. In many cases it is more important to know the effect of treatment and services on the quality of a person's life than it is to know the p value of the difference of before and after measures (McKechney 1989). This is not to deny the importance of appropriate, rigorous methodology and analysis in basic research or clinical trials, but to suggest that this is not the only way to evaluate services.

The aphorism that statistics can be used in the way that a drunk uses a lamppost, for support rather than illumination, reminds us that it is illumination we seek, not merely support for a preconceived position. A brief drive through any city, however, shows us that illumination comes in many colours and intensities. One person's clear blue light can be another's dim golden glow.

This chapter provides an overview of the main issues confronting the person seeking to evaluate services. In a chapter it is only possible to cover such topics in a limited way. The issues involved in consumer evaluation alone could fill a book. In a market economy it is assumed that market forces will determine factors such as quality, price and availability. There is not the space here to debate whether this is an appropriate paradigm to apply to the provision of health and social services in community care but it does seem reasonable to take the consumer, either as patient, client, resident, user or informal carer as the central figure in the evaluation of services (Ward and McHale 1985). Thus the second part of the chapter describes the responses of clients and their relatives to the psychiatric service they have received and some of the problems of doing this kind of study.

WHY DO WE NEED EVALUATION RESEARCH?

The Hippocratic oath commands doctors first to 'do no harm', and the evaluation of treatments, clinical skills, preventive measures and other services provides feedback as to whether this is the case. Although good research will provide more than simple reassurance of 'no harm', for many practitioners this is their first, and sometimes only, requirement. Such information should also encourage the further education of those into whose hands we place our health (Barlow, Hayes and Nelson 1984). Although other professions may not have the formality of the oath, the principle still applies.

The time when the only people interested in outcome measures were doctors and their patients has long gone, and the growth of the welfare state, and public provision of services, has led to a growing need for public accountability (Holland 1983). Financial constraints have led to the development of measures of cost-effectiveness which sometimes gets translated into 'cheaper is better' (Mumford 1987). An argument long put forward for the popularity of community care with governments and health boards is that it is a cheaper option than in-patient treatment. This is certainly true when current provision in the community means that many people do not get the services they need. Neither are costs easily evaluated. There may indeed be saving to the health service through not having to maintain the hotel services of hospitals, but the same individual living in the community has other costs on the public purse, not least of which is housing. It is very difficult to assert, as Falloon et al (1984) do, that a community service is more cost effective than an in-patient one, when taking the broader view.

Public accountability increasingly demands that treatment programmes or preventive measures demonstrate that they work. Evidence questioning the efficacy of certain psychotherapies may not always influence the individual client, paying privately for therapy, but will influence its provision on the NHS or reimbursement for such interventions by insurance companies. This begs the question of whose evaluation of services is most appropriate and we will return to this.

Although it might be assumed, or even hoped, that evaluation research would lead to informed decision making as to the utility of providing certain services, this is not always so. Wider political pressures may either influence the kind of questions asked, or ignore unpalatable evidence altogether (Barnes 1979, Pattison and Player 1990). The government's perceived need to be seen to be doing something about issues of public concern such as drug abuse and AIDS has lead to health education campaigns that are of questionable value in changing behaviour in 'at risk' groups at the individual level (Stimson 1990). The utility of evaluative research needs to be questioned if there is unwillingness to modify services and delivery systems as a result of research.

Much service evaluation is small scale, locally targeted research aimed at influencing local decision makers (Abramson 1984). The reasons for doing the research may then encourage not just overt outcome questions such as 'is the programme clinically effective?' or 'is the programme cost-effective?' or even 'do the consumers like it?' but include covert aims which have to do with continued funding of the programme and thus continued employment for staff, expansion of the programme and thus expansion of the sphere of influence for the programme leader, improved resource allocation for the existing programme (possibly at the expense of other programmes) or even protection of a particular discipline's involvement in certain tasks. If these are the 'true' aims of the research, then the importance of the research will be seen to depend more on its influence (that is, on whether it is acted upon locally) than on scientific questions of rigour or generality. And the reasons it is acted upon may have nothing to do with scientific value but everything to do with political expediency. Some may argue that research is of no value unless it is acted upon, but this would be to deny to the researcher the importance of publications as against the practitioner, who may be looking for more tangible outcomes (Barnes 1979).

This apparently trivial point in fact highlights some of the problems in evaluation research which centre around who does it and why. Milne (1987) suggests that 'evaluative research is what interested practitioners do'. This means that 'far from there simply being a rare breed of scientists who conduct evaluations, all members of a service can contribute. This is so because it is not essential that every evaluation is always rigorous and precise. Rather, we can view each evaluation as a step towards the next more careful evaluation, both in terms of the individual practitioner and in terms of the programme'. Milne highlights the distinction which can be drawn between 'basic' research and 'evaluative' research. The latter is more likely to be 'messy' (or 'uncontrolled') and less likely to be published.

This raises the question of whether there are, around the country, numerous groups of service providers busily reinventing the wheel because of a blinkered attitude by the scientific community to the utility of 'quick and dirty' research. 'Basic' or scientific research, in its attempts to control as many variables as possible may end up no more generalisable or useful than a more uncontrolled evaluation which dealt with practical issues involved in running a service as they arose.

Public accountability may lead service providers only to engage in, or commission, research that is likely to provide them with publicly acceptable answers, whether regarding clinical outcome or cost effectiveness. Research in politically sensitive areas, which asks unpopular questions, or is likely to have major resource implications may be side-stepped by practitioners and may only be tackled by researchers outside the practitioner system who may be less susceptible to the political fall-out. The impact of such research will depend on its dissemination and the publicity it attracts (Abramson 1984).

WHOSE VIEWPOINT?

The 'success' of a service depends on the person being asked to evaluate it. Why an evaluation is being carried out will determine whose viewpoint is elicited as much as what is measured. Service providers will be interested in cost-effectiveness and appropriate services and practitioners in clinical, behavioural or social outcome for individual patients. Practitioners and managers may also be interested in how services affect them, their work load and style, ease of manoeuvrability within the system, autonomy, responsibility and so forth. Evaluation of services can overlook these considerations (Barnes 1979).

The latest group whose views are sought in evaluation are the consumers: the direct consumers, the patients or clients who are users of the service, and the indirect consumers, the families of users who fill the role of informal carers (WHO 1989). To know what the users of a service think and feel about such a service is clearly an important part of evaluation. It has been argued that consumer evaluation has to take precedence as accountability to clients has higher priority than accountability to agency or profession (Wallace and Rees 1988). If concern for client evaluation is to be more than a fashion some account must be taken of methodological limitations and wider issues.

Parker and Thomas (1980), in pointing out some of these problems, suggest that although consumers may be 'the most easily accessible, logically direct and seemingly functionally relevant source' they are also 'the most apocryphal'. As they remind us, research in social psychology demonstrates the wide range of variables which influence perception, evaluation, memory and reporting on events, whether as observers or as participants. One of these is the halo effect. This occurs when positive (or negative) feelings or attitudes attaching to one aspect of what is being evaluated get transferred to all aspects. This is probably most commonly seen when services are rated highly by consumers because of a personally-liked professional. Another is response set, as when a respondent starts saying 'yes' or 'no' (or even 'don't know') to the first few questions and will then continue with the same answer to all questions.

Such methodological problems do not relate only to consumers, however, but to everyone involved in evaluating programmes and then evaluating the evaluations. At every stage of the process biases influence both the form the evaluation takes, the way it is interpreted and the use to which it is put (Corrigan 1990).

Brandon (1988) points out that '10 years ago, *consumerism* was still thought of in terms of washing machines/vacuum cleaners/cars/and holidays and *not* in the context of *services*, particularly services which are publicly provided'. Consumer evaluation and the consumer perspective is now, if not exactly commonplace, well established as a necessary part of an evaluation package (Holcomb et al. 1989).

The leap to the concept of patient or client as consumer, which has been encouraged, loses sight of a number of pertinent problems. It is not appropriate here (nor is there space) to discuss the impact of labels and changes in labelling people, but words such as 'user' and 'consumer' are often employed to de-medicalise a person's position. Whilst this may be a laudable aim it presents other problems, some of which affect evaluation.

The term 'user' implies an active participation on the part of the individual with the service and for many patients or clients 'recipient' may be more appropriate. In some groups of patients there is low compliance with treatment programmes and a loss to the services which in no way implies 'cure' or even improvement (McCabe 1988). A 'consumer' evaluation should, of course, involve 'non-users' of services who, by definition of service providers, *should* (or could) be recipients. Different methods of survey will affect the response rate of different groups (Burgoyne et al. 1977).

The use of the term 'consumer' itself brings with it the suggestion of choice in a market place filled with a variety of services (at least to western minds). That the client in community care is not in this position does not mean that their input is not valuable, but it can mean that it has limited perspective if not all options are known or understood. Clients may well have valuable information about services which are lacking and which they think they would find helpful, but there may be options which no one knows they want until they have been presented with the idea.

The most basic form of consumer evaluation is 'voting with their feet'. Services or goods not wanted by customers, whether because of price, quality or simply not wanted/needed/valued are not bought. Consumers of services provided under the umbrella 'community care' may not have any choice between 'take it or leave it'. If they leave it there is no alternative. In such instances lack of compliance, missed appointments or non-takeup of services can be seen as practical instances of evaluation. The patient/client-run case management systems developed in parts of Canada and the United States under the heading 'brokerage' (Brandon and Towes 1989, Maclean and Marlett 1987) are examples of ongoing, practical evaluation of services and is the closest system currently available whereby receivers of services become more truly consumers. Morrison (1978) argues that 'client advisory boards' should be created 'so that the real consumers of mental health services will be able, on a regular basis, to evaluate all aspects of a mental health facility'.

Patients, clients, residents, depending on the community care service being evaluated, can provide information in three major areas. The first falls under the 'needs assessment' umbrella and is a quantification of *their* assessment of *their* needs. The second group of information concerns services; whether the 'right' services are provided, that is, services which meet their needs or the service provider's performance. Third, consumers can evaluate the service provider's objectives in terms of a more general appropriateness.

Following on from seeing patient or client as a user of services and then as a consumer, it does not take much to see the families of users also as consumers, particularly if they can be labelled as carers. This is particularly so since both the Griffiths Report (1988) and the White Paper (HMSO 1989) make it clear that families are expected to care for ill relatives and that services may be needed to support them in this task. Again, it is quite reasonable to ask such people their views of services but, once again, the context in which this happens, the types of questions asked, and the options open to people are limited. Carers rarely, however, become part of the system for planning or evaluation (Atkinson and Coia 1991).

Rarely, if ever, are members of the wider public asked about the services provided in their names, with their money. By using the term 'evaluation' loosely we can see widespread condemnation of many current community care policies in reports by investigative and campaigning journalists when they raise the plight of those living in the community but for whom no provision is made. As a voice for society such journalists are expressing a judgement on services and policy which is rarely elicited through research.

The problem in evaluating the health and social services with their multiple shareholders is, at least in part, one of differing viewpoints, differing expectations and differing responsibilities. Pluralistic evaluation (Smith and Cantley 1988) can be attempted, but to assume that any evaluation of community care can take account of all these factors to present one, coherent picture is to ask for more than resources or methodology can provide. For not only does the service have to be evaluated but the research itself will be judged according to the criteria of those reading it. At the end of the day it is most likely to be planners and budget controllers who decided the real weight to be given to evaluation by service providers, clinicians and consumers.

WHAT IS BEING EVALUATED?

As difficult as deciding who to ask to evaluate services is to decide what *should* be evaluated rather than what *could* be evaluated. Inevitably, the who and the what are interlinked. Services, projects, programmes or treatments can be evaluated in isolation and clinical evaluations usually fall into this category. A new procedure is compared with either placebo or the best current treatment. It either works better, or not. This tells us nothing about how the procedure is received, whether it costs more or less, if it costs more whether the benefits are worth it, how 'worth it' is defined, how many people need the service or even whether there is something else recipients would prefer.

Every solution proposed to deal with these issues brings with it a new set of questions, of decisions to be made, of evaluative blind alleys. Needs assessment and quality assurance are current buzz words. Quality assurance must go beyond a simple monitoring process if it is to be effective (Donabedian 1989). Needs assessment sounds straightforward. It is frequently taken to mean 'the needs of particular populations will be assessed so that relevant services can be provided'. In health and social services needs seems inexhaustible. New problems replace old ones, people's expectations of their quality of life increases, needs proliferate. Where finances are limited is there any point in looking fully at needs assessment? Traditional expenditure is unlikely to be reduced overnight so the budgetary possibilities for providing new services is small. It can be argued that needs assessment can only inform decisions on the fringe of service development (Knight *et al.* 1980).

One controversial area of needs assessment arises over the definition of 'need'. By only allowing consumers to identify needs which can be met, whether by current resources, current technologies or current skills and knowledge, only the tip of a needs iceberg will be identified and even pressing needs ignored if they cannot be met. This raises the possibility of health and social services crashing, Titanic like, into the submerged mass of needs which have conveniently been forgotten.

It could be argued that the most basic need for a person with schizophrenia is a cure for schizophrenia. Since there is, currently, no cure, some assessments would deny this as being 'need', but would concentrate on what can be done, be it drug therapy, social therapy, rehabilitation, support, sheltered work, group homes or other housing. Such solutions do not make the basic 'need', a cure, go away, but may make service providers feel they are meeting needs if the basic issues are not allowed expression. Once again, this is not to deny that such services may fulfil useful functions, but to state that clear vision is needed to retain sight of need which cannot be met at present.

Poverty underlies many of the needs expressed by those in receipt of social services yet, as a basic problem, would not be measured by a system unable to do more than tinker with benefits. Needs assessment may describe the consequences of this but rarely presents the need as one which requires radical economic and political change.

If we cannot evaluate on a global scale, and needs assessment presents as many problems as it solves, what we are left with are more limited evaluative questions, such as appropriateness, effectiveness, equity, accessibility, efficiency and acceptability. Effectiveness is the traditional evaluative measure, while acceptability is a newer approach.

Effectiveness

Clinical effectiveness is one major criterion here, but evaluation needs to ask more than 'did the treatment work?', particularly when evaluating community programmes or services (Morrison 1978). If the goals of the programme are not clearly described then the question of evaluation is largely irrelevant. Three options suggested by Freeman and Sherwood (1965) are, guessing the programme's goals, insisting on project staff providing clear goals, or researchers assisting in identifying goals. Although the latter may lead to methodological biases (such as choosing project goals which are easy to measure rather than relevant) it is preferable to the outcome of the first two. Guessing leads to researchers being told when they have done the work that the goals they have selected are irrelevant, or were not the project's goals in the first place, whereas asking for specific goals means, according to Freeman and Sherwood, that 'the researcher should bring lots of novels to the office to read while he waits'.

Evaluating a programme's outcomes may be confounded by limitations put on tasks carried out by the programme. For example, by their own standards a rehabilitation team may achieve goals of independence as measured by the patient's behaviour, but because of community resistance, in housing, in employment and in social interaction, the patient may not get the opportunity to display such behaviour. Has the programme failed because it did not change community attitudes? Is this a legitimate task of any programme or should this be tackled separately? For the rehabilitation team the most effective measure of their success will probably be through using a standard assessment scale measuring various behaviours and criteria associated with discharge. This is unlikely, however, to be seen by planners as the sole measure of effectiveness of a programme.

Measurement is itself a thorny issue, and although well used and validated scales are usually the option of first choice, for many innovative projects these may not be appropriate and new scales or measuring instruments need to be developed, itself a long and difficult process (Morley and Snaith 1989, Streiner and Norman 1989). Assessment at this level can be costly in staff time and where resources are scarce may be one of the first tasks lost.

Even when change is measured, the question then arises, is this directly attributable to the programme. Experimental designs with control groups or systematically changing one parameter at a time should overcome such problems (Campbell and Stanley 1963) but are rarely applicable or available in project evaluation (Rutman 1977). Tied in with this is the issue of measuring outcome whilst a programme changes and develops.

Acceptability

In every part of evaluation research we are faced with circular questions. Here it is obviously 'acceptable to whom?' Wallace and Rees (1988) argue that 'the client is the ultimate expert on what kind of service is supportive and useful'. There are very few research instruments which measure quality or acceptability of care from the consumer's point of view. The WHO (1989) points out that, for consumers, 'a key index of quality of care... is the quality of life of those who receive the services'. This is not necessarily measured by acceptability of services. Depending on the type of evaluation measure used, consumers may find themselves evaluating services 'acceptable' in as far as the services go, but not in a position to point out that the services do not go far enough.

For a complete evaluation it is not enough to ask merely whether services helped, were satisfactory, accessible and so forth. If consumer evaluation is to be taken seriously and if measures of acceptability of service are to be incorporated into policy making then research instruments are needed which have consumer-defined parameters and consumer-defined priorities (Fitzpatrick 1991). This may take in not only views of treatment or services and outcome, but involvement in treatment management, involvement in administration and policy making and involvement in community education. 'Involvement' includes consumer opinion on budget priorities, staff recruitment, treatment policies, procedures, routines and complaints procedures (WHO 1989). Evaluating acceptability of a service means considering all such points.

CONSUMER RESPONSE TO SERVICES

As part of a wider project of evaluation of mental health services in east Glasgow,* patients, clients and carers were asked their opinions of services they had received over the past two years. In such a study the choices are either to opt for depth, that is, to ask questions in detail about a few areas, or breadth, which will entail a more superficial look at a large number of questions. In this part of the study it was deemed useful to find out what range of services clients were in contact with and what their general feelings were about these. This would be compared later with a new service and feelings about which services they thought would be helpful in the future. The clients interviewed were those nominated by a key worker to be referred to a new day care and home support service which was to be set up (Miller 1987). An evaluation of services by informal carers was also included.

Population

CLIENTS

One hundred and thirty one clients agreed to be interviewed (38 declined). Of those interviewed 68 were males and 63 were females. Their average age was 41 years with a range of 20–67. There were a number of different diagnoses. The largest groups were: people with schizophrenia 40 per cent, depression 25 per cent, anxiety problems (including phobias) 10 per cent, manic-depression 9 per cent, and other diagnoses 15 per cent. Within the 'other' category were people with head injuries, epilepsy, Huntington's chorea, social isolation, personality disorder and behaviour disorders.

CARERS

Of the 131 clients, 77 had relatives who were identified as carers and who agreed to be interviewed. Of these, 43 were female and 34 were male. This confirms approximately to national figures on sex of carers (Green 1988). Inevitably the definition of 'carer' causes some problems. Earlier we have mentioned the problems in defining clients as consumers or users, and some similar issues are involved in labelling relatives as carers. Some people who would view themselves as having a caring role are not viewed by their relative as a carer. Early research on the burden on families resulting from caring indicates that objective burden, or measurable, quantifiable aspects of caring do not necessarily correlate with subjective burden, or the feelings people have about caring (Hoenig and Hamilton 1967). Many people who fulfil a caring role do not live with their relative, but nevertheless spend many hours in activities related to care (Green 1988, Hicks 1988). In this study carers were those people who defined themselves as having a 'care role' in relation to the client and who were usually in contact with the client at least five days per week.

* The evaluation research was supported by a grant from the Mental Health Foundation. Our thanks go to Greater Glasgow Health Board and Strathclyde Region Social Work Department for their co-operation and access to patients and clients.

Reaction to Service

Clients were asked general questions about the services they had received and what help they had been, using a rating scale 'helped a lot', 'helped a little', 'did not help', and 'made worse'. (Only 3 'don't know' answers were recorded out of 1310 responses.) Carers were asked, using the same scale, what services their relatives had received and whether the service had helped the relative (10 'don't know' answers our of 770.) It was recognised that 'helped' did not necessarily imply satisfaction with services, nor does it investigate whether clients' and carers' expectations of a service are appropriate or realistic.

Services asked about were: hospital in-patient services (Inpt), hospital out-patient services (Outpt), general practitioner (GP), day centre (DC), day hospital (DH), social work (SW), community psychiatric nurse (CPN), hostels, LINK (a voluntary organisation) and medication (med). Although medication is not a service as such it seemed inappropriate not to ask about it.

The results can be interpreted in a number of ways depending on what type of questions need answering. For example, whether the whole client population is considered in terms of services provided to a community or only those who use each service. Rankings were obtained by calculating percentages so that variable numbers of clients using a service could be compared (no account is taken, in these rankings, of whether there are statistically significant differences between the ratings for services). Tables 10.1 and 10.2 give rankings for the use of services which 'help a lot', a 'combined help' category (a lot and a little), 'not helped' and 'made worse' for all clients rating services (Table 10.1) and for clients who used the services (Table 10.2). 'One' is the most positive ranking and '10' the least (i.e., for not helped and made worse '1' is the service with least problems).

Table 10.1 All Clients, Ranking of Services (n=131)

service	used	helped	help combined	not helped	made worse
inpt	4	4	4	4	9
outpt	3	3	3	8	5
GP	2	2	2	6=	10
DC	9	9	9	2=	3
DH	7	7	7	2=	5=
SW	5	5	5	8	5=
CPN	6	6	6	6=	7
Hostel	10	10	10	2=	1
LINK	8	8	8	1	2
med	1	1	1	10	9

1 – highest ranking
10 – lowest ranking

Table 10.2 Clients Using Services, Ranking of Services (n=variable)

| service | used | helped | Ranking services | | | n |
			help combined	not helped	made worse	
inpt	4	2	1	9	1	65
outpt	3	7	4	2	5	89
GP	2	10	7	3=	9	111
DC	9	9	9	7=	10	1
SW	5	4=	2=	6	2	53
CPN	6	6	8	5	6	48
Hostel	10	1	10	10	7	7
LINK	8	8	2=	1	3	16
med	1	4=	5=	7=	4	120

1 – highest ranking
10 – lowest ranking

Some immediate discrepancies appear. Using figures from all clients, help equates with the amount a service is used. The range for use of services was 120 out of 131 for medication down to 16 out of 1431 for LINK or 7 for hostels. This is reflected in Table 10.2, where services are rated only by people who use them. Clearly, the smaller the number of clients using a service the greater the weight each person's views have. Thus, although general practitioners drop in ranking dramatically, they are still providing a 'helped a lot' service to 35 per cent of the client population compared to 3 per cent by the hostel.

At the other end of the scale services can be rated as not helping at all, or making the problem worse, but here numbers have become very small. Out of 1310 responses (all clients, all services) 1 per cent of responses rated services as 'no help at all' and .02 per cent were rated as making the problem worse. If these responses are looked at from only those people who use the services then still only 2 per cent of responses rate services as 'no help' and .05 per cent as making the problem worse. These figures are important when looking at complaints. Traditionally, numbers of complaints are small and it may be that questionnaires or interventions which only deal with what is wrong are needed to identify problems. Thus of patients who had used in-patient services (ranked 1 on combined help) 80 per cent said it helped them compared to 9 per cent who said it did not help at all and 11 per cent who said it made the problem worse. The question now arises whether it is more useful to pursue questions on why the service helped 80 per cent or what was wrong for the 20 per cent.

Table 10.3 All Carers, Ranking of Services (n=77)

service	used	helped	Ranking of service help combined	not helped	made worse
inpt	4	4	4	8	6=
outpt	3	5	5	9	6=
GP	2	3	2	10	9
DC	8	8=	9	3	3=
DH	7	7	7	5	6=
SW	6	6	6	6	3=
CPN	5	2	3	4	3=
Hostel	9	8=	8	1=	1=
LINK	10	8=	9	1=	1=
med	1	1	1	7	10

1 – highest ranking
10 – lowest ranking

Table 10.4 Carers Whose Relatives Use Services, Ranking of Services (n=variable)

service	used	helped	Ranking of service help combined	not helped	made worse	n
inpt	4	5	5	7=	7	42
outpt	3	9	7	7=	5=	47
GP	2	7	8	9	5=	70
DC	8	8	10	10	10	4
DH	7	10	9	8	8	23
SW	6	6	6	6	3=	28
CPN	5	2	3	4	3=	36
Hostel	9	3	1=	1=	1=	2
LINK	10	1	1=	1=	1=	1
med	1	4	4	3	9	73

1 – highest ranking
10 – lowest ranking

Responses to open-ended questions were recorded verbatim and coded afterwards. The types of answers given on why in-patient services were useful were: 'it improves my condition' – 20 clients, 'someone to talk to who listens/sharing problems' – 10 clients, 'it gives me a break' – 8 clients, 'sorts out medication' – 5 clients, 'makes me independent' – 4 clients, and 'practical help' – 3 clients. The negative responses were: generally apprehensive, including 'don't want to mix with others worse than me' – 7 clients, 'it makes no difference' – 3 clients, 'makes me dependent' – 1 client, and 'dismal surroundings' – 1 client.

If the carers' views are also taken into account, Tables 10.3 and 10.4, the picture blurs further. There are some discrepancies, but it is more a question of slight variation than major shifts of opinion with clients. Comparing percentages of clients who have used services, clients are more positive about seven of the services than carers – in-patient and out-patient services, GP, day centre, day hospital, social work and medication – while carers are more positive about CPNs, hostels and LINK.

Although a structured interview was used, which did have the freedom of allowing respondents to explain their answers and make additional comments, such 'extra' information tends to be lost in an analysis of group results. The dilemma is then whether to build up a good picture of the individual, their needs, views and aspirations which can be used clinically, or simply to look at group views, a 'common denominator' approach to services. The service which was ranked highest as 'made worse' (by a small number of respondents) was medication. It also ranked highest as the service of most help by the majority. The person versus the group is the challenge of evaluation and planning of services.

CONCLUSIONS

There are no easy, straightforward answers, or even paths to take when it comes to the evaluation of services. Such issues as the group versus the individual, quantitative versus qualitative measures, practitioners versus researchers are only the beginning of the issues in assessing outcome. Whose opinion – service planner, provider, staff or client – is another dimension. Maybe the first rule should be to ask 'why is this project/programme/treatment/service being evaluated?' and 'who (if anyone) will act on the findings?', followed by 'and how might they act?' This might give some insight into the type of evaluation best suited to these questions, taking into account political as well as scientific or research considerations. If evaluation is to be employed to support a position which will be adhered to no matter what the findings, evaluators might then question whether they really want to be involved in such an exercise. If the purpose of evaluation is to improve the service to patients and clients, in the first instance, this determines the parameters. If, however, cost considerations are of prime importance then the way in which questions are asked, as well as the questions themselves, will be different. It would be a step forward simply to recognise that evaluation, while all things to all people, cannot be such in each individual piece of work.

REFERENCES

Abramson, J.H. (1984) *Survey Methods in Community Medicine.* London: Churchill Livingston.

Atkinson, J.M. and Coia, D.A. (1991) Carers, the community and the White Paper. *Psychiatric Bulletin, 15* 763–764.

Barlow, D.H., Hayes, S.C. and Nelson, R.O. (1984) *The Scientist-Practitioner.* London: Pergamon Press.

Barnes, J.A. (1979) *Who Should Know What.* Cambridge: Cambridge University Press.

Brandon, D. (1988) User involvement in mental health services: the service provider's perspective. Introduction. In Report of Common Concerns: International Conference on User Involvement in Mental Health Services. London: MIND.

Brandon, D. and Towes, N. (1989) *Free to Choose. An Introduction to Service Brokerage.* Community Living Monograph.

Burgoyne, R.W., Wolkon, G.H., Staples, F., Kline, F. and Powers, M. (1977) Which patients respond to a mental health consumer survey. *American Journal of Community Psychology, 5,* 355–360.

Campbell, D.T. and Stanley, J. (1963) *Experimental and Quasi-experimental Designs for Research.* Chicago: Rand McNally.

CCETSW/PSSC (1980) *Research and Practice. Report of a Working Party on a Research Strategy for the Personal Social Services.* London: CCETSW.

Corrigan, P.W. (1990) Consumer satisfaction with institutional and community care. *Community Mental Health Journal, 26,* 151–165.

Donabedian, A. (1989) Institutional and professional responsibilities in quality assurance. *Quality Assurance in Health Care, 1,* 3–11.

Falloon, I.R.H., Boyd, J.L. and McGill, C.W. (1984) *Family Care of Schizophrenia.* New York: Guilford Press.

Fauman, M.A. (1990) Quality assurance monitoring in psychiatry. *American Journal of Psychiatry, 146,* 1121–1129.

Fitzpatrick, B. (1991) Patients' views in a long stay ward for the elderly. Paper presented at Consumer-led Quality Assurance, West of Scotland Health Services Research Network, 27th Feb.

Freeman, C. and Tryer, P. (1989) *Research Methods in Psychiatry. A Beginner's Guide.* London: Gaskell/Royal College of Psychiatrists.

Freeman, H.E. and Sherwood, C.C. (1965) Research in large scale intervention programmes. *Journal of Social Issues, 21,* 11–28.

Green, H. (1988) *Informal Carers.* London: HMSO.

Griffiths, Sir R. (1988) *Community Care: Agenda for Action. A Report to the Secretary of State for Social Services.* London: HMSO.

HMSO (1989) *Caring for People. Community Care in the Next Decade and Beyond.* London: HMSO.

Hicks, C. (1988) *Who Cares. Looking After People At Home.* London: Virago.

Hoenig, J. and Hamilton, M.E. (1967) The burden on the household in an extra-mural psychiatric service. In H. Freeman and J. Farndale (eds) *New Aspects of the Mental Health Services.* London: Pergamon Press.

Holcomb, W.R., Adams, N.A., Ponder, H.M. and Reitz, R. (1989) The development and construct validation of a consumer satisfaction questionnaire for psychiatric inpatients. *Evaluation and Progress Planning, 12,* 189–194.

Holland, W. (1983) *Evaluation of Health Care.* Oxford: Oxford University Press.

Knight, B., Wollert, R.W., Levy, L.H., Frame, C.L. and Padgett, V.P. (1980) Self-help groups: the members' perspective. *American Journal of Community Psychology, 8,* 53–65.

McCabe, E. (1988) The lost schizophrenics. A retrospective cohort study of discharged patients. *Health Bulletin, 46,* 18–25.

McKechney, N. (1989) What's in a fix. *Community Care* August 3rd 15–17.

Maclean, H. and Marlett, N. (1987) Service brokerage: the promise of consumer control. *Just Cause, 5,* 18–21.

Miller, P. (1987) Putting the pieces together. The Greater Easterhouse Mental Health Pilot Project. In N. Drucker (ed) *Creating Community Mental Health Services in Scotland.* Vol II. Edinburgh: SAMH.

Milne, D. (1987) Evaluating Mental Health Practice: an introduction. In D. Milne (ed) *Evaluating Mental Health Practice. Methods and Applications.* London: Croom Helm.

Morley, S. and Snaith, P. (1989) Principles of psychological assessment. In C. Freeman and P. Tryer (eds) *Research Methods in Psychiatry.* London: Gaskell/Royal College of Psychiatrists.

Morrison, J.K. (1978) The client as consumer and evaluator of community mental health services. *American Journal of Community Psychiatry, 6,* 147–155.

Mumford, E. (1987) Assessing consumer benefit: cost offset as an incidental effect of psychotherapy. *General Hospital Psychiatry, 9,* 360–363.

Pattison, S. and Player, D. (1990) Health education: the political tensions. In S. Doxiadis (ed.) *Ethics in Health Education.* Chichester: John Wiley & Sons.

Reid, W.J. and Hanrahan, P. (1981) The effectiveness of social work: recent evidence. In E.M. Goldberg and N. Connelly (eds) *Evaluating Research in Social Care.* London: Heineman Educational Books.

Rutman, L. (1977) *Evaluation Research Methods: A Basic Guide.* New York: Sage.

Smith, G. and Cantley, C. (1988) Pluralistic evaluations. In J. Lishman (ed) *Evaluation, 2nd edition.* London: Jessica Kingsley Publishers.

Streiner, N. (1989) *Health Measurement Scales.* Oxford: Oxford University Press.

Stimson, G.V. (1990) AIDS and HIV: the challenge for British drug services. *British Journal of Addiction, 85,* 329–339.

Thomas, N. (1988) Evaluation research and the personal social services. In J. Lishman (ed) *Evaluation, 2nd edition.* London: Jessica Kingsley Publishers.

Tillotson, K.J. (1939) The practice of the total push method in the treatment of chronic schizophrenia. *American Journal of Psychiatry, 95,* 1205–1213.

Wallace, A. and Rees, S. (1988) The priority of client evaluations. In J. Lishman (ed) *Evaluation, 2nd edition.* London: Jessica Kingsley Publishers.

Ward, D.J. and McHale, P. (1985) Medical audit and patient satisfaction. *Irish Medical Journal, 78,* 323–325.

WHO (1989) Consumer Involvement in Mental Health and Rehabilitation Services. *WHO/MNH/MEP/89.7.* Geneva: WHO.

Conclusion
The New Agenda for Action

Mike Titterton

The chapters contained in this collection have addressed key issues for the new welfare, as embodied by the arrival of the Caring for People White Paper and the implementation of the NHS and Community Care Act 1990. The Griffiths report on community care called for an 'agenda for action', some of which was adopted by the government as the basis for Caring for People. Following the implementation of the Act however, a new agenda is required. What follows is based on the main points emerging from the preceding chapters.

1. RESPONDING TO NEW NEEDS AND DEVELOPING NEW SERVICES

- Service providers have to think again about how needs are defined and who defines them (chapters 4, 5, 6, 7, 8, 9 and 10).
- Assessments of needs should be user-led (chapters 8 and 9).
- Tinkering with services is not enough – major changes are required in their planning and delivering (chapters 4, 5, 6, 7 and 8).
- For local authorities to become genuinely enabling, they must fully engage users and carers (chapter 1).
- Transitions from old models to new models of working have profound implications and have to be managed with care (chapters 1, 2 and 3).

2. BUILDING GENUINE PARTNERSHIPS

- The challenge of multiagency working must now be confronted by caring agencies (chapter 1).
- The role of the NHS in community care has to be clearly addressed (chapter 2).
- Major tensions threaten collaboration between health and social service agencies (chapter 3).
- Housing agencies have to be more fully involved (chapter 6).

- The difficulties that voluntary organisations face must be acknowledged by statutory authorities (chapter 9).

3. EMPOWERING USERS AND EMPOWERING PROFESSIONALS

- Those planning and delivering services must listen closely to what users have to say (chapters 6, 8 and 10).
- People with mental disabilities face particular problems in getting their views heard (chapters 4, 5 and 6).
- User-centred services will necessitate new organisational designs (chapter 3).
- Professional concerns about new roles and responsibilities have to be properly addressed (chapters 1, 7, 8, and 9).
- Professionals need clout to make things happen – for example, through devolved budgets (chapters 7 and 8).

4. TAKING STOCK

- It is essential to monitor and evaluate developments (chapters 6, 7 and 10).
- Consumers should be involved (chapters 6 and 10).
- Research is fundamental to appraising current developments and advising on future trends (chapters 5, 6, 7, 8, 9 and 10).
- Policy analysis has a role to play here (chapters 2 and 3).

5. MAKING COMMITMENTS

- Commitment means training and supporting those most involved – users, carers, care professionals and managers (chapter 1)
- The government must not only ensure that sufficient resources are made available, it must also acknowledge that a more coordinated approach to community care is required to prevent future planning blight (eg due to local government reorganisation) (chapters 2, 3 and 8).

Index